HAUDENOSAUNEE WOMEN LACROSSE PLAYERS

HAUDENOSAUNEE WOMEN LACROSSE PLAYERS

Making Meaning through Rematriation

Sharity L. Bassett

MICHIGAN STATE UNIVERSITY PRESS | *East Lansing*

Copyright © 2024 by Sharity L. Bassett

Michigan State University Press
East Lansing, Michigan 48823-5245

This project would not be possible without the Dissertation Fellowship for Underrepresented Populations from the Diversity, Equity, and Inclusion Office at South Dakota State University. Thank you as well for the generous funding from the School of American Studies at South Dakota State University, Bader Philanthropies, and the Electa Quinney Institute for American Indian Education at the University of Wisconsin–Milwaukee.

Library of Congress Cataloging-in-Publication Data
Names: Bassett, Sharity L., author.
Title: Haudenosaunee women lacrosse players : making meaning through rematriation / Sharity L. Bassett.
Other titles: Making meaning through rematriation
Description: First. | East Lansing : Michigan State University Press, [2024]. | Includes bibliographical references and index.
Identifiers: LCCN 2023056804 | ISBN 9781611865073 (cloth) | ISBN 9781611864991 (paperback) | ISBN 9781609177683 (pdf) | ISBN 9781628955286 (epub)
Subjects: LCSH: Iroquois women—Social conditions. | Lacrosse players—North America—Social conditions. | Lacrosse for women—North America. | Iroquois Indians—Social life and customs.
Classification: LCC E99.I7 B2348 2024 | DDC 305.897/550082—dc23/eng/20240212
LC record available at https://lccn.loc.gov/2023056804

Cover design by Anastasia Wraight
Cover image is of Ashley Cooke. Photo courtesy of Lee Nanticoke.

Visit Michigan State University Press at *www.msupress.org*

CONTENTS

VII   FOREWORD
XV   PREFACE
XXI   ACKNOWLEDGMENTS
XXV   INTRODUCTION

1   CHAPTER ONE. Haudenosaunee Women Lacrosse Players and Healing
29   CHAPTER TWO. The Community Speaks: A Shifting Conversation
61   CHAPTER THREE. Wood, Plastic, and Gender: Crafting the Stick
89   CHAPTER FOUR. Rematriation: A Turn toward Love and Land

111   CONCLUSION
117   AFTERWORD
121   GLOSSARY
127   NOTES
147   BIBLIOGRAPHY
155   INDEX

FOREWORD

As Haudenosaunee, we are taught as children that women do not play lacrosse. At first glance, this may appear to be a gender restriction placed on young girls in a male-dominated world. This teaching, however, comes from a place that is completely different than what you may think. Women among the Haudenosaunee are uplifted as lifegivers who give rise to our powerful nations.

Our Haudenosaunee Confederacy and way of life, united under the Great Law of Peace, was the model that the U.S. Founding Fathers emulated when they created the U.S. Constitution. Further, it was Haudenosaunee women and our elevated status that provided inspiration for the Founding Mothers in creating the suffrage movement. The Haudenosaunee also gave the world the game of lacrosse—one of the fastest growing sports played by people of all genders around the world. With global contributions that have had great influence in the world—including modern democracy, women's rights, and lacrosse—how is it that the Haudenosaunee Confederacy is not more well known?

The answer lies in the male-dominated, patriarchal, and colonial institutions that continue to hide these truths away from history books and bury our influence.

Generations of genocidal policies and erasure of our voices, stories, and histories are no accidents and, despite all of this, *we are still here*. The Haudenosaunee Confederacy has coexisted as multiple, united Indigenous Nations, living together in peace and democracy for more than one thousand years, and we continue to exist as such to this day.

As the Haudenosaunee, we have sophisticated forms of peacemaking and ensure that all voices are heard and considered in our decision making—from the blades of grass to our children to the trees to the waters to the birds to the future generations. It is said that we can see the faces of those yet unborn coming up from our Mother Earth. In this coexistence, Haudenosaunee women are central to the lifeways and decision-making of our nations. We have inherent authority over the land, our children, our homes, our food, our bodies, and our democracy.

I accepted Sharity Bassett's invitation to be editor for this book for the same reason that I founded the nonprofit Rematriation, out of a deep sense of responsibility as a Haudenosaunee woman to uplift Haudenosaunee and Indigenous women's voices, and to combat inaccurate portrayals of Indigenous women in media with true stories of our resilience, strength, and vision for the future. In editing this book, I sincerely hope that public narratives about Haudenosaunee women lacrosse players are truer and more respectful of our women, our culture, and our people.

The westernized, male-dominated culture that brought violence to our communities, displaced us from our lands, and tried with all its might to separate us from our traditional ways, is the same force that has pushed our women into seeking healing in a game that traditionally we do not play. The dialogue among our people about women playing lacrosse is vital to the wellness of our own democracy. I ask for your openness to truly contemplate what is said and not to place your own lens on these stories; rather, try to hear what you are being told. This book and the voices of the people shared within it are evidence of our ability as Haudenosaunee to coexist amidst disagreement and to evolve and grow together.

The first time I saw our girls play lacrosse, I was about twelve years old and attending the Seneca Allegany Powwow. I saw Seneca girls, girls I knew personally, and some of whom are featured in this book playing on a local lacrosse team. I remember feeling shocked and thinking, *Wait, this can't be . . . ? I should not be seeing this. Shouldn't these girls know that we're not supposed to play? Shouldn't they get off the field? What is happening?*

From that day forward, I knew that some Haudenosaunee women play lacrosse. I also knew that their choice to play was a world apart from our teachings. I grew up on the Oneida Nation territory and often spent time on the Onondaga Nation territory. The Onondaga Nation is the Central Fire of our confederacy and a strong protector of our sovereignty and traditions. Oneida and Onondaga homelands are geographically close to one another and my family is from both communities. The teachings on lacrosse in both nations were very straightforward: women don't play.

As children, women are taught that it is very important not touch the men's wooden lacrosse sticks. This is because our medicine as women is powerful, and we must respect the medicine of the game. This understanding runs deep within our communities to this day. Lacrosse was given to our people by the Creator, where men play and women are part of the game but not directly playing on the field. My husband is a notable lacrosse player, and all of our sons have also played lacrosse. I have not touched the wooden lacrosse sticks that they use to play our ceremonial medicine game.

From a mainstream point of view, these teachings could be difficult to understand. I ask those who do not understand to start with this premise: it was Haudenosaunee women's status that inspired the suffragists to go out and fight for a status like they saw among the Haudenosaunee—absolute freedom, authority, and autonomy. Remember this as you read this book. The inspiration for women's rights in the United States is Indigenous, it is Haudenosaunee. Prior to European contact, Haudenosaunee women have never had to climb our way out of oppression in the face of patriarchal systems. This is an important point of distinction in understanding the discussion around Haudenosaunee women playing lacrosse, and why this discussion cannot be held in the context of western feminist paradigms regarding equality.

People will often say, "Haudenosaunee women are equal to men." Contrary to the western interpretation where men are the standard and women fight to be their equals, we hold an elevated and protected place among our people with regard to our connection to life. It is spiritual; it is sacred. Our Mother Earth is the ultimate lifegiver, and women are also lifegivers; we are connected to life in this way. We hold a special place among our nations and among our families with regard to our connection to life. It is important to also understand that there is no hierarchy among our people or among the people and the Natural World. We are all equal. As Haudenosaunee women and men, we are equal in our responsibilities to care for life. That is the well-being and peace of our people and our nations, and for all living beings—this includes all beings of life in the natural world. And within that realm, lifegiving is a sacred gift.

We are matrilineal people; our citizenship and names are given to us through our mothers, the uterine line—that is, the woman who you are born to. You are what your mother is. We are also matrifocal—meaning the women are in charge of our longhouses, the lands, foods, children, and important matters involving the well-being of our nations. We are also matrilocal—meaning a man moves into his wife's longhouse when they marry. He has to be on good terms with the women of her longhouse (that is, the women among her clan family) otherwise he will be asked to leave with only his personal items. Any children stay with the woman's family. As you can see, women hold a very prominent place within our culture and our nations. Violence against women did not exist within our communities; women are protected as the lifegivers and central to our way of life.

As lifegivers, Haudenosaunee women are connected to the lifegiving force of Mother Earth. We are also led by Grandmother Moon, the keeper of time and the leader of water, women, and children coming into the world. Every twenty-eight days, Grandmother Moon cycles from a new moon to a full moon and back again. Women follow this same cycle, and our menstrual cycle, our time of bleeding, is called our "moon time." This phase is associated with the full moon and a time of shedding and letting go. From moon phase to moon phase, women are connected to these two great life forces, our Mother Earth and Grandmother Moon. I have learned from the Women's Moon Lodge that a woman receives information from her ancestors and Creation for the well-being of all her people during this time. This is why she is sacred; this is why her medicine is powerful.

Men follow and emulate the sun for our families and our people. Every day, our Elder Brother the sun rises in the east and sets in the west, bringing the strength of his light and warmth for life on Mother Earth to grow healthy and strong. When you step into the light and warmth of the sun, your spirit also feels good. Every day our men bring that same light and warmth for our families, and in their presence, our spirits feel good and feel safe and supported to grow healthy and strong. The men tend to the internal fire of our families and our nations that holds us together. Our responsibilities as people are to care for each other and live in balance. These understandings are powerful and in today's context define rematriation, of returning the sacred to the mother and uplifting our voices and our teachings.

In Braiding Sweetgrass, Potawatomi botanist Robin Wall Kimmerer compares the Haudenosaunee matrilineal worldview that begins with Sky Woman in our Creation Story to the Judeo-Christian story of Eve.[1] Sky Woman's story uplifts women and our lifegiving gift that all Haudenosaunee hold central to our worldview and continuation of our way of life. The story of Eve, made from Adam's rib, forever condemns women with the pain of childbirth and bleeding as a burden because Eve ate an apple from the tree of knowledge. These viewpoints play themselves out in the beliefs and behavioral patterns in westernized societies over the past five hundred years. Laws in the United States, carried over from Europe, subjugated women as the property of her husband. Women had no rights to their children if they left their marriage, and a woman could be physically beaten or raped by her husband. This violent way of life was imposed upon Indigenous peoples by force, policy, and erasure of our stories.

Readers familiar with Indian residential schools know that our Indigenous children across Turtle Island were forcibly removed from our families and sent to these schools as a form of genocide. The mission of the schools was to assimilate Indigenous children into white, Christian society. It was believed that our children would choose not to return to our families on the reservations and instead blend in with white society. This did not happen; most returned home. They returned home carrying deep traumas that were eventually shared among all our peoples throughout the generations. At residential schools across the United States and Canada, physical and sexual abuse was rampant. Thousands of children died in these schools, and their remains are still buried in unmarked and unknown locations. These horrifying experiences of our children being stolen from our communities lasted for over one hundred years. These schools were sanctioned and run by both the U.S. and Canadian governments and their militaries, and by Christian missionaries and Catholic nuns and bishops.

In an 1892 speech, Richard H. Pratt, founder and superintendent of the Carlisle Indian Industrial School in the United States said: "A great general has said that the only good Indian is a dead one, and that high sanction of his destruction has been an enormous factor in promoting Indian massacres. In a sense, I agree with the sentiment, but only in this: that all the Indian there is in the race should be dead. Kill the Indian in him, and save the man."[2] Bishop Vital-Justin Grandin, who lobbied for the development of Indian residential schools in Canada in 1875, described the goal of residential schools: "We instill in them a pronounced distaste for the native life so that they will be humiliated when reminded of their origin. When they graduate from our institutions, the children have lost everything Native except their blood."[3]

The intergenerational trauma passed through generations of boarding school children cannot be understated. Epigenetic studies show that trauma, like the horrors endured at Indian residential schools, is transmitted through one's DNA to their children.[4] Through my work, I have learned that these intergenerational traumas can be healed. It takes dedication, support, and deep work emotionally, physically, spiritually, and mentally. Oneida health and wellness coach Heather Dane calls those of us who decide to do this healing work generational cycle breakers.

When I was a young girl, I was sexually assaulted by an individual close to my family who used our cultural practices as a doorway to harm me and other young women. Threats of harm and death of my family members silenced me from saying anything or from seeking help. As I grew older, I came to the realization that our Creator would not allow such harm to happen within the realm of our culture that he gave to us. Coming from a very loving and supportive family, I anticipated that the women in my family would support me when I shared what happened. Instead, I was met with silence. This left me confused and shaken for years.

Decades later, I learned that their silence was unresolved trauma from having been sexually assaulted within their lifetimes. They had never healed from their traumas, and their lives were impacted daily because of them. I was the first to give this voice within my family. I went on my own healing journey and sought ceremony and western therapy. Sometimes these would help, and sometimes they did not. After more than twenty years searching for anything that would make me feel an ounce better from the pain I carried within, I finally found transformation through a process of an Indigenous-based forgiveness. (Out of respect for the community, I refrain from naming this form of healing.) This process resembled the teachings of my own people's story of peace, forgiveness, and transformation. Since then, I have looked to my own culture more deeply along my healing journey. The Haudenosaunee Confederacy was created through a transformative process of healing, forgiveness, and peace.

Through my lifetime, I've witnessed a world where the words "trauma" and "healing" were unrelated concepts in our Indigenous communities. Today the awareness of trauma healing has become deeply embodied and transformative among many Indigenous nations. This movement of healing largely happened because the women within our Nations said "enough"; the cycles of trauma had to be broken. Women decided it was time to heal. Core and central to our way of life, our families, and our nations, women began this shift of healing intergenerational trauma that touches all aspects of our lives and ways of being.

In 2016, I watched the film *Keepers of the Game*, and my perspective on women playing lacrosse changed. In the film, young Mohawk women faced pushback from their community when they formed a girl's high school lacrosse team. A Clan

Mother is faced with holding the line for the sake of tradition or supporting these young women, including her daughter, who all show her that there is something greater at stake. Two sisters reconnected to their culture, transcending Christian assimilation that their family endured, and being shunned by their own community because of this. The Clan Mother's own daughter attempted to end her own life but found her healing and a reason to live through playing lacrosse. This changed me, and I thought, "Who am I to know what is the right path for others to find their own healing?"

Lacrosse may be their medicine, and it may not be mine—and maybe that is okay. Who's to know what Creator intends by women playing lacrosse? I cannot say, but certainly women are being called to play and are finding something for themselves in the game.

Haudenosaunee women lacrosse players are aware they are not playing the men's medicine game but are participating in a contemporary version of our game that thousands of men and women around the world now play. Haudenosaunee women are finding healing, stepping up as ambassadors for our game and our culture, and asserting our sovereignty as people of the Haudenosaunee Confederacy on the world's stage. Our women lacrosse players are playing on sports fields across Turtle Island, on lands that once belonged to our people, and traveling on our Haudenosaunee passports engaging in international diplomacy. They are asserting their presence on lands we've been denied access to, and in the process of rematriation, they are reconnecting to our Mother Earth in these spaces.

Many non-Native male lacrosse players talk about the healing that the contemporary game of lacrosse has brought them, and they have learned about the cultural origins of the game and the Haudenosaunee Confederacy from our male lacrosse players. I have come to understand that a lot of non-Native women lacrosse players know less about the Haudenosaunee roots of the game and even less about who the Haudenosaunee are. The growth rate of women lacrosse players across all nationalities worldwide is rapidly exceeding the growth of the game among men. This means there are less Haudenosaunee women interacting with other women players to help share the knowledge that Haudenosaunee men have shared among other male players for several decades. By playing and being a visible presence on the fields, Haudenosaunee women lacrosse players are changing this, proudly standing up as ambassadors for our people under our Haudenosaunee flag.

The Haudenosaunee Nationals Men's Lacrosse team, formerly the Iroquois Nationals, recently changed their name. From what I have learned, they did so to match the name of the Haudenosaunee National's Womens Lacrosse team. I am proud of our men for making this change. Yaw^ko, a grand thank you. We are standing together united in this game. The International Olympics Committee recently added lacrosse to its games, but it has been resistant to granting admission for the Haudenosaunee to compete. Our Haudenosaunee lacrosse teams are seeking to represent together under our flag, playing our game, in the Olympics.

Watching women among our nations claim their healing and sharing it with our families and nations assures me that our future generations will know us for this. May the stories in this book provoke your thinking. While Haudenosaunee women are now playing lacrosse, our traditions and teaching still exist to be true and will continue to be so.

I asked my twelve-year-old niece Sequoia, who is Onondaga, what she felt about women playing lacrosse. She said, "I don't play lacrosse. I was taught that we don't play. My cousin plays. But I guess it is up to everyone to decide for themselves."

Michelle Schenandoah
Oneida Nation Wolf Clan
Founder of Rematriation

PREFACE

"Please remind me again why you chose to do this project," said Akwesasne Mohawk Clan Mother Mommabear, a gentle but firm reminder that I would not be able to publish this work without a clear statement up front about my proximity to and interest in it. Why would a non-Indigenous woman who has never played lacrosse participate in a decade-plus-long project with Haudenosaunee communities about Haudenosaunee girls and women playing lacrosse?

Birth. I was drawn to this project in 2011 because of the experiences I had with the birth of my son in 2003, and this project deeply informs the experience I had with the birth of my daughter in 2014. The birth of one of my sons yielded a healthy child but nearly killed me due to a combination of hemorrhaging and neglectful medical staff. Unconsciousness marked this birth, much like the powerlessness I felt during a sexual assault I experienced years before. In the eleven years between these two births, I researched the history of childbirth in the United States, the history of midwifery, and how western medicine quelled midwifery in the United States and Europe. I found contemporary maternal and fetal statistics for homebirths and hospital births as well. This inquiry led to

American Indian women because healthy homebirth has happened on Turtle Island since time immemorial; the land has memory of this. In 2013, when my Anishinaabe, Bear Clan daughter came to me in pregnancy, I realized one very big reason why I had engaged this inquiry. Violet Luna was born at home, a second-story apartment over a print shop in Onondaga Territory, and it was the most powerful healing of my life. This birth healed many things including my family, and possibly births that my mothers and grandmothers experienced. This inquiry and the subsequent thirteen-year project fill and shape the space between the birth of my son in 2003 and the birth of my daughter in 2014.

"We don't want to be discussed as though we are not in the room," said Michelle Schenandoah (Oneida, Wolf Clan) as we examined these questions: How can I as a non-Indigenous woman, steeped in feminist thought, represent the set of questions in this book? What kind of language can I use throughout that recognizes my subjectivity and foregrounds Haudenosaunee voices without positing some sort of universal or generic Haudenosaunee reality? Is it really me who is arguing, demonstrating, or claiming these things? Or is it what I have come to understand through the time I've spent with Haudenosaunee people and communities? Michelle's main concerns centered around my position as a scholar, how much presence I had in the argument versus the voices and the narratives of the women I interviewed.

My response strove to relay what I have come to understand, but taking myself out as the active analyst runs the risk of a slippage into Eurowestern universalism and objectivity. This slippage could be applied by readers onto Haudenosaunee culture, communities, and people. Put more frankly, my fear is that without naming myself as the one making the analyses, (non-Indigenous) readers could assume an objective Haudenosaunee culture, communities, and people that I happened upon, and I am simply representing an objective set of realities. Furthermore, every person engaging in the work would draw the same conclusions and represent the same analyses. This is not my intention. I did not do this work on my own, draw the conclusions alone, or choose the representational lenses alone; rather, I co-labored with Haudenosaunee community members over time. Still, this book is ultimately my work, and as such, I take full responsibility for the representations and analyses laid out in it. My hope is that this work opens dialogue and uplifts narrative, and that any challenges the reader may have with its analyses and representations be addressed to me. This is the longer, drawn-out version of *any mistakes are my own.*

My academic training in global gender studies reinforces that a writer's perspective is part of the narrative, and that Eurowestern universalism and objectivity are *a* perspective. Inserting the "I" into academic work is a feminist move, rooted in feminist standpoint theory, and led by women of color and Indigenous women who have disrupted the erroneous claims to objectivity present in academic disciplines, a part of which includes Eurowestern feminism. The insertion of "I" as a woman of color or an Indigenous woman revolutionizes academic discourse. I am not a woman of color or an Indigenous woman. What does it mean for me to insert my "I" into this project? This is the crux of the conversations between Michelle Schenandoah and me, conversations that deeply inform and disrupt how I navigate the self throughout this book. In the solutions that Michelle Schenandoah and I sought to find together, the question emerged, What is the space between "I" and "we"?

The truth about stories is that they are all that we are.[1] We carry the stories of our communities and ancestors on our bodies, and we carry those bodies into spaces that we share with another's stories. The space between any "I" and "we" is stories. This book foregrounds Haudenosaunee stories, as they have come to me through conversation and relationship, and are mitigated through my intergenerational stories, academic training, my female body, marked by some of what that entails, such as birth, menstruation, sexual assault, and deep love.

Next to the familiarity of my own intergenerational stories, Haudenosaunee stories sit newly on my body. Entering one-on-one interview space with a Haudenosaunee woman was a commitment to still my own stories, the stillness that I demanded of my body reflective of what I asked my perspectives, assumptions, and stories to do. I came to understand the interview space as one of an immense gift and responsibility. I kept my body still, my voice soft, my stories to myself for fear that an abrupt outburst of "me too" or "wow" would derail the narratives. I left interviews with muscle stiffness and headaches. These were not my stories, but they were with me. In this process of engaging with Haudenosaunee community members, I have learned how to radically listen *with the body*. I learned how to take Radhika Mohanram's critique of Locke's mind/body split seriously. For each interview, as the new stories ruminated, I would not say or write a word of analysis about the narratives for several days. Once, when my spouse (an Anishinaabe cultural theorist) greeted me after an interview, he had questions. I answered with a description of how the stories were sitting within my body. The body is a location of cycles that take time, the mind a part of the body. The generative space of analysis comes from the space of my body. I did not know that this would become my process until I lived into it. I did not know the effect that being with Haudenosaunee people and stories would have on me, how it would change my cells, inform how I raise my children.

I am not an expert in Haudenosaunee anything, but I have come to understand a great deal through the interstitial space between your stories and mine.

This work is a product of co-laboring with Haudenosaunee community members and leaders. I began this research in 2011 as part of a year-long course in qualitative methods. Dr. Theresa McCarthy (Onondaga, Six Nations, Beaver Clan), director of Indigenous studies at the State University of New York, Buffalo, and Dr. Dawn Martin-Hill (Mohawk, Six Nations), founder and former director of the Indigenous Studies Program (now Indigenous Studies Department) at McMaster University, deeply inform the ethics and methodology of the project. Through multiple conversations and shared drafts, we worked to elevate voices of Haudenosaunee women. These scholars confirmed the need for telling these narratives, but they were not, themselves, in a position to do so. Their work is focused on the immediacy of suicide prevention and water protection, for example. Additionally, there is risk to Haudenosaunee women who work and live in their communities to address openly sensitive matters, since it involves their daughters and granddaughters. And so, they entrusted me with the work under their close eye.

In a conversation on September 21, 2020, Dr. Martin-Hill reminded me that this is relational research, the analysis shaped by the geographic location of Haudenosaunee territory, and by the friendships and relationships developed throughout the project. These relationships were established over time, through multiple conversations and cycles of cultural vetting of the work. They developed despite the mistakes I made along the way. These relationships developed as my capacity to hold the effects of colonization expanded, to hear and feel them. My mentors sent me articles about the trauma for the researcher associated with this kind of work, which kept me going. We co-labored to hold the space to uphold these stories.

I shared draft analyses at Haudenosaunee research symposia and with Haudenosaunee women lacrosse players. We co-labored to articulate meaning; I brought the perspective I was developing based on a horizontal slice, and they brought the depth of their experience. One moment sings out as propelling the project forward. I was presenting chapter 2, "The Community Speaks: A Shifting Conversation," at the annual Haudenosaunee Research Symposium at SUNY Buffalo (2018). Since by that time I had moved from Haudenosaunee to Dakota Territory, I was presenting virtually. There was a technical hiccup and while attendees could hear and see me, I could not hear or see them. During the question-and-answer period, someone in the room was typing questions that attendees had for me. There was a long delay and then the person began typing that one of the Haudenosaunee women lacrosse players in chapter 2 was in the audience. She was sharing with the room what it meant for her to have her stories represented in this way. Corinne Abrams told me later, "I told the audience that I wanted to tell my story anonymously because I didn't want to bring shame to my family. But I said, nearly ten years have passed. I'm an adult now. I'm confident, educated. I'm not scared anymore to fully share who I am." I had been in contact with Corinne earlier that year and asked for her feedback on chapter 2, which she gave, and I incorporated before the presentation. These are some of my favorite moments of co-laboring on the project.

Some of the most important work that has come from co-laboring has set the parameters and limits for this project and cycles back to the theme of birth. Between 2003 and 2014, I learned as much as I could about midwifery, which brought me to Jeanne Shenandoah (Onondaga Nation). Jeanne Shenandoah has been a midwife in her community since the 1960s and grew up with stories about her grandmother and midwifery, stories she heard during a time when homebirths had been made illegal in New York State. My desire to have a homebirth for my daughter led me to my midwife, Susan Derby. Imagine my delight to find out she had studied with Jeanne Shenandoah for nearly a decade at the Onondaga Nation. It was only because of the friendship between Jeanne and Susan that Jeanne agreed to have an interview with me for this project. The interview would become a cornerstone in how I understand the limits of this project and how I understand and teach ethical research when co-laboring with Indigenous communities.

The following narrative is one I've shared multiple times, especially in trainings and classes about Indigenous methodologies, ethnographic refusal, and research ethics. Jeanne Shenandoah was reluctant to have an interview with me, and I understood that it was important that she establish the boundaries. We met around a conference table in the Onondaga Nation communications office. Early in the interview, Jeanne shared that traditional lacrosse is so important for the Haudenosaunee and difficult to talk about with outsiders. I was slow in hearing this message and a couple of questions after this statement asked, "Can you tell me more about traditional lacrosse?" Jeanne scolded, "What did I just tell you?" and went on to describe the piece of colonization that involves researchers coming into Indigenous communities, extracting information, and then leaving with it, as though it belongs to them to do with whatever they want. It was an incredibly important pushback and boundary. This was not my first interview, and I had read enough anticolonial work to recognize the need for this resistance. We sat in silence for what felt like minutes, but was more likely seconds. I cautiously said that I wasn't sure what to ask next, to which Jeanne replied, "Good. That is how I want you to feel." One might think that this was the end of the interview—and I am convinced that it most certainly could have been had I in any way tried to defend myself or a history and contemporary reality of academic extraction in Indigenous communities—but it was just the beginning. Jeanne shared two hours of her time with me, very much informing this project.

Another poignant example of establishing the scope of this project comes from conversations I had with Michelle Schenandoah regarding ceremony. Haudenosaunee ceremony, even as it relates to lacrosse, is not the scope of this project but one of its boundaries. The questions that Michelle Schenandoah and I co-labored over helped to create a buffer in my writing to protect that space. We co-labored over questions like, To what extent does using the term "ceremony" conjure curiosity for the non-Indigenous reader that could provide an avenue for consumption and exploitation? Since Haudenosaunee players and community members publicly talk about lacrosse as a ceremony, is there risk in not naming it as a boundary in the project? I open the introduction with the words of Berdie Hill, Cayuga Clan Mother. Her words are a poignant caution for the non-Haudenosaunee reader that help to provide the buffer around Haudenosaunee ceremony.

What I hope this book will be in the world is first and foremost for Haudenosaunee women and girls. I hope that the Haudenosaunee women lacrosse players I interviewed will be proud of the representations herein and that current and future generations will be uplifted and inspired by their stories. I hope that Indigenous and non-Indigenous women will find ways to see themselves as powerful and beautiful through the narratives, perspectives, and analyses therein. I hope that my daughter, sons, and students experience three-dimensional beauty in the following pages. Upon first seeing the image that graces the cover of this book, my then four-year-old daughter asked in utter awe, "Is she real?" I responded, "Yes, she's very real. Isn't she so powerful and beautiful?"

ACKNOWLEDGMENTS

Haudenosaunee lacrosse players' desire to tell their stories drives this project and is only possible because of their participation. I am so thankful to Corinne Abrams (Tuscarora), Amber Hill (Tuscarora), Tsiotenhariio (Beautiful Corn Silk) Herne (Mohawk), Ashley Cooke (Mohawk), Star Wheeler (Seneca), and the several others who decided to remain anonymous for sharing their time and love for their culture and lacrosse. Thank you to Jacky Snyder (Seneca) for sharing insights about language revitalization and lacrosse. I am incredibly grateful to the Haudenosaunee Elders who shared time and wisdom with me and whose knowledge frames and theorizes this project, namely, Louise McDonald (Akwesasne Mohawk), henceforth identified as Mommabear, Berdie Hill (Cayuga), Jeanne Shenandoah (Onondaga), and Diane Schenandoah (Oneida). Thank you to Sandy Jemison (Seneca), Western New York Lacrosse Hall of Fame inductee (2018), who provided a detailed memory of Haudenosaunee women's lacrosse. Thank you to all who interviewed and provided such incredible insight.

I am deeply indebted to the Haudenosaunee community members who gave sage insight and read drafts. Jonel Beauvais (Mohawk, Wolf Clan) and Dr. Theresa McCarthy (Six Nations of the Grand River, Onondaga, Beaver Clan) ground this project in Haudenosaunee lifeways and worldviews. Theresa and Dr. LaKisha Simmons and Dr. Susan Cahn all read early drafts and offered painstaking feedback. Dr. Dawn Martin-Hill (Mohawk, Six Nations of the Grand River) opened windows into Haudenosaunee lifeways and wisdom. Michelle Schenandoah (Oneida, Wolf Clan), whose words open this book, spent countless hours serving as an editor and ultimately helped this become a kinder, more culturally relevant book.[1] Thank you to Neal Powless (Onondaga, Eel Clan) for sharing important insights about the world of lacrosse. Mommabear ends this book as the final word. Any paucity of Haudenosaunee cultural understanding is my own.

My ability to engage in this work as a non-Indigenous scholar is only possible because of scholars and activists who in very real and important ways blew my mind and broke my heart. Dr. Alexis DeVeaux pushed me to think harder and do better; her encouragement is gold. Drs. Tink Tinker, Mark Freeland, Theresa McCarthy, and Dawn Martin-Hill handed me a lifeline in the form of Indigenous frameworks of thought after Drs. Albert Hernandez and Katherine Turpin put books in front of me that deconstructed colonizing ways of knowing, or, in other words, broke my mainframe.

I am deeply grateful for the support of the School of American and Global Studies at South Dakota State University, whose financial support helped the project turn a corner toward completeness. Immense gratitude for the final student readers of this project, Paige Cain (Flandreau Santee Sioux), Erin Smith, Ronan Carpenter, and Eliza Faeh, fantastic students, and humans, in whose hands the future is bright. A special thank you to Michelle Lietz (Yaqui), Dr. Timothy Pearson, Dr. Catherine Cocks, and the blind peer reviewers for close readings and edits of this book. Thank you to Dr. Christine Stewart, who gave poetic edits to the preface. Thank you to Ronan Carpenter for both the suggestion for and a first draft of the glossary.

Miigwech to the amazing staff at the Electa Quinney Institute for American Indian Education at the University of Wisconsin, Milwaukee, and for the faculty research funding through the Bader Foundation and the College of Letters and Sciences at UWM that brought the project across the goal line, including trips to Haudenosaunee territories to ask for final permissions. Thank you to Sam Krueger (Wisconsin Oneida) for providing administrative support on one of those trips. Much gratitude to my colleagues in Women's & Gender Studies at UWM who help carry the vision that this is more than a book, but a community-facing-community-serving endeavor that has scholarly, political, and social impact. Thank you to my dear friend

Dr. Wendy Felese for seeing the optimism in these pages and being the first to teach them in her courses.

Thank you to dear friends and family who checked in throughout the years as I worked toward completion, providing a net for myself, my spouse, and our children. My apologies because there are too many to name, but I want to start with Sharon Bassett, Mindy Niles, Clay Bassett, Adam Walborn, Zach Walborn, Aubrie Entwood, Jim Entwood, Patrich Soch, Angela Bradley, Darren Bradley, Linda Freeland, Jim Freeland, Paul Reed, Luis Rodriguez, Laverne White Bear, Dr. Becky Kuehl, Dr. Marlene De La Cruz-Guzmán, and Dr. Sana Illahe. Miigwech to Susan Derby, my midwife and champion of doing difficult things.

Thank you to my mother, Aleta Reed, and my father, Everett Bassett—my first writing and ethics teachers. Thank you to Mark, Niwiidigemaagan, and to the people who raised this kind, Anishinaabe inini, Donna and Jim Freeland. Mark's support included holding onto the vision that I could complete this long before I believed it, weekends away with our young children so that I could work, and many discussions of ways to apply the incisive theory of Indigenous worldview present in his own scholarship. Without him, I would not be the one to write this book. This is for our children—Payton, Lian, Gavin, Violet, and Giizhik—especially for Lian who will one day put his story into the world.

INTRODUCTION

There are just some things that I am going to say that you are going to have to accept." This is one of the first things that Cayuga Clan Mother and Elder Berdie Hill said when I sat down at the diner on the Tonawanda Reservation to interview her in 2011 about why she believed Haudenosaunee girls and women should not play lacrosse.[1] I knew of the conversation within Haudenosaunee communities regarding girls and women playing the game of lacrosse, a game well documented as originating with the Haudenosaunee. I had read about the conversation, written as a controversy, in a 2007 *New York Times* article by Aimee Berg titled, "Lacrosse: Cradle of a Sport Has Crossed a Gender Line." I had chosen to investigate what Berg presented as a controversy in a year-long class on qualitative research methods. I was concerned that Berg's representation of Onondaga Clan Mothers holding back young women from progress was problematic in its incompleteness, simplicity, homogeneity, and how it superimposed western feminist tropes onto Haudenosaunee cultural complexities.

Berdie Hill agreed to interview with me for this project on the one condition that there would be some things that I would need to hear at face value and not question. I agreed. Berdie was the first person I interviewed for this project. My western feminist sensibilities were challenged by her emphatic proclamations that Haudenosaunee girls and women could cause damage to themselves and, by extension, to their communities if they played lacrosse. Western feminism has held up Haudenosaunee culture as privileging and valuing women, especially politically. Sally Roesch Wagner writes and speaks prolifically on the influence that Haudenosaunee women and society had on Eurowestern feminists of the early twentieth century. This influence is noted by Roesch Wagner, for example, in her essay "Haudenosaunee Influence on the Women's Suffrage Movement," showing up at the United Nations at a panel titled "Haudenosaunee Influence on the Women's Rights Movement."[2]

There is this seemingly glaring contradiction when it comes to prohibiting Haudenosaunee women and girls from playing lacrosse. Berdie was incredibly effective at relaying the depths of what is at stake for Haudenosaunee communities, and I left with a glimpse of an understanding of why Berdie and others felt that Haudenosaunee girls and women should not play. More accurately, I should say, I felt a glimpse of what is at stake for Haudenosaunee communities in holding onto their cultures and traditions: the future of the community, loss of culture, assimilation. More than anything, I felt Berdie's love, compassion, and sense of responsibility. I took seriously Berdie's understanding that Haudenosaunee girls and women play because "they don't know [why it is against our culture that they play]. If they knew, they wouldn't play."[3] The depth with which Berdie conveyed what is at stake for Haudenosaunee communities, as well as the deep roots that lacrosse has within Haudenosaunee culture and tradition, informs this project. Her voice—her power and conviction—is in my head when I present on this material, and when others echo her belief. What she withholds in our interview becomes as crucial as what she shares.

I take on the task in these chapters of relaying that which is so critically important to Haudenosaunee women regarding Haudenosaunee cultural survival and flourishing and demonstrating how rematriation frames these efforts. In this project, I examine how what at first glance seems a paradox—women holding great authority while being restricted from participating in lacrosse—is best understood through a framework of rematriation. For Haudenosaunee communities, rematriation involves reconnecting to the authority over lands, bodies, minds, children, and governance, breaking through the surfaces of colonization to deep, cellular healing found "all the way down through the earth and back up again."[4] Rematriation weaves throughout this work as a way of grounding the discussion of Haudenosaunee women lacrosse players within a broader cultural context of healing, belonging, and claiming conceptual and theoretical spaces. Importantly, there is no *one* Haudenosaunee women's perspective.

The representations of lacrosse in this book describe a slice of the experiences of Haudenosaunee women lacrosse players from the 1980s to the present. More prevalent in the analyses than the timeline is the space in which the narratives occur, mostly Haudenosaunee land, and relationships to that land. Though there are a few narratives of grandmothers and great-grandmothers playing pickup games of lacrosse throughout, the question of whether Haudenosaunee girls and women were playing precontact is not taken up in this project. References to historical, medicinal, and traditional lacrosse are in service to more deeply understanding contemporary lacrosse. Any mention of the reclamation of Haudenosaunee lacrosse regards the 1980s and after.

Debates about professionalism and amateur status in sports informs the one-hundred-year ban on Indigenous men playing lacrosse in amateur, international competitions. This professional-amateur debate was imported from England in the nineteenth century and was employed to marginalize Indigenous, working-class, and athletes of color. In England, elite men who were part of universities or just had more leisure time played amateur sports, except they were not called amateur athletes, but "gentlemen." Mike Cronin enunciates the ideals present in historical debate in *Sport: A Very Short Introduction*: "Caught up in these blanket ideals were the specific beliefs that sport should inculcate in its players a respect for the order of rules, the leadership of the captain, the belief in fair play, and the tying together of mind and soul in the practice of muscular Christianity."[5]

This divide affected not just lacrosse or Canada. When elite athlete Jim Thorpe (Cherokee) was divested of his Olympic medals in 1912 for allegedly playing professional baseball (in the past, only amateur athletes were allowed to compete), a primary source articulated not only the colonial importing of the professional-amateur debate but demonstrated the racism surrounding this debate. The Chicago newspaper *The Day Book* articulated how the professional-amateur debate was a colonial tool targeting working-class athletes: "No man who worked with his hands would ever get into athletic games in England except as a professional. All the amateurs were 'gentlemen.' The idea was imported to the U.S. and instead of calling the classes 'gentleman' and professionals we call them 'amateurs' and professionals. And we haven't changed our style since."[6] While *The Day Book* criticized this debate for being somehow un-American, it illuminated colonial racism through its representation of and call to (non)action toward Jim Thorpe. Aligning with colonial racism across continents, *The Day Book* articulates, "The *London Daily Citizen* sums the situation up correctly in an editorial, which shows insights into American athletics. It says: 'There is no reason for the hysteria exhibited in America. We would hesitate to dub Thorpe a sham amateur. He seems to be suffering severely from unsophistication and faithful indiscretion. There is no doubt that the American committee acted properly, but we wish they had not started in on a poor Indian.'"[7] Jim Thorpe's Olympic medals were returned posthumously in 1982. Of note, the Iroquois Nationals men's team (now the Haudenosaunee Nationals men's team) was "the ceremonial host of a ... pre-Olympic reconciliation event celebrating the return of Jim Thorpe's 1912 Olympic medals."[8]

The professional-amateur divide informed a "ban that had been brewing for some time" against Indigenous men playing in amateur lacrosse leagues.[9] The National Lacrosse Association of Canada (NLA) began in 1875 and started with segregation of Indigenous teams. There was an initial understanding that those teams would accept travel funds from the ticket sales. (Where were the rest of the sales going?) In 1876, NLA targeted Indigenous teams when it revised the rules so that no teams could accept money for travel, as colonization put Indigenous communities in a position where they were not able to secure funding in other ways. In 1880, NLA became the National Amateur Lacrosse Association of Canada (NALA) and banned Indigenous men outright.[10]

The decade of the 1980s marks a particularly important moment for Haudenosaunee lacrosse, after much activism in the 1960s and 1970s, led by Oren Lyons (Onondaga, Turtle Clan, Faith Keeper, founder of the Iroquois Nationals team), resulted in an elimination of the ban. Haudenosaunee men reclaiming lacrosse in the 1980s inspired Haudenosaunee women to play during the same period. (The medicinal game never left some of the communities.) This project focuses on how lacrosse is enacted by Haudenosaunee women on Haudenosaunee land, and how they carry their relationship to land when they play in various spaces.

In this book, when referencing women's lacrosse, I am speaking specifically of contemporary field lacrosse. Some women I interviewed discussed themselves or other girls and women playing box lacrosse, which is played in an arena, with pads, helmets, and checking allowed. When girls and women play box lacrosse, they are playing on co-ed teams. When this is the case, I name so specifically; otherwise, women's lacrosse refers to contemporary field lacrosse throughout.

Some Haudenosaunee people believe that women's lacrosse is even more aligned with the traditional game, focusing as it does on offense, agility, a more expansive field, and that there is no checking—meaning no pads or helmets required. This point of view is present in the following narrative given by Six Nations Mohawk scholar Dawn Martin-Hill:

> D: At the same time, I was watching [my daughter's team] play, a lot of old men used to come out when the girls were playing. And I used to wonder, why are these old guys here? And I'd say, do you have a granddaughter playing? No. And then I would kind of be like, ew. I'm not sure I like this. I didn't know what was going on. And then I noticed more old men coming. One of them followed [my daughter] to every game. He was her biggest fan. So, we were parked next to each other at one game, and I asked him why do you come to the women's field lacrosse when there's the men's? And he said because the men aren't playing it with the spirit anymore and the women are.
>
> S: Wow.
>
> D: Yeah. He said this is the way it was meant—look at their skill. They're doing amazing things, jumping. He said they're playing the game the way it was intended, not for money and adulation. It's not the reason these girls are out there. It's the real deal.

Martin-Hill continues to describe the Elders' admiration for the girls' and women's grace and skill with the ball, saying that watching it was "peaceful and beautiful" without "swearing or scrapping."[11] Her narrative is a further example of how Haudenosaunee girls and women playing lacrosse in increasing numbers is calling Haudenosaunee communities to discuss meaning more deeply when it comes to defining this contemporary game in cultural terms, specifically historical and traditional.

Methods and Methodology

For this project, I interviewed thirty Haudenosaunee women, and two Haudenosaunee men, coming from four generations, spanning from eighteen to eighty-plus years of age. The two Clan Mothers I interviewed, Berdie Hill and Mommabear, lay the theoretical and cultural groundwork for much of this project, offering the depth and breadth within which the conversation regarding Haudenosaunee women playing lives. I interviewed past, recent, and current lacrosse players, community leaders, and Elders who come from Six Nations of the Grand River Reserve in Ontario, Canada; Akwesasne Mohawk Territory in the Adirondack region of New York State; Onondaga Nation near Syracuse, New York; Oneida Nation in Oneida, New York; Tuscarora Territory south of the Onondaga and Oneida Nations; and Cattaraugus Seneca Nation near Irving, New York. The community members whom I interviewed offered diverse experiences regarding the conversation over their playing.

In some cases, such as women from Tuscarora, they did not know of the teaching around their playing until they picked up a stick at Onondaga Nation. In two cases, young women reflected on forging their mothers' signatures as young girls so that they could play. Others, from Cattaraugus Seneca Nation and Six Nations Reserve, had the full support of their communities within the traditional Longhouse. I interviewed two women who had played on the team in the mid-1980s that disbanded after being asked not to play at Onondaga, one of whom did not know that was the reason they stopped playing. I interviewed two coaches and one referee, as well as two men who play the traditional medicine game, one of whom played for the Iroquois Nationals men's team. I interviewed a community leader from Six Nations Reserve, two scholars from Six Nations Reserve, two additional Elders without formal leadership in their community, and an Onondaga midwife and Elder. Those I interviewed represent all corners of the internal conversation over girls and women playing lacrosse. Some adamantly oppose their playing; others once opposed their playing and now range from tolerating it to emphatically supporting it. Some did not know it was a conversation for a time, and others knew of the conversation and supported their playing despite it. I interviewed community members from every Haudenosaunee Nation but not all territories such as the Cayuga Territory or Oneida, Wisconsin. Each person interviewed lent to the knowledge production regarding Haudenosaunee lacrosse.

Oral history, as accessed through qualitative interviews, maintains its strength and legitimacy when it does "not suppress conflicting voices in order to force a single and collective narrative but instead to embrace multiple voices and conflicting points as inevitable."[12] Oral history presents the possibility of nuance (through multiple interviews) regarding difficult topics such as tradition and women's roles.

Ethics in a qualitative endeavor involves holding carefully and with great respect the stories that others have offered. Trust is key. After sharing difficult stories about his parents, Cherokee scholar Thomas King says, "stories can control our lives, for there is a part of me that will be chained to these stories as long as I live."[13] King then describes how stories remain within Indigenous communities as well. The process of writing this book means asking to be invited into a matrix and memory of stories long held within communities.

Thomas King and Linda Tuhiwai Smith (Māori) inform how I represent the interviews. King states, "The truth about stories is that that's all we are."[14] Qualitative researchers cannot reduce someone to one characteristic. When I spoke with Berdie Hill, she shared a piece of her collection of stories, to some of which I had an internal reaction. It was complex. My stories stayed silent except for how they interacted with hers inside of me. In this work, I aim to give a fleshed-out version of Haudenosaunee women's stories and the land and lifeways to which they are connected. I work to craft representations that trouble the binary categories of western thought and avoid "claiming an authenticity which is overly idealistic and romantic, and simply engaging in an inversion of the colonizer/colonized relationship which does not address the complex problems of power relations."[15] However, my own biases as a researcher are present, as is my intention to center Haudenosaunee women lacrosse players and give them an opportunity to articulate meaning about their playing to their communities. What this methodology allows for is the centering of women's voices in a matrilineal culture in the process of decolonizing western impositions of patriarchy, a form of rematriation.

Field Observations

I grew up on and spent much of my adult life on Haudenosaunee land. Over the past many years, my relationship with that space included that of a researcher. I spent time at and near Haudenosaunee nations and territories in the United States and Canada, in the role of both observer and participant-observer. I attended lacrosse games, community educational events, film viewings, and participated in activism events organized by the Onondaga Nation, such as the Sgeññoñh Unity March in solidarity with Standing Rock water protectors. I visited and took extensive field notes at the communication offices at the Onondaga Nation and

Tonawanda Seneca Territory, as well as the cultural center located at the Oneida Nation. I spent time in diners at Akwesasne Mohawk Nation, Onondaga Nation, and Tuscarora Territory. I visited Sally Roesch Wagner's brainchild, the Matilda Joslyn Gage Museum in Fayetteville, New York. I participated in educational events hosted by the Neighbors of the Onondaga Nation. This included the public conversation between Onondaga midwife and Elder Jeanne Shenandoah and Sally Roesch Wagner titled, "The Influence of Haudenosaunee Women," held as part of the Onondaga Land Rights and Our Common Future series at Syracuse University between February 2010 and February 2011. I attended one session of a language immersion class at the Cattaraugus Seneca Nation. Time spent at Haudenosaunee nations and territories was almost always a result of an interview I had scheduled and was reflective of the reality that if the interviews were going to happen, I would be traveling to Haudenosaunee nations and territories. Building relationships with community members facilitated a level of trust. A methodology that recognizes all Haudenosaunee land, not just that which has been parsed off into reservations, territories, and reserves, also promoted trust.

Each of these field experiences lends to understandings of how Haudenosaunee communities are engaging the conversation about girls and women playing lacrosse. The rich qualitative material from interviews informed how I experienced the games. To hear how vital lacrosse is to Haudenosaunee women, and then attend women's college games where they make up one or two of the entire team, presents itself as a surprise, but a surprise in Black feminist Kathrine McKittrick's use—that the surprise is that the thing observed is surprising at all. Being present for an opening address of thanksgiving at the Sgeñnoñh Unity March at Onondaga Nation and watching as a Haudenosaunee community member asked a participant to stop filming the thanksgiving address taught me about respect in the process and asking permission at every step. By going to Haudenosaunee territories repeatedly and developing field notes on the differences between when they invited me and when I just showed up, I developed a methodology of respect, times of appropriate silence, and process. Riding to Albany with people from the Onondaga Nation to protest hydrofracking informed a knowledge of relationship to land. Through my fieldwork, I developed a methodology of relationality, foregrounding the importance of trust for those I am interviewing, as well as the relationships I observed between Haudenosaunee and non-Indigenous people. In sum, this project is only possible with the intentional and frequent movement across Haudenosaunee lands and in and out of the colonial impositions of the space of territory that are held intensely by Haudenosaunee peoples. In fact, in order to complete this project, I needed to come home from Dakota to Haudenosaunee territory, where the words once again flowed.

Presentations

The several times that I presented on this project over the course of thirteen years serve as primary research for the critical interactions that occurred between myself and the audiences or the interactions among audience members. Presenting at Haudenosaunee research symposia at the State University of New York, Buffalo, to mainly Haudenosaunee audiences, proved incredibly helpful in gaining perspective on this complex conversation occurring within Haudenosaunee communities. I was able to observe gender dynamics that raised questions for me about matrilineality and colonial impositions of patriarchy. Why, for example, at one symposium did only men respond to my presentation for the first several minutes, and women comment very little? I wondered, based on my reading about the Haudenosaunee, if this was related to colonial impositions of western patriarchy or Haudenosaunee traditionalism whereby men speak publicly what women leaders have instructed them to say. Alternatively, why in another symposium did men stay silent after a young woman brought up the colonization of the power held in women's bodies? These presentations facilitated probing questions, informing a methodology that works to hold open, rather than foreclose on inquiry.

Other presentations I have given serve this project differently. The presentation at SUNY Oswego, where most of the women's lacrosse team was in attendance, allowed me to assess how informed non-Haudenosaunee lacrosse players were about the origins of lacrosse. Presenting to a variety of classes brought questions such as, Are the Haudenosaunee just trying to replace one set of gender norms with another? Are Haudenosaunee women not supported in lacrosse in the same way as women, in general, have struggled in sports historically? What is at stake if Haudenosaunee women keep playing? Stop playing? This fieldwork informs a methodology of situating fields of questions within particular contexts, a trajectory that informs how this project works to firmly situate lacrosse within a Haudenosaunee historical, traditional, and cultural context.

Materials Produced by Haudenosaunee Peoples

For this project, I worked with archives at the Charles B. Sears Law Library at SUNY Buffalo and the Seneca Nation Library to access historical perspectives from the 1980s to the present on Haudenosaunee women and lacrosse. I examined the historical periodical *Turtle Quarterly*, which gives Haudenosaunee perspectives through news, commentary, artwork, and stories. Several films and documentaries produced, directed, or informed by Haudenosaunee people have come out about lacrosse, such as *Crooked Arrows* (2012), *Sacred Stick* (2013), *Keepers of the Game* (2016), and *Spirit Game: Pride of a Nation* (2017). I engage these for the way that they are moments of solidification, a particular narrative told by some in Haudenosaunee communities, atop shifting ground. They serve a methodology interested in how the solidified moment of film declares specific realities, both real and hoped for, that articulate the present and future. Also informing this project for the ways that it speaks to matrilineality and the importance of Clan Mothers, and women more generally, is the emerging online publication *Rematriation*, with over two hundred contributors. The magazine produced a short documentary, *An Indigenous Response to #MeToo*, which informs discussions regarding Haudenosaunee women's power and colonization.

Collectively, these methods work to inform a methodology that foregrounds Haudenosaunee women's perspectives and meaning making. Through the experiences of interviewing Haudenosaunee people, spending time over meals and on their homelands, observing and participating in what matters to them, and learning from relationships they have established with their non-Indigenous neighbors, I have worked to offer a project rooted in a methodology of close listening, emerging trust, and deeper understandings of the rematriation of Haudenosaunee women's social and political power.

Describing Lacrosse

In September 2015, the Onondaga Nation, adjacent to Syracuse, New York, hosted thirteen nations for the men's World Indoor Lacrosse Championships (WILC), the Iroquois Nationals coming in second place. The Onondaga Nation hosting WILC—after the NLA placed a ban on Haudenosaunee men playing internationally in 1880, and the Iroquois Nationals not being able to travel on Haudenosaunee passports to compete (2010)—marks a critical moment in Haudenosaunee sovereignty. Lacrosse is one of the fastest growing sports in North America, and although Haudenosaunee communities are overwhelmingly supportive of their men playing and publicly laying claim to the game as their sport and ceremony, there exists an internal conversation over whether Haudenosaunee women and girls should play, and what it means when they do. The Haudenosaunee Creation Story locates lacrosse as a healing ceremony, given so that men can provide medicine for the communities and settle disputes. Haudenosaunee men currently play the medicine game of lacrosse during ceremonies or whenever there is a call for healing. Haudenosaunee women are central to the medicine game, weaving the balls and stick nets, and throwing the ball in the middle of the field to start the ceremony. Haudenosaunee communities agree that only Haudenosaunee men should play the *medicine game* of lacrosse.

This book considers what the internal conversation regarding Haudenosaunee women and girls playing says about lacrosse as a Haudenosaunee game as a source of healing, how definitions of "traditional" and gender are worked out, and how women enact sovereignty through the game. The concept of rematriation plays an important role in structuring how different enactments of the game of lacrosse are understood and articulated toward meaning making. A process of rematriation lends an understanding of how Haudenosaunee women's bodies heal through their playing lacrosse and, as I have come to understand through conversations with Haudenosaunee knowledge holders, how that healing is connected to Sky Woman in the Haudenosaunee Creation Story. Rematriation speaks to the generative authority that Haudenosaunee women have, intergenerationally, to name where healing resides in the game. Rematriation speaks to the colonial histories that severely limit the land base on which lacrosse can be played, which informs how that land is understood today, while looking toward the healing of land, water, and bodies. Rematriation is about the returning of and to Haudenosaunee land, which holds healing for its Haudenosaunee women lacrosse players.

In this section, I describe different kinds of lacrosse, as I have come to understand them through conversations with Haudenosaunee community members working through the definitions. However, how these iterations overlap and the degree to which Haudenosaunee community members articulate the iterations as distinct or not distinct informs this project. The contemporary games of field and box lacrosse have their roots in historical lacrosse. The contemporary rules for men's field lacrosse have their origins in a pamphlet distributed by Montreal dentist William Beers in 1860. Box lacrosse originated in Canada in the 1930s and is dominated by men's teams, though several women whom I interviewed have played on box lacrosse teams and more women's box lacrosse teams are emerging.[16] The contemporary rules for women's field lacrosse come not from North America, but from Scotland in 1890. All lacrosse involves quick reflexes, strong hand-eye coordination, agility, and speed. The differences between women's field lacrosse, men's field lacrosse, and box lacrosse center around contact. While in all iterations, stick checking is a legal form of contact, bodily contact is allowed only in men's field lacrosse and men's and women's box lacrosse, precipitating the need for pads and mouth guards. Box lacrosse, played exclusively indoors, has smaller boundaries, more checking, and focuses more on defense. Women's field lacrosse focuses on agility, speed, and offense. Notably, none of the participants I interviewed dispute that the historical and contemporary traditional medicine game is played only by Haudenosaunee men.

Claiming Lacrosse amid Worldwide Growth

In discussing the conversation within Haudenosaunee communities regarding women and girls playing lacrosse, it is necessary to explain its growth as a contemporary sport and its impact on the international stage. The 1980s mark the growth of lacrosse in two ways relevant to this project. First, the 1980s mark the decade when Haudenosaunee communities endorsed the Iroquois Nationals men's team to play at the international level, the same decade that the International Lacrosse Federation (ILF) lifted a one-hundred-year ban on their playing internationally (described below). Haudenosaunee communities came together to support their playing as an essential expression of national sovereignty. Secondly, the decade marks a precise moment when some Haudenosaunee leaders made clear statements against Haudenosaunee women and girls playing the game, especially internationally and in any way that would represent Haudenosaunee nationhood. When the Iroquois Nationals women's team disbanded before the third international World Women's Championship in 1989, a competition for which they were preparing, women's lacrosse was continuing to grow worldwide. It was not until 2007 that Haudenosaunee women joined international competitions as full contenders and members of the Federation of International Lacrosse (FIL).[17]

Kim Clause (Tuscarora) was part of the Iroquois Nationals women's team that was preparing for the 1989 World Championship. The night before the team was to play an exhibition game against a prominent high school girls lacrosse team in the Syracuse area, their coach, Sandy Jemison (Cattaraugus Seneca Nation), received a call informing her and her team not to pack because they were not going to be allowed to play.[18] Twenty-two years after Kim Clause was part of the team that could not play near Onondaga, her daughter, Corinne Abrams, was part of the Haudenosaunee women's lacrosse team that played in 2009, in the team's first World Championship in Prague.[19] In those two decades, women and girls continued to play lacrosse, just not as a team endorsed to represent the Haudenosaunee at an international level.

For a time, women's international teams grew at a faster rate than men's international teams. By the time the Haudenosaunee women's team made it to the international lacrosse scene, different nations had played in seven prior World Lacrosse Women's Championships (called the World Cup until 2022), beginning in 1982.[20] Between that first World Championship and the 2005 World Championship, four more nations joined the World Women's Championships.[21] In the 2009 games, the Haudenosaunee women's team was joined by Austria, Denmark, Ireland, the Netherlands, and South Korea as first-timers.[22] The 2022 World Championship was held in the United States.[23]

Over nearly four decades, women's lacrosse has grown from being an international sport involving six nations to involving thirty, with others on deck to become part of the scene. But in 1987, the Haudenosaunee women's team disbanded due to pressure from various traditional Haudenosaunee community leaders. When I asked Sandy Jemison when women started playing again after this moment in the 1980s, she responded that they never quit. That is when Sandy began the Seneca Girls Lacrosse Club in which, over the decades, several hundred have participated.[24] During the late 1980s through the mid-2000s, girls' and women's lacrosse had grown within Haudenosaunee communities to the point that over sixty young women tried out for the team that played an exhibition game at the 2005 World Championship in Maryland, and then four years later played at their first World Championship in Prague. This growth in Haudenosaunee women's lacrosse is part of calling lacrosse back to communities, after the one-hundred-year ban on Haudenosaunee men playing internationally.

The growth of men's lacrosse as an international sport mirrors the World Women's Championships, with some distinctions. Men's international competitions started earlier, and as of 2023, there are more nations participating in men's lacrosse (54) than women's lacrosse (34). However, men's lacrosse was slower to involve more nations than women's lacrosse. During the same decade when the Iroquois Nationals women's team was asked not to play on Onondaga Territory, the Iroquois Nationals men's team that began in 1983 was gearing up to play in the 1990 World Lacrosse Championships in Perth, Australia. Before the first World Women's Championship in 1982, the men's world lacrosse championship had occurred in 1967, 1974, and 1978. Whereas the first World Women's Championship hosted six different nations, the World Lacrosse Men's Championships hosted the same four nations—Australia, Canada, England, and the United States—for the first five championships. The Iroquois Nationals men's team can boast being the first Indigenous team to join the international arena in 1990, infiltrating a competitive space cornered by the same four nations for nineteen years. By the time the Haudenosaunee women's team competed in its first World Championship in 2009, fifteen nations were already competing. Given the layered ways in which the historical record ignores Haudenosaunee women in the shared, international space in which they find themselves engaging their cultural game, and the internal conversation over their playing, Haudenosaunee women insert themselves into the world of lacrosse in profound ways, the focus of this project.

The centrality of Haudenosaunee women in international lacrosse playing is an important part of Haudenosaunee claims to lacrosse. Haudenosaunee claims to lacrosse on the world stage begin with the fight to play internationally again, led by Oren Lyons (Onondaga). Reporting on the lift of the ban, David Treadwell said, "The Iroquois have long yearned to return to international lacrosse competition. When their white-and-purple flag with its wampum belt emblem is unfurled along with the banners of the United States, Canada, Britain, and Australia, it will mark what many Iroquois see as the opening of a new era."[25] Haudenosaunee claiming of lacrosse includes acts of sovereignty and unequivocal visual representations of lacrosse as originating with the Haudenosaunee.

Examples of sovereignty as part of the claiming include the Iroquois Nationals men's team (2010) and the U19 (under age 19) Haudenosaunee women's team (2015) not traveling on U.S. or Canadian passports after their Haudenosaunee passports were declined by England and Scotland respectively. A profound reclamation of lacrosse includes the opening ceremonies of the WILC in 2015, which included an enactment of lacrosse within the Haudenosaunee Creation Story, traditional opening addresses in Haudenosaunee languages, traditional singing and dancing, and Haudenosaunee protocols of welcoming foreign nations to their homelands. (This included the more contemporary act of stamping passports.) The film *Keepers of the Game* (2016) offers another example of visual reclamation of Haudenosaunee lacrosse, in this case, a girls' team and supporters sharing narratives that connect their playing with their participation in the coming-of-age ceremony Ohero:kon (under the husk).

Sovereignty and reclamation are unevenly recognized by the international lacrosse community. For example, when the men's Iroquois Nationals were not invited to play in the 2022 World Games—because they were not recognized as representing a sovereign nation—over fifty thousand (mostly non-Indigenous) individuals signed a petition, helping to overturn the decision. When this posed a problem of an uneven number of teams, Ireland pulled out of the competition, making room for the originators of the game."[26]

Traditional and Medicinal Lacrosse

Traditional and *medicinal* are often used interchangeably within Haudenosaunee discussions of lacrosse. Lacrosse is present in critical locations of Haudenosaunee worldviews, such as the Creation Story and the Great Law of Peace, underscoring its cultural significance. In his chapter, "The Kayeneren:kowa (Great Way of Peace)," Mohawk scholar Brian Rice shares the narrative of a young man called the Peacemaker, who brought a message of peace and governance to the (from east to west) Mohawk, Oneida, Onondaga, Cayuga, and Seneca communities over one thousand years ago, a message that still continues today. After the five nations joined the Great Peace, the Peacemaker shared with them a message and governance structure that became known as the Great Law of Peace.[27] Rice tells of the Peacemaker scolding some boys for playing lacrosse in a way that indicated that they were preparing for war. The Peacemaker yelled to them, "Stop what you are doing! Why do you continue to play games of war? Did not anyone in the village tell you that using the Creator's game to prepare for warfare was against the will of [the Creator of human beings]?"[28] Later, when Ayenwatha (Hiawatha) becomes ill, men of his village are called in to play a lacrosse game "in order to amuse him and lift up his spirits."[29] Throughout his relaying of the Great Law of

Peace among what would later be called the Haudenosaunee Confederacy, Rice reminds the reader of the profound cultural and cosmological importance of lacrosse to the Haudenosaunee.

Lacrosse as it sits in the Haudenosaunee Creation Story and the Great Law of Peace is simultaneously traditional in the ways it holds and reflects culture for future generations, as well as medicinal in its function for Haudenosaunee people as a ceremony. Today, Haudenosaunee men play the medicine game of lacrosse during ceremony and when there is a specific call for healing. It is a ceremony that starts when a woman throws the ball and is played by men for the benefit of specific community members who may need the healing ceremony, as well as for the community's general well-being. In his book *Creator's Game: Lacrosse, Identity, and Indigenous Nationhood* (2018), Allan Downey (Dakelh) engages perspectives from Haudenosaunee community members to craft understandings of how lacrosse functions as medicine. Through oral history, Downey states that the lacrosse stick is an important location of medicine within the game of lacrosse for the Haudenosaunee. Drawing from an interview with Rick Hill (Tuscarora), Downey offers: "From a Hodinöhsö:ni' [Haudenosaunee] Longhouse perspective, the lacrosse stick was, and continues to be, more than just a piece of sports equipment; rather, it is alive and is a form of medicine that allows the game to heal, whether for an individual, a community or a nation."[30]

Lacrosse and Sovereignty

It is essential to name some of the colonial limits and prohibitions that have interfered with Haudenosaunee people playing their game of lacrosse and to distinguish these colonizing factors from Haudenosaunee cultural protocols regarding lacrosse. I outline colonizing limits and prohibitions here so that when I talk about Haudenosaunee cultural protocols that appear only to limit and prohibit, we know, first, that I am working to not conflate these cultural protocols with colonizing limits, but also, that I am not leaving specific cultural protocols alone. The cultural protocols that were shared with me—such as the protocol that women are not to touch a man's lacrosse stick—importantly contribute to the conversation. The colonizing limits and prohibitions discussed below—the one-hundred-year ban on men playing internationally, imposed requirements to be part of leagues, and issues with Haudenosaunee passports—are meant to give a greater understanding about how and why lacrosse functions as a vehicle for sovereignty in Haudenosaunee communities.

The 1980s mark a pivotal moment when Haudenosaunee communities claimed lacrosse as a location of sovereignty amidst a history of assimilationist policies in the United States and Canada against Indigenous peoples. The Iroquois Nationals men's team formed just four years before the ILF lifted restrictions on Haudenosaunee teams playing lacrosse internationally. In 1880, the NALA of Canada banned all professional teams from membership, targeting Haudenosaunee teams. Up until that point, Haudenosaunee men's teams from both sides of the U.S./Canadian border had played in international and regional exhibitions, such as in England, New York City, and Boston. Often these exhibitions charged an entrance fee for observers, some of which would go toward Haudenosaunee teams' travel. This was interpreted as the players taking money for playing, during a time when distinctions were being made between amateur and professional play by umbrella sports associations. Haudenosaunee teams were also outstanding, often defeating opposing all-white teams while playing with fewer players and a far smaller pool of players from which to draw.[31] Individual Haudenosaunee men continued to play on both U.S. and Canadian teams after their expulsion from NALA, but it wasn't until 1987 that the ILF accepted the Iroquois Nationals men's team as a member, the first sports' governing body to recognize Haudenosaunee national sovereignty.[32]

Through their use of Haudenosaunee passports, both the Iroquois Nationals men's team and the Haudenosaunee women's U19 teams exert international sovereignty. The Haudenosaunee Confederacy first issued their own passports in 1923 and continue to push for the recognition of their international sovereignty.[33] In 2010, England denied the Iroquois Nationals men's team from flying on Haudenosaunee passports for fear that the United States and Canada would not let them return. Secretary of State Hillary Clinton offered the team, coaches, and managers expedited U.S. passports (for those on the team within U.S. borders). In collaboration with Haudenosaunee communities and leadership, the team declined the passports that would reflect forced U.S. citizenship and did not play.[34]

Haudenosaunee community support of the 2015 WILC held at the Onondaga Nation, just three months after the Haudenosaunee women's U19 team could not fly to the UK on Haudenosaunee passports, demonstrates a position for sovereignty through lacrosse. I asked Onondaga midwife and Elder Jeanne Shenandoah what that was like:

It was nice in the fact that [thirteen] different countries came here, and we stamped their passport. Because we have our own passport, you know? And England who had given our teams so much trouble a couple years previous—that was a whole political wrangle.... They were not able to go, and when they came here, England was the first country to show up to get their passports [pantomimes stamping]. And I know it because I stamped them.[35]

A similar moment happened in 2015 with the U19 women's team as they prepared to travel to Scotland, discussed more in chapter 4.

World Lacrosse, which oversees WILC as well as both men's and women's international lacrosse championships, has strict codes regarding the kind of arena that must be available for the host nation. When the Onondaga Nation won the bid, they needed to build a new arena, which they did in just five months.[36] It is not the first time the Onondaga Nation has had to do this, reflecting another limit that Haudenosaunee teams run up against when trying to compete in their sport. Jeanne Shenandoah elaborates:

> We have this arena next door. The story about that is, we have an outdoor lacrosse box. Lacrosse was an outdoor game, down on the other road. Well, people started complaining about having to play outside. That's the honest truth. Started complaining, said it was dirty, blah, blah, blah. They called it the dust bowl. So, the league that we were in, without our consultation, passed a rule that you must have an arena. All ages of our people here, from five years old, you know six, begin playing, right up to elderly men. So, this league changed the rules. We had to go way over in Camillus and rent an arena for our games because they would not play in the dirt. Is the dirt that bad when you're playing a traditional game that gives thanksgiving for Mother Earth? And your feet are on the ground. They wanted an arena, so we built an arena.[37]

Amid these restrictions, prohibitions, and limits, Haudenosaunee peoples continue to play their game. In relationship to contemporary lacrosse, I begin with the moment in the 1980s when the Onondaga Clan Mothers asked the newly formed Iroquois Nationals women's team not to play in their territory. Against the backdrop of this moment is a long history of Haudenosaunee men fighting to play their game within the colonial contest over sovereignty. The chapters reflect a Haudenosaunee cultural theory as it relates to women's lacrosse by centering the voices of Haudenosaunee women lacrosse players and community members. These community members range from holding traditional teaching that only men play lacrosse to an evolving understanding of Haudenosaunee tradition that can come to hold space for women playing.

Defining Haudenosaunee Women's Lacrosse

Haudenosaunee women lacrosse players I interviewed struggle to name what exactly lacrosse means in their lives. Some women speak with ease about the historically Indigenous game, giving details about its scope and significance within their nations. They clearly articulate the importance of the game to their culture and communities and do not dispute that the medicine game, played both historically and today, is played only by men for the whole of the community. My observation is that the articulations become more uncertain when they try to explain the significance of playing lacrosse to their own lives, to their healing and connection to culture.

Often, Haudenosaunee women who play lacrosse play or have played a variety of other sports as well. For the women who work to give language to its meaning, lacrosse sits somewhere between being more than a just a sport and not precisely a medicine game—but certainly incredibly meaningful in their lives for how it connects them to their culture and is part of their healing. Haudenosaunee women claim lacrosse against a background that works to exclude them both as players and as producers of meaning around its cultural significance.

Haudenosaunee women claim lacrosse as their own while recalling its roots to their Creation Story and how the game is played as a medicine game, only by men. None of the women lacrosse players or their supporters whom I interviewed refute that only Haudenosaunee men play the medicine game. Haudenosaunee women who claim lacrosse as their sport are part of Haudenosaunee communities who have been claiming lacrosse as their own with fervor and conviction as the game has grown like wildfire in North America and across the globe since the 1970s for both men and women. This book addresses what it means for Haudenosaunee women to claim lacrosse as their game, drawing to the surface how Haudenosaunee women experience lacrosse as more than just a sport, playing it as a way of claiming their Haudenosaunee identity.

Representing Haudenosaunee Women Lacrosse Players

Around the time that Haudenosaunee women's lacrosse was gaining attention, Aimee Berg's article "Lacrosse: Cradle of a Sport Has Crossed the Gender Line" gave a brief account of the moment in 1987 when "the Onondaga Clan Mothers threatened to lie down on the field in protest." Berg tells a story of young women who are caught in the struggle between tradition and opportunity, placing "crossing a gender line," alongside the binary of tradition and opportunity, and opposition to Clan Mothers.[38] This framing of the conversation as controversy recasts the characters in this narrative onto certain western feminist "bad guys" (the patriarchy).

Pitting Clan Mothers and the lacrosse players against each other casts Clan Mothers as the traditional western patriarchy, thus holding young women back and keeping them firmly on their side of the gender line. Berg views young women playing as a victory along these western feminist lines. At the same time, this representation omits the power that western feminisms acknowledge Haudenosaunee women have had traditionally and historically. This omission points to the importance of the work of Sally Roesch Wagner and others in establishing Haudenosaunee influence on western feminism. Berg's representation as a controversy hides more than it reveals, squeezing how a few Haudenosaunee women lacrosse players feel about some Clan Mothers' protective responses to them into a western feminist framework of the "old guard" or tradition holding them back from "progress."

Such monolithic representations of Haudenosaunee women reflect a historical, cultural propensity in the west to erase the complicated lives and relationships of Indigenous women to their communities while ignoring Indigenous national sovereignty.[39] From Berg's perspective, Haudenosaunee women playing lacrosse puts them on track with women from all over the world who are also playing. Effectively, they now have the potential to catch up in the realm of progress and opportunity. Berg's representation falls in line with dominant representations of Indigenous people within settler nation-states, as being primitive and anachronistic, while hiding the paradox of western feminist fascination with Haudenosaunee women's power. The error of simplicity in this representation is that it misses the diversity of thought among Clan Mothers. The representation also misses the ways that Haudenosaunee women lacrosse players hold in high regard those who came before them to share cultural teachings.

This representation does not accurately or adequately depict this conversation or how lacrosse creates meaning within communities, thus erasing the interdependence that generations have on one another to hold and perpetuate culture. Throughout this project, I demonstrate how this internal shifting conversation over women playing lacrosse further embeds lacrosse into Haudenosaunee communities at a time when there is a risk of the Haudenosaunee roots of lacrosse being swallowed up in the international growth and fervor around the sport.

Uses of "Rematriation"

That there are matrilineal and matrifocal Indigenous societies all over the world, who have survived through countless colonial attacks, speaks to a deeper understanding of their being grounded in Natural Law. There is nothing "natural" about patriarchal law, as it is borrowed (stolen). Khoe-San scholar Bernedette Muthien, from Southern Africa, names this:

> Rematriation is rooted in contemporary reality and can no longer be considered utopian, since the number of gender egalitarian and/or matricentric societies that still exist today, despite centuries of patriarchal encroachments and colonization, remain a powerful testimony to the values of ancient sacred mother-centered and women-centered spiritual communities, across all continents: from the Akan of Ghana and Khoe-San of Southern Africa, to the Minangkabau of Indonesia; from the Mosuo and Lahu of China to the Khasi and Nair of India; from the Iroquois of North American and the Kuna of Panama, to the Saami of Scandinavia.[40]

Rematriation shows up in the British school of psychoanalysis in relationship to the psychology of creativity.[41] Bernedette Muthien credits the term to Mohawk/Blackfoot poet Susan Deer Cloud.[42] Barbara Alice Mann also credits Deer Cloud in her short discussion of "Rematriation of the Truth."[43] Executive director of the Indigenous Law Institute Steven Newcomb (Shawnee/Lenape) asks, "what term do we use to refer to the 'home countries' that are themselves, in many cases, now being 'held captive' by the United States?" He turns away from the term "repatriation," and to "rematriation" to hold "culturally essential places [such] as Mt. Graham, the Black Hills, the Wallowa Valley, Lyle Point, the lands of the Havasupai, the

Western Shoshone lands, and many others."[44] Eve Tuck (Unangax̂, Aleut) began using rematriation in 2011 in relationship to curriculum, describing it as "the work of community members and scholars in curriculum studies who directly address the complicity of curriculum in the maintenance of settler colonialism."[45]

Rematriation as a Framework for This Project

To discuss rematriation as a framework for this project, it is important to name the cultural starting place. Since rematriation is heavily imbued with an impetus to *returning*, it is critical to name that which is being returned to. Michelle Schenandoah's foreword names the starting place for this book by invoking Haudenosaunee lifegiving. Paraphrasing and quoting Schenandoah here serves as an important reminder of the context that invokes rematriation. A non-Haudenosaunee reader might struggle with the fact of women's power and crave more of an understanding. "A small, helpful explanation is that this power is related to the lifegiving energy of Mother Earth that flows through all women who are lifegivers." Schenandoah describes the dance where women are honored for this gift by the men who sing for them. As the men sing, "women caress the earth with our feet, reaffirming this lifegiving energy that we hold between us to bring life to this world. This is the same dance that Sky Woman did on the Turtle's back and made the land grow. She danced, and the earth grew."[46] Rematriation has been in use by Haudenosaunee communities "for quite some time."[47] Schenandoah, (Oneida, Wolf Clan) founder of the nonprofit organization Rematriation (formerly *Rematriation Magazine*), dedicated to uplifting the movement of rematriation, shares that Haudenosaunee midwife Katsi Cook began using it in the 1970s to describe the indigenizing act of reuniting placenta with the earth after a child is born. Schenandoah, in collaboration with Mommabear and wanting to ensure that the word makes its way into the dictionary, created a definition of the concept of rematriation as "returning the sacred to the mother."[48] Schenandoah nuanced this definition during a conversation I had with her:

> The mother gives us all this life—we get our food, we get our water, our breath, from the mother. And so, when we understand that sacred relationship—to me when I say returning the sacred to the mother, I actually don't think of humans first. I think

of our mother earth. Rematriation is a process in which all humans participate, including men, who are to uphold and project the sacred that gives us life.[49]

At the 2019 "Indigenizing Spaces: Rematriating Leadership and Land" symposium at South Dakota State University, Akwesasne Mohawk Clan Mother Mommabear credited Katsi Cook with the following definition: "Rematriation describes the process of returning sacred human and biological remains, production of women's bodies, including breast milk, ovum, and other genetic materials to their place of origin."[50] I engage these articulations of rematriation in this project for how they speak to the relationship between Haudenosaunee women's corporeal integrity, and the ancestral land that longs for their return and continuous connection to cultural knowledge.

Meanwhile, Haudenosaunee communities are more clearly defining "medicinal" and "traditional" lacrosse because of the growth of Haudenosaunee women playing lacrosse since the 1980s. Where the professional-amateur debates excluded women, Haudenosaunee women playing contemporary lacrosse further roots—rematriates—the discussion of lacrosse within the community. It is because of their playing that communities work to more clearly and carefully define the boundaries that define medicinal, traditional, and contemporary lacrosse. As I will demonstrate throughout, rematriation is at the heart of Haudenosaunee lacrosse.

These articulations connect to larger conversations within Haudenosaunee communities regarding the power that women hold and rematriation of that power, a concept woven throughout the project. Mommabear defines rematriation as the returning of the sacred to the mother, or the return to mother-law.[51] For a matrilineal society, Mommabear and others such as Michelle Schenandoah, Jonel Beauvais (Akwesasne Mohawk, Wolf Clan), and Chelsea Sunday (Akwesasne Mohawk, Turtle Clan) call for a rematriation of the power that goes along with being matrilineal, rather than in name only.

In chapter 1, I discuss rematriation in connection to violence against Indigenous women, and how rematriation is engaging Haudenosaunee cultural skills toward healing. I position the incongruity over Haudenosaunee women and girls playing lacrosse within a contemporary reality whereby Indigenous women and girls are particularly affected by social ills within settler national space. To do this, I center Mommabear's reflections that Haudenosaunee women have two choices: to fall prey to a great many social ills, or to participate in the best that Haudenosaunee culture has to offer, including lacrosse. Chapter 1 demonstrates how the social ills that befall Haudenosaunee women at a disproportionate rate from other groups of women are not the end of the story. Lacrosse is rematriation in motion, not just for Haudenosaunee men and communities, but particularly as coming from Haudenosaunee women playing. I do not probe why only men play the medicine game both historically and contemporarily, mainly because everyone I interviewed agrees that only men should play the medicine game. The discord lies in girls and women playing contemporary lacrosse, played with plastic sticks. Mommabear explained to me that what makes the wooden stick sacred is that it is made from a tree. It is a relative, where plastic sticks are manufactured and are not a direct resource from the earth. However, because of the significance of the lacrosse stick for the medicine game, Haudenosaunee communities discuss whether even, in some cases, the plastic stick is equipment Haudenosaunee women should not touch.

In chapter 2, I discuss rematriation in relationship to the concept of "traditional," and how western patriarchy has influenced Haudenosaunee conceptions and meanings of tradition. This chapter focuses on why there are divergent viewpoints, what different views say about definitions of "traditional," and the connections of these perspectives to colonization. I examine my observations of how Haudenosaunee community members sometimes talk about the historical game and traditional lacrosse interchangeably and how that might lead to understandings of tradition that are relegated to the past. When those within Haudenosaunee communities harken to a definition of traditional lacrosse that centers the past, they compromise the political and future-oriented potential of tradition. Chapter 2 works to distinguish between historical and traditional lacrosse. I examine questions about whether girls and women are playing the traditional game of lacrosse while demonstrating how their playing at all encourages their communities to define traditional anew. Haudenosaunee women and girls playing calls for an articulation of the distinctions between historical and traditional lacrosse to define the future potential of tradition and rematriation. Chapter 2 is centrally concerned with how Haudenosaunee communities claim lacrosse as their own; how historical, traditional, medicinal, and contemporary lacrosse are being defined; the overlaps and distinctions therein; and how women and girls playing informs these discussions.

In chapter 3, I engage rematriation through discussions of gender construction and illuminate the way the prohibition around women touching a man's lacrosse stick is intended to function as a way of preserving gender balance and ceremonial space. When Haudenosaunee community members invoke the protocol, they often follow it with an explanation that it is because women hold power on account of of their ability to give birth and have a moontime. In this chapter, I look at the ways in which gender balance has been misinterpreted, positioning the protocol as a source of oppression rather than a reflection of balance. I also examine how Haudenosaunee women's power has been romanticized and firmly placed in the past by western feminists. Finally, I look at how the protocol works to name and claim lacrosse as a contemporary medicinal ceremony, profoundly connecting lacrosse within Haudenosaunee culture. In chapter 3, I analyze gender balance within Haudenosaunee communities both as a prescriptive solution to incomplete or misrepresented traditional Haudenosaunee gender constructs as well as to tease out how both Haudenosaunee and non-Indigenous romanticized representations further limit the potential power of balance.

Finally, chapter 4 theorizes lacrosse as a rematriating project, this time looking at the way Haudenosaunee women enact sovereignty through the game. The Haudenosaunee are claiming lacrosse as a way of claiming a distinct Indigenous identity and as a way of claiming sovereign national space. In chapter 4 I develop the theoretical and analytical category of embodied sovereignty through essential narratives by and about Haudenosaunee women who travel through space to play the game and carry with them their nationhood and connection to communities. I attend to the various ways embodied sovereignty travels, carries homeland, and claims sovereignty, disrupting and decolonizing western spaces through the action of the body, in part, because of the space the body occupies.

In this book, I have observed how the internal conversation regarding Haudenosaunee women playing lacrosse has rematriation at its center, and more deeply roots lacrosse as a Haudenosaunee sport both within and outside of Haudenosaunee communities. As we move into chapter 1, I juxtapose the narrative of Haudenosaunee women's power with the contemporary lived violence that Indigenous women face both from outside and within their communities. Often this gross disparity is met with denial and omission as historical renderings of matrilineal power are used as a discursive mask for maintaining the colonial status quo at the expense of the women they report to be influential and respected.[52] The theoretical and methodological emphasis on the voices of Haudenosaunee women works to shed much-needed light on their contemporary lived reality. This project then is grounded in the ongoing rematriation of Haudenosaunee cultures, as evidenced by ceremonies such as Ohero:kon discussed throughout the book.

CHAPTER ONE

HAUDENOSAUNEE WOMEN LACROSSE PLAYERS AND HEALING

By the time I interviewed Mommabear for the first time I had already spoken to many Haudenosaunee women lacrosse players who struggled to articulate just how important lacrosse is in their lives, how it connects them to their culture, and what that means in their communities. During our first conversation at a diner in the Akwesasne Mohawk Nation, Mommabear narrated her own process of embracing the daughters and granddaughters of her nation playing lacrosse. Before Mommabear and I officially began our interview, she met my young daughter. Toward the end of our time together, she asked me, "You as a mother want what's best for your daughter, right?"

"Absolutely. I get that," I replied.

"And I want the best for my daughter. And I want the best of what our culture has to offer her." She continued,

1

Would you choose to have your daughter be trapped in silence, being abused by an abuser, caught up in an addiction, be incarcerated, be caught up in the social ills of our [communities], or would you have her be participating in something that makes her feel good about herself, so that she is driven and determined to be greater than she is? That's the choice.[1]

The choice she names, of course, is no choice at all. Taking something that is so healing—lacrosse—away from Haudenosaunee girls and women, when their bodies are systematically disenfranchised by settler nation-states, is not an option. In settler logic, Indigenous women pose a specific threat to colonial projects and the settler state's ongoing desire for land. Mommabear's words provide the basis for this chapter on Haudenosaunee lacrosse and healing, as Haudenosaunee women play their cultural game on their ancestral lands, disrupting settler colonialism.

As a Clan Mother, Mommabear speaks directly to her Haudenosaunee community when she articulates the unambiguous question, "Would you choose to have your daughter be trapped in silence, being abused by an abuser?" Her question speaks to Haudenosaunee communities that know all too well the risks and dangers that Haudenosaunee girls and women face in settler society and is rooted in the cultural knowledge that Haudenosaunee women historically have represented the law of the land in their communities. That she asks me, a non-Haudenosaunee person, this question invites all of us into a deeper consideration of how settler society has positioned Indigenous women in relationship to land because of this connection to land.

When Mommabear names these choices for Haudenosaunee women, she is saying several things at once. She is invoking the memory and current reality of how colonization and settler nation-states limit Haudenosaunee women's choices regarding traditional identity, community connection, and the integrity of their bodies and the disasters that result. Simultaneously, she bursts open what is possible for Haudenosaunee women through the game of lacrosse. Her statement is as expansive as the fields on which young women play, the colleges and universities they attend to do so, the miles they cover to play, sometimes crossing continents, and the choices they make on behalf of their daughters, mothers, and communities. Mommabear's statement simply and directly demonstrates what is at stake for Haudenosaunee women, and Indigenous women more generally. It also demonstrates that the effects of colonization are not the end of the story for Haudenosaunee women.

This chapter examines two intimately connected realities of Haudenosaunee women: the specific ways in which settler nation-states continue to colonize Indigenous women's bodies, and the healing potential of crucial Haudenosaunee cultural components, specifically lacrosse, drawn from Haudenosaunee worldviews and lifeways. Whereas the social ills that Indigenous women face are firmly rooted in the logics of settler colonialism, solutions are embedded within Haudenosaunee cultural structures as found in the Creation Story, clan system, and ceremonies. Within a context of settler colonialism that systematically dispossesses Indigenous women's bodies, lacrosse emerges as deep healing for Haudenosaunee women, rematriating land and bodies. I follow Mommabear's lead by pointing out how Haudenosaunee worldviews and lifeways, found in the Haudenosaunee Creation Story and ceremonies such as lacrosse and the coming-of-age ceremony Ohero:kon, hold ancestral knowledge of how to address the social ills that Haudenosaunee women face. By engaging Haudenosaunee knowledge keepers, scholars, poetry and fiction written by Indigenous women, and lacrosse players, I demonstrate how lacrosse is connected to Haudenosaunee ceremony and cultural wisdom. Through lacrosse, Haudenosaunee women disrupt layers of colonization by engaging in their history and tradition on the land that belongs to them and in international spaces where they represent their nationhood. Haudenosaunee women who play contemporary lacrosse defy the settler nation-state by healing their bodies and disrupting colonial landscapes, restoring the Haudenosaunee worldviews and relationships to land. Thus, playing lacrosse becomes a process of rematriation.

Gender Balance and Rematriation

To describe how balance functions within an Indigenous worldview, I turn to Mark Freeland's (Anishinaabe) analysis in *Aazheyaadizi: Worldview, Language, and the Logics of Decolonization* (2021). A logic of balance and a web of relatedness are central to an Indigenous worldview. One location where worldview is articulated is in creation narratives. Looking at Indigenous creation narratives, we can see how balance and relatedness are central to the narrative and shape worldview and lifeways. In the Lakota Creation Story, when humans emerge from Wind Cave in the Black Hills, it is their older siblings, the buffalo, who help them to survive.[2] In the creation narratives of the Algonquian and Haudenosaunee peoples, it is the birds and water animals and turtle's back that save Sky Woman's life as she falls from Sky World, and later gives birth, leading to one of her grandsons who will create human beings. This understanding of humans' placement in relationship to all other animals differs from the Judeo-Christian creation narrative whereby a hierarchy is established in the two versions of the narrative in Genesis. In Genesis 1, the deity tasks humans with dominion over the natural world. In Genesis 2, the woman is created from the man. Indigenous creation narratives establish a web of relatedness among all the animals—including humans. The Judeo-Christian creation narrative establishes a hierarchy with humans closest to the deity.

Creation narratives structure the shape of society. A primary difference between Indigenous creation narratives and the Judeo-Christian creation narrative is between a web of relatedness and a hierarchy. In the web of relatedness if one strand is pulled too tightly, the rest become distorted. In other words, if one part of the web gains too much power, the rest suffer. In a hierarchy, imbalanced power is normalized and expected. Consider gender in relationship to how creation narratives shape society. In a hierarchy, one gender being above another would be naturalized. Western feminism works diligently to dislocate what has been naturalized, gendered hierarchy. Within an Indigenous worldview, one part of the web having too much power weighs down the system by throwing it out of balance. Restoring balance becomes the priority, while mitigating the pervasive power and ubiquity of the present western hierarchy.

Freeland moves away from the tired religious concepts that pervade cultural theory surrounding Indigenous communities, and instead turns to scientific concepts. Like homeostasis, the dynamic process of restoring and keeping balance is "a complex system regulating itself towards the goal (or goals) of equilibrium."[3] Furthermore, Freeland articulates gender as a web of relatedness, rather than a scaled binary.[4] This understanding of gender is expansive and inclusive. Indigenous gender balance is but one goal of Indigenous logics of balance. This logic of balance also applies to how communities engage with animal and plant relatives (how much to harvest and hunt, for example). Additionally, a logic of balance includes the balancing of life and death, Freeland stating, "Balance is achieved through having life and death alternating. Life and death balance each other out in the yearly cycle of birth, growth, senescence, purity, and rebirth. The cycle is balanced by having both life and death built into it."[5] An excess of death is reflected in taking more than what is needed (greed), taking without reflection (selfishness), and structures that are too male (patriarchy). A turn toward the female (in a complex gender structure) is a move toward balance.

Haudenosaunee communities' desire to maintain balance drives an understanding of why only men play the medicine game of lacrosse. As a purveyor of cultural knowledge, Mommabear provides the context of the medicine game:

> When you actually take it to a ritual space, that's when the women overpower the ritual. And because in our culture men deal with death and women deal with life, that's the reason why the game is played, to deal with grief, to settle disputes, to bring medicine to somebody who is sick. It's the mental health and wellness in our community, so men are supposed to take care of that. It's their job. It's their responsibility. And we have a rightful part in it, but it's they who carry the burden of it.[6]

Here, Mommabear gives an understanding of why the community agrees only men play the medicine game. Mommabear does, however, open space to consider the death that colonization has imposed upon Haudenosaunee women's and girls' bodies and how their playing lacrosse, while not *the* medicine game, is *a* medicine to heal themselves.

Haudenosaunee enjoyed complex political, social, and economic systems long before the advent of the settler nation-states of the United States and Canada. Rematriation describes a process whereby Haudenosaunee women rediscover their connection to or reinforce their relationship with their culture and lands, restoring the balance that settler colonialism disrupts. Michelle Schenandoah places lacrosse as a connection to culture such as planting traditional foods, claiming land and planting seeds, and home birthing.[7] When Haudenosaunee women play lacrosse, they change the narrative of colonization with their bodies. When Haudenosaunee women traverse the globe to play their sport, they carry their land and their narratives with them. Haudenosaunee women, as coming from a matrifocal society in a patriarchal world, are uniquely and importantly positioned to share these narratives and shifts at a communal and global level.

Through colonization, specifically settler colonialism, nation-states were imposed onto Turtle Island, which, imbued with an ideology that all citizens are members of the same community, worked to erase and eliminate Indigeneity and absorb racial and ethnic differences within a multicultural understanding of diversity.[8] The "state" is defined both by its formal institutions (e.g., courts, central banks, schools) and by civil society (e.g., home, social interactions and relations, and volunteerism). Formal institutions act upon civil society, together creating a complex system that perpetuates the colonial project. Nevertheless, cultural theorists Daiva Stasiulis and Nira Yuval-Davis demonstrate how settler colonialism is never absolute:

> This is important because while agents both of the state and from within civil society may engage in regulation, coercion and control of populations within (and entering) a given territory, it is usually the state which generally has legitimate authority to exercise control over such matters. However, in many societies, especially in settler and developing [sic] societies, the state cannot penetrate effectively certain social and ethnic enclaves, and other, customary systems of control have retained their legitimacy.[9]

In other words, settler nation-states create colonial realities for Indigenous peoples but never absolutely. Haudenosaunee communities continually find ways to retain their worldviews and lifeways. Haudenosaunee women demonstrate healing on their land, even in "settled" spaces.

Settler nation-states perpetuate a colonized reality on stolen land. Legislative measures such as the Indian Act, which defines who is legally considered Indigenous in Canada, impose the patriarchal nuclear family and dispossess Indigenous women of their Indigenous status. Legal loopholes create a vacuum of justice for sexual and other violent crimes against Indigenous women, suppressing Haudenosaunee worldviews and lifeways. Such measures illustrate the settler nation-state's ongoing anxiety about Indigenous women's relationship to land and therefore the need to control their bodies in order to dispossess Indigenous peoples of their land. Settler nation-states cannot function without land, and Indigenous women are deeply connected to that land. Indigenous women must, therefore, be disenfranchised, silenced, and dispossessed. The result is an ongoing and systemic attack on Indigenous women's bodies that results in missing and murdered women, the imposition of western patriarchy in Indigenous communities, and the intergenerational trauma created by residential (boarding) schools. Mohawk scholar Audra Simpson and Muscogee Creek scholar Sarah Deer critique the use of terms such as "phenomenon" or "epidemic" to describe this violence against Indigenous women, arguing instead that the apparatus of the nation-state is historically and contemporarily set up precisely for the sustained and systematic success of said violence.

The prevalence of missing and murdered Indigenous women in the United States and Canada is not a surprise to Haudenosaunee people but is "explained by . . . dispossession of Indian people from land." Audra Simpson eloquently articulates the relationship between land and Indigenous women's bodies in the settler-colonial imagination:

> Indian women "disappear" because they have been deemed killable, able to be raped without repercussion, expendable. Their bodies have *historically* been rendered less valuable because of what they are taken to represent: land, reproduction, Indigenous kinship and governance, an alternative to heteronormative and Victorian rules of descent. Theirs are bodies that carry a symbolic load because they have been conflated with land and are thus contaminating to a white, settler social order.[10]

Simpson reveals the severe tensions between a settler nation-state that renders land and women's bodies invaluable while doing all it can to subjugate both to its own desires. Simpson unmasks the word "settled" in reference to settler society, meaning, "done," "finished," "complete." As Simpson contends, "This is the presumption that the colonial project has been realized: land dispossessed; its owners eliminated or absorbed."[11] Rather, Simpson contends, settler anxiety remains over that which has not been settled, what is undone, unfinished, incomplete. Indigenous women bear the brunt of this anxiety on their whole beings, and the sovereignty that Haudenosaunee women embody is particularly threatening to the ongoing project of colonization, which masks Haudenosaunee land as settled.[12]

Colonial Tactics and Internalized Eurowestern Patriarchy

Settler nation-states, with the systemic help of church organizations (self-proclaimed do-gooders), took measures to distort and sever Haudenosaunee women's corporeal integrity and decision-making authority in relationship to land. The imposition of the reservation/reserve system, the authority of the Bureau/Department of Indian Affairs, Indian agents, forced assimilation, and private ownership of land have all decentered women within the family and imposed a hierarchy that places men at the head, moves the home from communal and visible to private and hidden, and changes land from shared to privately owned.

Within Eurowestern patriarchy, there is a separation between the home and public life. This split began with the onset of nation-states and sovereignty from the crown in sixteenth- and seventeenth-century Europe. Women have historically been sequestered to the home space while men occupy the space of the public.[13] This split does not translate onto Haudenosaunee communities where the space of the home is both public and private. Activities associated with the home, like raising children and cooking and growing food, have been understood in Eurowestern thought as less than, but this is not the case in Haudenosaunee communities. These are activities of power within the realm of lifegiving force. However, the impositions of a Eurowestern public/private split and the nuclear family, plus the devastation that resulted when children were removed from their communities and sent to residential schools, led to domestic violence and addiction issues in Haudenosaunee communities. Mohawk scholar and mother of a Haudenosaunee woman lacrosse player Dawn Martin-Hill explains in an interview:

> Traditionally, in my Nation, the Haudenosaunee women did not "stay home alone with children." They worked in the fields harvesting and preparing foods and clothing.
>   Children were raised by the mother's clan (her extended matrilineal family), usually by the Elder women. The mother's brothers were also responsible for rearing the children, and her husband was expected to maintain his role and responsibilities with his mother's clan and in rearing his sister's children. *This left little room for spousal or child abuse, since young families were never left in isolation.* . . . *That is the western tradition, and it is based on the nuclear family, which isolates the mother from her extended family and leaves her and her children vulnerable to her husband's authority.*[14]

This reordering of the space of home, moving from communal (visible) to private (hidden), was accompanied by Eurowestern hierarchical organizations of gender that disrupted Indigenous gender balance, including for the Haudenosaunee. When land went from shared to owned, Haudenosaunee men internalized a gender hierarchy that made them the heads of households. Outside the purview of the community, in the private home, under state-sanctioned marriage, violence bred, just as in Eurowestern patriarchal systems where women could be legally beaten and raped within marriage.

But, according to colonial logic, Haudenosaunee communities had moved "from 'primitive' matrilineal to 'civilized' patrilineal law."[15] For example, at a 1917 meeting of the Associated Executive Committee of Friends on Indian Affairs, Rayner Wickersham Kelsey reported that in 1796 three Friends (Quakers) had "settled among [the Oneida Nation] and began the experiment of teaching them the ways of civilized life.... Premiums were offered with good effect to excite competition among the Indian men in the raising of crops and among the women for the weaving of woolen cloth."[16] Kelsey described the "success" of this mission:

> Spinning, weaving, knitting, cooking and general house work were the arts taught to the Indian women. Thomazine Valentine was one of the most devoted of the women Friends engaged in this work and one of her letters of 1866 portrays the progress that had been made at that period: "I have felt comforted in visiting the Indians this time, and feel there is cause of thankfulness, that the Lord has opened the hearts of the Indian women so generally to attend to what has been told them in regard to keeping better houses, and not taking offense." ... Speaking of the progress of her people in agriculture [Lydia Jackson, teacher among the Indians] cites the following examples: "Thomas Jemison of Cattaraugus Reservation who raises annually a thousand bushels of wheat, John Mt. Pleasant of Tuscarora Reservation who raised last year fifteen hundred bushels of oats and sixteen hundred bushels of wheat ... he has a beautiful farm of two hundred acres. ... His wife who is a Seneca woman keeps the house neat and in order."[17]

In short, farming was for men, the home was the domain of women, and the home was private. For Michelle Schenandoah this "success" "was an introduction of patriarchy into a very ancient matrilineal system that I don't think needed any fussing with."[18] In this Quaker mission, the deep, ancestral connection that Haudenosaunee women held with the land had been disrupted by the imposition of Eurowestern agriculture and the gendering that came with it. Schenandoah further explained to the fall 2018 sessions of the New York Meeting of the Religious Society of Friends (Quakers) that

> because of all of this land loss there was a desire to help our men to learn a new lifeway, and agriculture was what the Quakers felt would be important for our men to learn. But that was the domain of the women, and it always had been because the land is a woman and the connection to land goes all the way back to that

Creation Story ... when [Sky Woman] danced on the turtle's back. Our women still do that today.[19]

For Haudenosaunee community members on the Canadian side of the (imposed) border, a male head-of-household model was imposed through the Gradual Enfranchisement Act (1869) and solidified through the Indian Act of 1876. Again, the Indian Act defines who is legally an Indigenous person in Canada; through this act, "status Indians" (those identified as First Nations individuals by the act) and their land became the legal responsibility of the Canadian government. The government regulated their lives by legislating who was considered Indigenous, who could live on reserves (solidified through the British North America Act, 1867), how they educated their children, and how they handled their estates. Status Indians were defined as "any male person of Indian blood reputed to belong to a particular band ... any child of such person ... any woman who is or was lawfully married to such person." A person lost status if they became a Christian minister, doctor, or lawyer, graduated university, or—if they were a woman—married a nonstatus person. In 1951 the Indian Act was amended and further solidified the patriarchal structure of gaining status by adding that any status woman who married a status man was no longer a member of her own band, her band membership tied instead to her husband's. Furthermore, a status woman lost her status if she was widowed, divorced, or was abandoned by her husband. First Nations men who married non-Indigenous women, however, did not lose their status, nor did their children.[20] Bill C-31 (1985) allowed for women who had lost their status to regain it, but not their children.[21] For Audra Simpson, the Indian Act has always been about decreasing the land base, resources, and identity of First Nations people in Canada.[22]

Through these and similar colonial impositions, Indigenous communities internalized Eurowestern patriarchy in ways that extended to the broader community. Cultural theorist Luana Ross (Salish and Kootenai) argues that "the consolidation of male power within tribal councils and communities has created a situation within tribes that fosters the disregard and perpetuation of sexual violence against Native women."[23] In her article, "She No Speaks: And Other Colonial Constructs of 'The Traditional Woman,'" Dawn Martin-Hill describes how male leadership addressed a perpetrator of rape by bringing him to the sweat lodge. When this response was questioned, the leadership said that punishment was not traditional practice, so the answer was to take him to the sweat lodge.[24] Eurowestern gender roles were even reinforced at the height of the American Indian Movement in the 1970s. Renya

Ramirez (Ho-Chunk) points to the American Indian Movement as contributing to Indigenous women's reticence toward addressing sexism in their communities for fear of usurping work toward national sovereignty, stating:

> Indigenous women were placed in subservient roles as cooks and helpers, and at times were expected to attend to the sexual needs of the male leaders of the movement. Native women were, therefore, taught that Native men should be in control. Within this sexist context, indigenous women were supposed to defend a Native nationalism that ignored their own needs to be liberated from misogyny and sexism.[25]

Through personal experience, Martin-Hill elucidates how expectations of women's subservience, reinforced during the 1970s, have carried on. While organizing an event for Elders and spiritual leaders in 1995, Martin-Hill rejected the overt sexual advances of one of the presenters only to have him admonish her publicly at the event for not having adequate organizational skills.[26] There are consequences for Haudenosaunee women who speak out against these imposed stratifications.

Intergenerational Trauma

Alongside the internalization of Eurowestern patriarchy comes the intergenerational trauma experienced by communities forced to assimilate into Euro-Christian society. Roman Catholic Bishop Vital Grandin stated about Indian boarding schools in 1875: "We instill in them a pronounced distaste for the Native life so that they will be humiliated when reminded of their origin. When they graduate from our institutions, the children have lost everything Native except their blood."[27] Boarding or residential schools used by the nation-state had devastating effects on Indigenous communities, causing intergenerational trauma. Maria Yellow Horse Brave Heart (Hunkpapa/Oglala Lakota) engages the category of intergenerational trauma to explain the effects of colonization on Lakota communities, defining it as a "cumulative emotional and psychological wounding across generations, including the lifespan, which emanates from massive group trauma."[28] In her seminal work, "Dealing with Shame and Unresolved Trauma: Residential School and Its Impact on the 2nd and 3rd Generation Adults" (2000), Rosalyn Ing (Opaskwayak Cree) identified fifteen categories of impact on subsequent generations of residential (boarding) school survivors, which includes disruption of Indigenous identity through denial and shame, poor self-esteem, family silence, difficulty communicating, expectation to be negatively judged, controlling father, experiences of racism, physical and/or sexual abuse in family, and addiction.[29] At the time of this publication, multiple Indigenous networks, organizations, scholars, and community leaders use intergenerational trauma as a way of holding nation-states accountable for a history of boarding (residential) schools and their effects.

The opening of the first boarding schools—the Mohawk Institute Residential School in Brantford, Ontario, 1831, the Yakima Indian Reservation in the state of Washington, 1861, and the Carlisle Industrial Indian School, Carlisle, Pennsylvania, 1879—was part of the official U.S. and Canadian governments' assimilation policies to *kill the Indian, save the man*.[30] In order to do this, reformers worked to destroy social practices and gender constructions and to impose Victorian patriarchal systems and norms.[31]

Between 1819 and 1969, the United States, with the help of fourteen church denominations, operated 408 boarding schools across the country, including twenty-one schools in Alaska and seven in Hawaii.[32] Between 1831 and 1996, Canada operated 140, placing around 150,000 (30 percent) of First Nations children in residential schools, where at least 6,000 children died.[33] In the 1990s, survivors of boarding schools began collectively sharing their stories. American Indian Leader Dennis Banks (Ojibwe) shared his narrative of not being allowed to return home for six years. When he did, he asked his mother why she had not written him, to which she responded that she had written him many letters. Federal records confirmed that she had indeed written many times to him and a couple of times to the school director, and even sent bus fare for him to visit home.[34] The documentary *We Were Children* (2012) painfully and powerfully depicts the experiences of malnutrition, sexual assault, and loneliness of Canadian residential school survivors Lyna Hart (Nisichawayasihk Cree Nation) and Glen Anaquod (Muscowpetung First Nation). In one sequence, the camera zooms in on a photograph of a classroom in one of these schools, revealing the forlorn faces of First Nations children and the words *thou shall not tell lies* written on the blackboard behind them. Lyna Hart says, "When I hear people who firmly believed that nothing happened in these schools, I can tell them my story; I can tell them, this is what happened."[35] Stories are in fact what drives a discussion of residential (boarding) schools.[36]

The boarding school era peaked in 1931 in Canada, and the last one closed in 1996. However, the end of boarding schools did not mean the state ceased systematically taking Indigenous children from their homes. Researcher for the Canadian Council on Social Development Patrick Johnson coined the term *Sixties Scoop* in a 1983 report to describe how Canadian child welfare services removed Indigenous children from their homes in the 1960s on the slightest pretext. A massively disproportionate number of First Nations children were taken from their homes, often with no warning, and placed in white homes. These children were not exposed to their culture in any way and were often adopted out to white families.[37] Sixties Scoop survivors won a class action suit against Canada in 2017 for $750 million. As of April 2022, 20,167 claims had been approved and 1,864 were being actively assessed.[38] Some recipients call the $25,000 in compensation a "slap in the face" considering the intergenerational trauma that ensued due to systematic cultural loss and physical and sexual abuse.[39] The United States engaged in the same systematic practice during the 1960s and into the 1970s. During this time, between 25 and 35 percent of Indigenous children were taken from their homes and placed in institutions, foster care, or adoptive homes. Ninety percent of those homes were non-Indigenous. Many of these children would never see their families again.[40]

Propaganda in news outlets and women's magazines fed governmental policies undergirding these removals. One particular advertisement from the time depicts a child being held by a white woman and the text: "Once this child's life and future was uncertain, lonely. He faced the problems of a Métis child growing up without parents to guide him. Now he lives in a home full of love, free from prejudice."[41] Thick in the space of these three sentences is a myth of the emptiness of Indigenous communities that facilitates settler colonialism— empty lands, empty kinship. During COVID-19, I attended several virtual moon lodge ceremonies, healing events led by Haudenosaunee women. Because these were virtual, women from all over Turtle Island attended. A few times during introductions, we learned that a participant had been part of this removal and was on a path to return home to Indigenous ways of knowing and being. Their pain and loss—and resiliency—were palpable. In the United States, it was not until 1978 with the Indian Child Welfare Act (ICWA) that American Indian parents gained the legal right to deny their children's placement in off-reservation/reserve schools. ICWA safeguards against Indigenous children in the foster-care system being placed in non-Indigenous homes.[42] Even with ICWA, however, Indigenous children are not fully protected. Like the American Indian Freedom of Religion Act passed in 1978, it is legislation that is difficult to enforce and hard to hold people and organizations accountable when it is violated.

Haudenosaunee Daughters: Silence and Abuse

My first introduction to the violence that Indigenous women face in settler societies was through their printed words. It is the ways that Indigenous women have spoken into the silence of violence to their bodies with fiction, short stories, essays, and poetry that I hope to capture here.

In her poem "To the Spirit of Monahsetah," Charlotte DeClue (Osage) pays reverence to Monahsetah, the daughter of Cheyenne Chief Little Rock. Monahsetah (1850–1922) and fifty-two other women and children were taken by the U.S. Seventh Cavalry under General Custer's command after her father was killed in the Battle of Washita River. DeClue brings together generations of Indigenous women who have suffered violence, rape, and dispossession (of land and body) through colonization, obscuring time, and centering colonized space.[43] The first lines of the poem read,

> To the spirit of Monahsetah
> and to all women who have
> been forced to the ground.

By connecting a historical battle over traditional territory, and the mass kidnapping and violence that ensued, to the ongoing violence that Indigenous women experience, DeClue connects Indigenous women's bodies with settler desire and the need to occupy stolen land.

In her novel *The Round House*, Louise Erdrich (Ojibwe) illuminates through the character Geraldine the vacuum of justice that exists for Indigenous women when they are sexually assaulted. When Geraldine's husband, Basil, and son, Joe, take her to the emergency room after a violent rape by (we later learn) a white man, Joe asks his father which police they are awaiting, to which Basil responds, "Exactly." The passage speaks to the challenge of jurisdiction:

Three men came through the emergency ward doors and stood quietly in the hall. There was a state trooper, an officer local to the town of Hoopdance, and ... the tribal police. My father had insisted that they each take a statement from my mother because it wasn't clear where the crime had been committed—on state or tribal land—or who had committed it—an Indian or a non-Indian.[44]

In the space of three sentences, Erdrich introduces the vast complexity of jurisdiction pertaining to sexual assault against Indigenous women.[45]

Angeline Boulley speaks to the challenging decisions that young Indigenous women face in her novel *Fire Keeper's Daughter*. This novel takes on issues of dating violence and stalking, as well as intergenerational trauma and associated substance abuse. When her main character, Daunis, loses her best friend to drug-related violence, Daunis wrestles herself away from her mother's medicine cabinet and reaches instead for cultural healers:

> I close the medicine cabinet and go to the table next to the front door. Gramma Pearl's birchbark basket in the shape of a blueberry. A pinecone hangs from each point of its flared crown. I reach inside for a pinch of loose-leaf tobacco. My bare feet touch cold concrete steps and then grass slick with dew. The bumps and dents of the lawn remind me of dancing in my moccasins. Drumbeats reverberating from uneven ground, up my legs and into my heart ... I hold the semaa in the palm of my left hand, the one closest to my heart. Release it to the poplar where I always begin my day. After my introduction, I inventory the Seven Grandfathers—love, respect, honesty, humility, bravery, wisdom, and truth. Which one will help with this unfathomable anguish?[46]

Taken together, these three Indigenous writers tie together a history of violence against Indigenous women for the purpose of securing settler society, the ways that settler justice systems perpetuate this violence, and the struggle that Indigenous women endure in finding and engaging in their cultural practices toward healing.

The violence with which rape is inflicted on Indigenous women's bodies is tied to the settler anxiety to keep stolen land. The colonial legal system enables such crimes to occur largely with impunity, thus clearing a path to Indigenous women's bodies, and through them to land. In a short documentary about sexual violence on Rosebud Reservation an unnamed Lakota woman states, "Men [rape] because they can. That's the bottom line."[47] Within these two sentences is a world of historical and legislative context. In the United States, at least 86 percent of reported cases of rape or sexual assault against Indigenous women are committed by non-Indigenous men. Among other groups, interracial rape is relatively rare; for whites and African Americans, the majority of perpetrators are of the same race, 65.1 percent for whites and 89.9 percent for African Americans.[48] There is a nexus of race, gender, and land that drastically affects Indigenous women—violence tied to settler anxieties to keep stolen land and get away with it.

Amnesty International published a report, titled *Maze of Injustice: The Failure to Protect Indigenous Women from Sexual Violence in the USA* (2007), in which they demonstrate how

> [sexual violence against Indigenous women] has been compounded by the federal government's steady erosion of tribal government authority and its chronic underresourcing of those law enforcement agencies and service providers which should protect Indigenous women from sexual violence. It is against this backdrop that American Indian and Alaska Native women continue to experience high levels of sexual violence, a systemic failure to punish those responsible and official indifference to their rights to dignity, security and justice.[49]

The 1978 U.S. Supreme Court decision *Oliphant v. Suquami* protects non-Indigenous men from prosecution for raping Indigenous women by divesting tribal courts of criminal jurisdiction over non-Indigenous peoples, even those who are members of their territories. Muscogee Creek Indian Law scholar Sarah Deer calls the combination of this court ruling, the Major Crimes Act (MCA), and Public Law 280 (PL 280) a *vacuum of justice* for Indigenous women.

The MCA, a federal law passed in 1885, works to convolute justice through "concurrent jurisdiction." MCA prohibits tribal courts from prosecuting felony violent crimes, including rape and murder. It is not merely that the federal government prosecutes these crimes on behalf of sovereign tribal governments. Instead, tribal governments and the federal government have concurrent jurisdiction. Deer illustrates how concurrent jurisdiction results in a vacuum of justice for Indigenous women by pointing to interpretations of the legal language as well as how the law is applied (or denied) on the ground. She says, "Tribal nations have successfully sustained authority over rape (and other major crimes) arguing that the doctrine of inherent sovereignty requires Congress to divest tribes of concurrent jurisdiction in clear language. The MCA never explicitly divested tribal nations of authority over the enumerated crimes."[50] How this plays out on the ground is that "many tribes do not pursue cases against rapists, or will wait until a declination from a federal or state prosecutor before proceeding with an official tribal response."[51] This vacuum of justice is further complicated by the shame and fear of retaliation Indigenous women (like many women) feel after an assault.[52] All of these jurisdiction questions result in obscuring and confusing the routes a Haudenosaunee woman can take after a violent assault of any kind. In sum, the ability of Haudenosaunee women to find justice in cases of violence ends up being only as good as the relationship between tribal and local, state, and federal governments. Saint Regis Mohawk Tribe Chief Beverly Cook illustrates this point: "Our community and governmental issues are as complex as they are numerous. Ongoing conversations such as these are essential to the process of developing respectful relationships between law enforcement agencies, governmental bodies and communities."[53] In her chapter, "The Enigma of Federal Reform: The Tribal Law and Order Act and the Violence Against Women Act," Sarah Deer demonstrates her confidence in the knowledge that Indigenous communities hold in eradicating rape. Deer argues that while both pieces of legislation have improved the safety of Indigenous women, in order to "truly end rape" full jurisdiction to tribal governments is what is needed.[54]

Haudenosaunee Daughters, Mothers, and Grandmothers: Healing and Lacrosse

Violence against Indigenous women is not the end of the story, and Haudenosaunee women and communities turn toward their lifeways and worldviews to address it. What follows is an articulation about (1) how the Haudenosaunee Creation Story names both lacrosse and a web of relatedness as ways of addressing violence against women and (2) how the Haudenosaunee clan system enunciates the efficacy of intergenerational approaches to solving community problems. These two articulations lead what this chapter aims to portray—that lacrosse is a traditional healing for women, and Haudenosaunee women's defining of that healing through lacrosse is imperative to Haudenosaunee communities claiming lacrosse at a global level.

Addressing violence against women begins for the Haudenosaunee in the Creation Story, and lacrosse is an important—if oft forgotten—part of Sky Woman's narrative. Mommabear's telling of the Haudenosaunee Creation Story in *A Clan*

Mother's Call: Reconstructing Haudenosaunee Cultural Memory (2017) rematriates the part of the narrative where a lacrosse player brings love and joy into Sky Woman's life.[55] When the jealous Sky Chief learns of their relationship, he punishes Sky Woman and shakes the tree of life so vigorously that it uproots, creating a hole from Sky World to turtle's back and the water world. Sky Woman either falls through the hole, jumps, or is pushed by Sky Chief, depending on the telling.[56] As she plummets toward all that will become the Mother Earth World, a collection of animals ponders the best way to break her fall, save her life, and sustain her being. They accomplish this on turtle's back (Turtle Island). Embedded within this part of the Haudenosaunee Creation Story is the understanding that (1) lacrosse is a source of joy, life, and well-being for the community and (2), if and when a woman endures violence, a whole community of beings will work to restore her health and well-being.

When Sky Woman falls toward turtle's back, water animals and birds convene and consider the best way to save her life. Birds decide to break her fall and lower her safely. Water animals realize that she will need earth in order to grow the seeds that she took with her from Sky World. Several animals take a turn, diving deep to the bottom of the sea to retrieve soil. All give their lives in the attempt, a sacrifice to sustaining life. All but muskrat, who successfully brings earth to turtle's back. This earth spreads across all of turtle's back, creating Turtle Island (North America). Sky Woman plants her seeds, which sustain her life, the life of her daughter whom she is carrying, and future generations. The Haudenosaunee Creation Story articulates an intimate connection between soil and the sustainability of humans, as mitigated by water and water relatives.

Sky Woman's survival on Turtle Island and the subsequent generations that experience flourishing demonstrate connections to ancestral land, water, and life. Where colonization disrupts those relationships, rematriation calls the relationships back. When discussing the rematriation of some Oneida land, Michelle Schenandoah talked about what Heather Dane-Fougnier (Oneida) calls Indigenous connections to ancestral lands and water *cellular healing*.[57] When the revitalization of ceremonies and gatherings occurs on Haudenosaunee land—when Haudenosaunee women sink their toes into the damp earth—the land remembers, too. About a gathering of women from three Oneida communities that took place in 2018 on rematriated Oneida land, Dane-Fougnier says:

> In my work with epigenetics and health, I began to realize that the soil is the connective tissue of the individuals that make it up. It's all the structures that give us

shape and allows for strength and wellbeing. What I felt when we were together on our land was the kind of healing and strength that comes from repairing connective tissue.... I'm sure our ancestors were speaking to us [during the gathering], reminding us to always remember this connection.[58]

As described at the end of this chapter, Haudenosaunee women lacrosse players struggle to articulate why lacrosse does not feel like any other of the sports that they have played. Embedded within the Haudenosaunee Creation Story is the web that lacrosse, land, and water create toward well-being. The mechanism for working through how lacrosse is defined by and for Haudenosaunee women and girls is also embedded in Haudenosaunee worldviews and lifeways. What follows is a description of the establishment of the Haudenosaunee clan system, which illuminates an intergenerational approach to solving problems.

Young people and Clan Mothers have especially important leadership roles among Haudenosaunee people. The Creation Story shows how the Haudenosaunee have cycled through periods of flourishing and balance, followed by periods of excessive illness, death, and neglect or loss of ceremonies. Each period of difficulty is met with help from Sky World, usually with a new ceremony, ceremonies such as for strawberries, the Three Sisters (corn, bean, and squash), and coming-of-age (Ohero:kon—under the husk). During one of these cycles caused by an expanding population, it becomes clear that a new political and familial organization is needed. The clan is a method of social organization that helps facilitate systems of balance. Clan not only mediates intrahuman relationships, such as who can marry whom, it also facilitates relationships between humans and other-than-humans by assigning subgroups responsibilities for a group of relatives, as indicated by their clan's name (e.g., deer, beaver, turtle). In this way the clan system is a structure for mediating a complex set of relationships for the purpose of flourishing for all of life.

Brian Rice (Haudenosaunee), in his work on traditional Haudenosaunee culture, explains how the clan system developed to meet this challenge. First, the Elders came together to work out a solution, but when they could not come to a consensus, they decided, "Let the women, or even the youths, be the ones to do it if they can, so that our children and our grandchildren may continue to live and have a future." They assigned the task to a young man, Okweta:she, who looked to the earth for a solution since "she is the mother who has given birth to all the things that grow."[59] Earth as mother connects to woman as mother:

The young man answered them, "... Tomorrow at noon, all the people will assemble themselves together. At that time, I will try to arrange something so that the clan system will work. Those who are female will be the principal persons involved in this process. That is because they are the ones who give birth to the new onkwe:honwe on earth. The woman who is the oldest of each of the families will be the head of the entire clan that I will develop."[60]

During the process to establish clans, "the young man then took hold of the vine and began to cross the river. Many of the onkwe:honwe (people) followed the young man and began to cross the river one by one, as quickly as possible holding onto the vine."[61]

The next morning Okweta:she visits the eldest matron of each of the families gathered on both sides of the river, asking each what she saw when she went to the river for water. Each matron answers by identifying the animal she saw, which becomes her clan, followed by, "I then departed for my lodge where I prepared some food to feed my children and grandchildren." Okweta:she then says to all of the matrons, "You ancient ones, the eldest women of the clans, are to be in charge of this matter."[62] The eldest women were responsible for gathering the water for the evening meal, dipping in the ladle, and letting the young man know what they had seen—deer, bear, wolf, turtle, hawk, sandpiper, beaver. This story demonstrates important relationships of interdependence among generations as well as the role of Clan Mothers in naming social relations. The young men helped to establish the clans, relying on the Elder women to care for the people and maintain balance. Within Haudenosaunee worldviews, wisdom lives within acts of feeding and caring for future generations.[63] It is because of this capacity that Clan Mothers come to be and to hold the power. There is a precedent of young people and Clan Mothers working together to address issues. Also present in this narrative are the ways water, animals, and landscape are conduits for Haudenosaunee cultural knowledge.

As enunciated at the beginning of this chapter, Freeland's theory in *Aazheyaadizi* identifies creation narratives as one location whereby a culture's worldview can be found. The narrative of Sky Woman falling and how Haudenosaunee clans come to be articulate a deep cultural value placed on a web of interrelatedness among four-leggeds, younger relatives, the two-leggeds, birds, water, and land. This extends across and depends upon cross-generational approaches to well-being. The following describes how Haudenosaunee women and communities are engaging these Haudenosaunee principles—a web of relatedness and intergenerational work—to rematriate balance disrupted by colonization.

Michelle Schenandoah describes how Indigenous women's activism brought attention to violence against Indigenous women in the United States and Canada. She also talks about the patriarchal overtones that have made their way into Haudenosaunee communities, resulting in diminished accountability, especially for sexual abuse. Indigenous women are addressing this problem head on by calling out the ways in which male authority is consolidated in Indigenous communities that disenfranchise Indigenous women. For example, the mission of the Seven Dancers Coalition (SDC) of the Akwesasne Mohawk Nation is "to uplift the families of Indigenous communities by educating and restoring traditional values with the purpose of strengthening self-confidence and dignity. We strive for an environment of peace and tranquility to heal all spirits." To "[restore] harmony within Indigenous communities," SDC specifically addresses domestic violence, teen dating violence, sexual assault, stalking, and sex trafficking in ways that take seriously a cultural system of gender balance.[64] Outreach Coordinator Jonel Beauvais (Akwesasne Mohawk) describes how SDC has been very thoughtful in addressing violence and considering solutions that are culturally relevant.

Part of this means also addressing men's health and well-being. Harvey Herne and Pray Lazore (both Akwesasne Mohawk) have created a program for men at SDC that "goes to the trauma places" in order to stop cycles of violence. In this way, "nobody is left out or neglected," and all community members are called home.[65] In a film produced by Michelle Schenandoah, *An Indigenous Response to #MeToo*, Mommabear speaks to this reality saying, "Men have been missing for a long time and we need them to come home." Chelsea Sunday (Akwesasne Mohawk) explains that even when Haudenosaunee women have men in their lives, they are often left alone in the daily caretaking of their homes and families. In the film, Chelsea describes a ceremony that Akwesasne Mohawk women held for seven men in the community who were fulfilling their responsibilities, including helping women and children feel safe. The ceremony included the men's families and had the ripple effect of many more men saying, "we need to do this, too."[66]

Michelle Schenandoah says that prior to these direct initiatives, sexual assault was not talked about or dealt with because of the heavy influence and impact of residential schools. Today, Indigenous women say "enough; no more of this." This demand is not new, but rather a return to something very old where Indigenous women control their bodies, the connection of their bodies to land, and how infringements on their bodies and the land are dealt with.

Mommabear is deeply concerned for the young people of her community at Akwesasne. That is part of her role and responsibility as Clan Mother, to hold and care for the young people. Because of the long history of physical and cultural genocide against Indigenous people—systematic stealing of children to attend boarding schools, a gradual and persistent outlawing of Indigenous ceremonies—Haudenosaunee ceremonies went underground for several generations. Mommabear worked with her community to bring the coming-of-age ceremony Ohero:kon out from *under the husk*, first in 2003 with seven young people. Almost two decades later, nearly one hundred young people register to participate in the ceremonies each year at Akwesasne. The ceremony takes four years to complete. First-year participants prepare and fast in fields with no food or water for one day. Second, third, and fourth years fast in the woods for two, three, and four days respectively. Aunties, uncles, grandparents, mothers, and fathers all help in the preparations and teachings, and they camp nearby during the fasts. The fast is broken with a whole community celebration, the fourth years arriving by canoe. These moments, this cycle, are the embodiment of the revitalization of tradition focused on a communal reality.

The film *Keepers of the Game* (2016) relates deep intergenerational and ancestral Haudenosaunee relationships through lacrosse and Ohero:kon. On the first day of the fast for Ohero:kon, Akwesasne Mohawk lacrosse player Tsiotenhariio Herne is escorted into the woods by her father. They hug, and the camera lingers for long enough that the viewer may ask, Are they going to film her during her fast? But at the last moment the camera pans out and away, backing off as a reflection of its invasive history, or perhaps it was given a firm boundary to start. Instead, viewers see a time-lapsing sky spanning four days. And then they see something positively magnificent: a community of grandmothers, grandfathers, aunts, uncles, mothers, fathers, family, community all waiting on the shore as the young people who fasted for four days come around the corner with Elders in canoes. Every person is adorned in exquisite Mohawk dress. Traditional foods await. Everyone leaves the canoes and embraces those waiting on the shore. The landscape seems to sing and breathe deeply. There is a memory of Haudenosaunee ceremony embedded in the land here, reflected in how the clan system mirrors the natural world, as in the story above. There is a depth of meaning in this community near and traversing the water, a rightness that the land remembers. The ritual space and time of these ceremonies shift and remember the landscape.

Like Ohero:kon, lacrosse bridges land and cosmology. If bodies (land) are vessels of memory holding intergenerational trauma, lacrosse becomes a location of tremendous healing. Many matches in which young women play take place on traditional Haudenosaunee land. Because colonization has disrupted relationships to that land, as well as cosmology, a lacrosse game has the potential to restore these relationships. The diverse iterations of the Haudenosaunee Creation Story places lacrosse as an important ceremony. In Mommabear's telling, a lacrosse player crosses Sky Woman's path, which leads to a series of events that create the first humans. In Brian Rice's telling of the Creation Story, lacrosse takes place in the Sky World before humans are ever a part of the scene: Since the beginning of time, Tewaaraton, lacrosse, has been played by the onkwe:honwe as a form of amusement for the Creator. It involved many men from the villages and was played in the fields. The fields sometimes could go on for miles.[67] In Rice's account, lacrosse has always been there as a source of help and healing for the people. In John Mohawk's telling of the Creation Story, on the other hand, lacrosse comes as a ceremony to help the community, paralleling many other gifts given to the people, such as the Three Sisters (corn, bean, squash). Lacrosse is deeply connected to the cycle of ceremonies, gifts, and teachings given to the people whenever they struggle to find balance.[68]

In both Rice's and Mohawk's accounts, men specifically play lacrosse. However, in neither is there an explicit mention of women *not* playing lacrosse. According to Mommabear:

> So the evolution of the human being and the gift of lacrosse, it's changed. And in the beginning it was a brutal sport and it was intended for the men. But as we evolved and through the ages, where lacrosse was big and then it diminished, and then it reclaimed itself again. And part of the reclaiming, there became an attitude with it. Because the more that the men were unable to hunt and fish, the more that they were unable to go to war, the more that their own environment and their roles and responsibilities got diminished, *they had to hold fast to certain areas of the culture, and so lacrosse became a men-only sport.*[69]

A prominent player and recent graduate of Syracuse University told me in an interview that her great-grandmother (Onondaga Nation) used to play for fun and that "when she was young it wasn't taboo [for a woman] to touch a lacrosse stick."[70] Haudenosaunee women are defining lacrosse in ways that connect to their culture and are doing so despite great obstacles. Like Sky Woman in the Creation Story, Haudenosaunee women are creatively manifesting new realities against great odds, while honoring multiple points of view and processes. The world described in Haudenosaunee knowledge is large, multidimensional, full of processes, and capable of holding contradiction. It is a world unto itself. Colonization has disrupted that world, but Haudenosaunee people are very adaptable in how they access and preserve that world. In playing and defining lacrosse, Haudenosaunee women peel back layers of colonization and protect the world so intricately woven on Turtle Island, a world connected to the ancestral goings on of Sky World.

As producers of cultural knowledge and meaning, Haudenosaunee women lacrosse players often begin with what lacrosse *is not*. First and foremost, they are specific that what they are playing is not *the medicine game*. The medicine game refers to a game played during ceremonies and whenever there may be a call for healing. It is played only by men, and women players do not refute this. Nevertheless, a medicinal game of lacrosse, played with a stitched leather ball and wooden stick within the larger context of ceremonial space, cannot start until a woman tosses the ball. Every woman interviewed who plays or has played lacrosse, including Mommabear, agreed that what they are playing is not the medicine game. Amber Hill (Tuscarora) says that "obviously, women aren't supposed to participate. I would never ask to participate just because I play lacrosse, because I'm respectful."[71] Another player from the Oneida Nation (New York) asks, "Is this the medicine game that you're playing? No. It's completely different."[72] Given the importance of protecting ceremonial space for generating and regenerating Haudenosaunee culture, women who play lacrosse are careful to protect that space in their articulations of and participation in the game. By making a distinction between the medicine game and the game they play, Haudenosaunee women carve out space to play while protecting culture.[73]

Furthermore, lacrosse is also *not* just another sport for those Haudenosaunee women who play it. Many Haudenosaunee women play other sports as well but see differences in their meanings. For Amber Hill, "It's a different feel when you get out there. I've played a lot of sports. I've played softball, basketball, soccer. But when I play lacrosse, it's different. It's like a connected feeling. Your mind's clear."[74] Star Wheeler (Cattaraugus Seneca Nation, Turtle Clan), who played on a team in the 1980s that disbanded after Onondaga Clan Mothers drew a line about their playing on Onondaga Territory, echoes this when describing the sports she played in addition to lacrosse:

I played basketball too, and I ran cross-country. Basketball didn't do [what lacrosse did] for me. I think it was because it was lacrosse. It is our game. I think that was like a—I didn't have a sense of pride playing basketball, but I did playing lacrosse. Because it was our game and that I was doing something that made me more culturally connected, because obviously I wasn't culturally connected to basketball. But it did make me feel more connected with my culture.[75]

By defining contemporary lacrosse by what it is not, Haudenosaunee women create space to articulate what it is, and thus claim it as *their* sport. When one young player from Tuscarora Territory, who graduated from Syracuse University, faced disapproval from some of her community for playing lacrosse, her mother told her: "You know if they let the Australians play and they let people from all over the world play—not that they let them, but they do it. If they can do it, then so can you. And as a Native person, you have the right to because it's your game."[76] Another young player from Oneida Nation said: "I went to college and saw all of these girls playing lacrosse. And I wasn't going to sit back and let all these white girls play my sport and not play myself."[77] In response to the rapid growth of contemporary lacrosse internationally, these Haudenosaunee women lacrosse players are claiming the game as their own with deep cultural relevancies and origins. Playing a game that is played all over the world by a growing number of women helps Haudenosaunee women maintain its cultural connection. They serve as a reminder of the game's origins and cultural meanings.

Between Haudenosaunee women's assurances that the lacrosse they are playing "is not the medicine game" and their feelings that "it is everything" lies a deep struggle to name what it is about the game that is so essential to their lives. Mommabear helps to create space for a growing and deepening articulation of Haudenosaunee lacrosse that includes Haudenosaunee women by connecting it to Haudenosaunee culture and lifeways. She names Haudenosaunee women's bodies as both the site that needs medicine and the purveyor of healing when engaged in lacrosse. She calls on traditional Haudenosaunee frameworks:

> We have to consider the evolution of our people. When times [were difficult] and times got so brutal, and people moved beyond the level of integrity, we were given gifts in order to bring order to the chaos. And lacrosse was one of those gifts ... the conditions change over time. Our realities change. So does the culture. And to make the culture stagnant doesn't serve rightfully for the people. And

even in the frameworks of our Great Law of Peace, they put in there a provision that says, *when you come in times of change, and you need to change this law, you can add to the rafters.* So in the evolution of the human being and the gift of lacrosse, it's changed.[78]

Haudenosaunee culture already provides for adaptation and survival in trying times through the gifts of ceremony, including lacrosse. Colonization has hindered but not obliterated this. Tradition is living and breathing, not stagnant. The center of Haudenosaunee culture is the Longhouse. This is where teaching and ceremony take place. When the Peacemaker united the five nations of the Haudenosaunee over one thousand years ago, he began with one rafter and left room for more to be added as needs arose. Mommabear describes, "The Peacemaker decided to begin to build his Longhouse of One Family; it was time for him to put up the first rafter."[79] Mommabear's assertion that women's lacrosse adds to the rafters builds on this Haudenosaunee cultural concept and refutes any claim that it is a result of western influence. Rather, what has been traditionally male grows to include women within a framework of traditional Haudenosaunee culture. This framework gives new language to lacrosse as a healing game housed within the space of the Haudenosaunee woman's body, the ceremonial space within the body itself. As Mommabear says, "the woman can play the game if it's a medicine for herself."[80]

Here, she is saying to Haudenosaunee women who say their game is not *the* medicine game that it *is*, after all, *a* medicine. She assures Haudenosaunee girls and women, who are so cautious, that it is okay that the game is a medicine. Also embedded in this statement, she "can play the game *if* it's a medicine for herself," is a caution that Haudenosaunee women should not play without recognizing how lacrosse offers cultural medicine. She thus both reaffirms and expands a cultural boundary:

> I'd move heaven and earth to have our women more empowered, and if lacrosse can give that to them, then I support that. When it comes to that medicine, when you're doing a doctoring, the culture holds true to what a woman's place is inside that. Now if there would come a time, if there's no men capable of playing in our game, inside the medicine of that game, there's nothing to say that women can't play then. So it evolves, it adapts, it changes.[81]

Haudenosaunee men play the medicine game of lacrosse to help heal individuals and the larger community. Haudenosaunee women lacrosse players, with the help of leaders such as Mommabear, name that when girls and women play lacrosse, they help heal *themselves*. And when Haudenosaunee girls and women heal themselves, the community is uplifted toward healing.

Two Haudenosaunee lacrosse players describe the healing they experience through lacrosse. Tsiotenhariio Herne from Akwesasne describes how important it makes her feel to play, how it helps her to avoid poor choices, and how she loves feeling part of a team.[82] As if in a direct response to Tsiotenhariio, Star Wheeler says:

> To me it just provided an outlet for me to really come out of my shell. And I'm a turtle too! (Laughs.) So, because I was pretty introverted when I was younger, and I think that that really helped my self-esteem and form bonds of friendship with the other girls and really motivated me to do something better with my life. And I think that it does that with the girls now. I think it's a such a great way for them to build their self-esteem, and to get that connectedness with not only their culture, but other females. So, it was a big turning point for me playing lacrosse. I think it really helped me a lot. I really think that playing lacrosse did propel me to want to do bigger and better things. But I know there were other girls I had asked if they could play, and they said their parents wouldn't let them because girls aren't supposed to play lacrosse. And there was only a handful of us back then. Now there's like—it's exploded.[83]

Haudenosaunee girls and women playing lacrosse is part of recentering the cultural roots of the game. By providing an intervention into the elite game it has become, primarily played by white women, Haudenosaunee women and girls become cultural messengers and reminders that lacrosse is a Haudenosaunee game.

Conclusion

This chapter describes the land with which Haudenosaunee women engage and the interventions into colonization they make when they step onto the field. Settler colonialism cannot function and prosper with Indigenous woman's bodies and relationships to land and community intact. When Haudenosaunee women go out on the field to play lacrosse, they undermine colonial logics that deny their existence and dispossess their bodies from their Haudenosaunee homelands. Settler nationhood depends upon this dispossession, nonexistence, and disappearance. But as Mommabear and others contend, this is not the end of the story for Haudenosaunee women. Haudenosaunee women lacrosse players are intervening in the prescriptions of settler colonialism by placing their bodies, their whole beings, and their connections to their culture and lands onto the space of the field and into conversations around the game. Lacrosse is a source of healing for Haudenosaunee women that is rooted in their culture, worldviews, and lifeways. When their cleats sink into the soil, they invoke an ancestral world that began with Sky Woman falling onto the back of turtle. Young Haudenosaunee women who play lacrosse across Turtle Island are surrounded by ancestors and ancestral land that remembers and heals along with them, at a cellular level.

CHAPTER TWO

THE COMMUNITY SPEAKS: A SHIFTING CONVERSATION

n the film *Keepers of the Game*, members of the Akwesasne Mohawk Nation are depicted working through the delicate intricacies of Haudenosaunee high school girls playing lacrosse *and* being traditional. One central narrative in the film belongs to Tsiotenhariio Herne. As Tsiotenhariio is shown ice fishing and then lifting weights at the gym, her voiceover shares, "even though it's forbidden for girls to play, sometimes I can feel a presence there when I'm playing."[1] Since the time of this film, Tsiotenhariio has gone deeper into her culture and continues to play lacrosse. The central question of this chapter is, What understandings and articulations of *traditional* are available to Tsiotenhariio and others like her to make these reconciliations? Haudenosaunee people agree on the importance of sustaining the culture that has connected them across generations. However, sustaining culture looks different for different community members. For some of them, taking the culture seriously means "being real" about being a matrilineal society, as Akwesasne Mohawk Clan Mother Mommabear put it, and that in turn means putting the empowerment of women, including playing lacrosse, at the center of decolonization. Other community members come at it from a different angle, seeing girls and women playing lacrosse as a sure sign that they are out of touch with their Haudenosaunee culture as a direct result of colonization. From this perspective, girls and women playing lacrosse put this matrilineal society, land, ceremony, and nationhood in danger. These conversations demonstrate tradition as the process of engaging one another for the purpose of continuity for future generations, a process that is painstakingly intellectual and pragmatic.

It would be nine decades between the first contemporary women's lacrosse games and the first Haudenosaunee women's team. The contemporary women's game, with the rules that we know today, was first played in Scotland in 1890, the same year that Haudenosaunee men were banned from playing lacrosse internationally. Within a century of these first contemporary women's games, women's lacrosse hit the international scene with the first Women's World Cup in 1982, in England. As Haudenosaunee women were struggling to form teams and earn the endorsement from their nations to carry their flag internationally, women's lacrosse was growing in popularity in high schools, colleges, and universities. Haudenosaunee communities claim the contemporary game is an act of rematriation, an intervention in what might otherwise remain a game played mostly by non-Indigenous players at elite institutions of western education. Michelle Schenandoah (Oneida) discusses how lacrosse has become a game of white privilege and an appropriation of Haudenosaunee culture.[2] Haudenosaunee women players are positioned to educate non-Indigenous players, as what non-Indigenous women know about the cultural components of lacrosse mostly comes from what is learned from Haudenosaunee men's experiences.

Young Haudenosaunee women lacrosse players are responsible for more and more first-generation college students among their communities. Akwesasne Clan Mother Mommabear attributes this increase to the Thompson brothers who played for the State University of New York, Albany. "They started to create new veins of success. And colleges started to offer scholarships for lacrosse, it wasn't enough to do it for the boys, they had to do it for the girls."[3] One Haudenosaunee lacrosse player says that without lacrosse she doesn't know that she would have even thought of college.[4] The empowerment of women and being a matrilineal society is at the center of what the culture works to hold onto, and it connects Haudenosaunee communities across generations. Mommabear claims that rematriation has to include being real about being a matrilineal society: "Because of the undercurrents that have diminished those roles of women with colonization, we have gotten away from it. And we've lost focus and we've lost sight of the importance of a woman-led society."[5] Some Haudenosaunee community members agree with this but come at it from a different angle, seeing girls and women playing lacrosse as a sure sign that they are out of touch with their culture as a direct result of colonization. From this perspective, a matrilineal society, land, ceremony, and nationhood are in danger with girls and women playing lacrosse.

Whether or not Haudenosaunee women are a part of lacrosse is not the question, as they have always been involved, weaving the balls or netting for the sticks, at times being the reason the game is played for healing purposes, and more contemporarily, supporting the teams. However, as for playing? Some would say Haudenosaunee women and girls have always been playing lacrosse. One player recalls, "My great-grandmother, who is no longer with us, Phoebe Hill [Onondaga], said that when she grew up with girls and women playing lacrosse was not taboo. She remembers playing with the boys."[6] Mommabear echoes with, "I remember playing some pick-up games at the Kahnawake Mohawk Reserve in the late seventies. I think unofficially, girls have always been playing."[7] Women and girls were playing "unofficially" prior to the mid-1980s, when the Onondaga Clan Mothers drew the line, the team temporarily disbanded, and Haudenosaunee peoples wondered over whether or not girls and women can play contemporary lacrosse.

Within Haudenosaunee communities, no one disputes the protocol that women do not play the medicine game of lacrosse that is played as a ceremony for healing.[8] Out of respect for Haudenosaunee communities and the participants steering this project, I do not to delve into the Haudenosaunee medicine game beyond what Haudenosaunee community members shared about lacrosse with myself or other scholars. For example, Christopher Root, in his master's thesis for SUNY Buffalo, shares an interview with Haudenosaunee lacrosse player Pete Hill. Through this interview, Root learns that "most notably, medicine games are played in the autumn on the Tonawanda and Onondaga Reservations, but are closed to outsiders from participating or viewing."[9] One Haudenosaunee woman lacrosse player states, "There are games within communities where they do play for medicine. And obviously, women aren't supposed to participate. I would never ask to participate just because I play lacrosse, because I'm respectful. Obviously, only men compete."[10] Mommabear shares that the medicine game wasn't played by women and that a man's role has been and continues to be to deal with death and grieving.[11] When I asked one young player if she agreed with only men playing the medicine game, she responded, "Yes, I am in complete agreement with that. I don't know how to describe when things just make sense to you, in your mind. It just makes sense to me in my mind."[12]

The medicinal ceremony of lacrosse is so clearly not what the Haudenosaunee are working to define in traditional terms, and if they are, these conversations are not for the greater public. This chapter works to illuminate where and how the lines become blurred and complicated concerning how Haudenosaunee communities define medicinal and traditional lacrosse and the relationships between these definitions and contemporary lacrosse. I demonstrate in this chapter how Haudenosaunee women and girls playing contemporary lacrosse encourages communities to define more clearly what is traditional lacrosse, and how contemporary lacrosse intersects with traditional and medicinal lacrosse. I argue that Haudenosaunee women and girls playing lacrosse enriches understandings of tradition and medicine, propelling a traditionalism that reflects futurity through rematriation and intergenerational relationality, and is grounded in what is at stake for Haudenosaunee communities.[13] To carry this out, I engage Theresa McCarthy's (Onondaga, Beaver Clan) discussion of Haudenosaunee tradition in her chapter, "Unpacking the 'T' Word."[14] Specifically, I engage McCarthy's use of the late Seneca scholar John Mohawk's articulation of Haudenosaunee tradition as being a thinking tradition, rooted in the past, engaged in the present, with an eye to the future (futurity). Additionally, I engage McCarthy's analysis of Elizabeth Doxtater's (Six Nations of the Grand River) art installation *It Encircles Everything*, which helps articulate the role of intergenerational relationality in maintaining tradition for future generations. In this chapter, I examine the relationships between this conversation and definitions of tradition: how Haudenosaunee women articulate tradition, and how a nuanced understanding of the conversation combats simplified or romanticized representations of tradition.

Conceptualizing Tradition—Part One

Haudenosaunee culture has been methodically threatened to near extinction through colonial acts such as the Sullivan-Clinton Campaign, waged by President George Washington, that systematically burned Haudenosaunee agricultural fields, land grabs, the introduction of diseases such as smallpox, and later, the boarding school era. Part of survival, resiliency, and revitalization means that generations have fought hard to make definitive statements about what is and what is not traditional in the wake of colonial interference. Since the 1980s, lacrosse has increasingly become one location through which Haudenosaunee communities work out these understandings of tradition. What definitions of tradition do some apply when they make the statement that women who are playing lacrosse are not traditional? What definitions of tradition are being employed by those who are playing and claiming the identity of traditional? What are the limits of ontology concerning "traditional"? How is engaging in the questions themselves traditional? This is an incredibly complex set of questions that are being worked out, and overly simplistic explanations erase how Haudenosaunee communities are defining traditionalism and medicine through the conversation.

Indigenous scholars such as Jennifer Denetdale (Diné), Audra Simpson (Mohawk), and Theresa McCarthy make clear that Haudenosaunee communities should not relegate "traditional" to the past or make it synonymous with "precontact." Instead, the past is accessed and talked about in the present; it is an act that can only happen in the present, meant to inform the future. How this conversation about women's lacrosse is nuanced and connected to tradition is informed here by three Haudenosaunee women lacrosse players, Amber Hill (Tuscarora), Corrine Abrams (Tuscarora), and Tsiotenhariio Herne; a coach from the Cattaraugus Reservation of the Seneca Nation, Sandy Jemison; Onondaga Nation Elder and midwife Jeanne Shenandoah; Akwesasne Mohawk Bear Clan Mother Mommabear; Oneida community member Michelle Schenandoah; and Cayuga Clan Mother Berdie Hill. These eight Haudenosaunee women engage diverse definitions of tradition to articulate medicinal, traditional, and contemporary lacrosse. The collection of women represented in this chapter are all deeply invested in defining traditional lacrosse for their communities. Some embody sovereignty through playing, some through holding a hard line against women playing. Moreover, while some play it as a way of restoring their physical and mental well-being, and thus the health of their communities, and others see this as a sign of assimilation, all hold lacrosse as an essential vehicle for traditionalism for the present and future.

The following four examples are simplistic representations of the internal conversation over women and girls playing lacrosse. I share these first as a way of distinguishing them from more complex understandings of traditionalism that focus on futurity. As previously stated, Aimee Berg's representation is an outsider's perspective that limits the political role and potential of tradition within Haudenosaunee communities. In her representation in "Lacrosse: Cradle of a Sport Has Crossed the Gender Line," tradition is the enemy of progress. Berg uses the language of crossing a gender line and succeeding against the wishes of the Clan Mothers to portray young women "caught in the struggle between tradition and opportunity."[15]

Here, Berg recasts the characters in her piece into a narrative of western feminism, pitting Clan Mothers and lacrosse players against each other. In her lack of acknowledgment of women's power within Haudenosaunee communities, the Clan Mothers and traditionalism are cast as upholding oppressive western patriarchal structures, holding young women back and keeping them firmly on their side of the gender line. Berg establishes the young women playing two decades later as a victory along western feminist lines, while ignoring how their playing is attached to their being Haudenosaunee. Berg's representation omits a long history of sexism in sports and exclusionary realities for women athletes within mainstream dominant cultures. This depiction does not accurately or adequately represent this shifting conversation from the point of view of Haudenosaunee peoples. Even reference to Haudenosaunee cultural traditions can present overly simplistic representations and erasures regarding girls and women playing lacrosse, as with the next example.

While I was presenting the early set of questions to a mostly Haudenosaunee audience, a gentleman in the room asked me if I knew that lacrosse was part of *their* creation narrative (indicating that he was not Haudenosaunee). This question was meant to end the discussion with an overly simplistic analysis. All that needed to be understood was that lacrosse is a game that is part of the Haudenosaunee Creation Story, given by the Creator, and played by men. Knowing this should answer why women should not play because only men play the version of lacrosse that the Creator gave as a medicine game. The question, *are you aware that lacrosse is part of their creation narrative*, does, at least in part, explain why there is a conversation surrounding girls and women playing. However, it also points to a conflation of medicinal and contemporary lacrosse, and here is where definitions of tradition come into play. Within this logic—because there is a game given by the Creator as a medicine game for the community that is traditionally only played by men—the game that Haudenosaunee men play today is traditional, and therefore medicinal, and therefore only played by men. Two things never change in this understanding of tradition: the game of lacrosse and Haudenosaunee culture. Those employing this trajectory fix definitions of tradition and simplify the conversation within culturally rigid terms.

Another facet of this inquiry relates to the power Haudenosaunee women hold to give birth. Haudenosaunee women hold the culture alive through ceremony, their connectedness to creation, through giving and sustaining life, and as important repositories and purveyors of knowledge. This power is at times reduced in patriarchal and heteronormative ways, to simply the ability to give birth. At a research symposium, a young Cayuga man echoed an adage I have heard many times: "Women do not play lacrosse, or touch a man's stick, because of their ability to give birth and menstruate." One young woman lacrosse player echoes this: "So the way [it was explained to me], as women, as givers of life, our bodies are sacred."[16] Nancy Napierala's biographical dissertation of Pearl White (Cattaraugus Seneca, 1933–2012) iterates the long-standing perspective:

> When Pearl was young, girls were not allowed to play lacrosse, which was exclusively a male game. Pearl says the running and stick manipulation were thought to overdevelop the 51 muscles they would need for childbirth, making a barrier around the birth canal.[17]

At the same gathering where an audience member asked if I knew that lacrosse was part of the Haudenosaunee Creation Story, an Elder Haudenosaunee woman said that she had always heard that women do not play because it threatens their ability to give birth. She discussed the physical risk, a concern echoed by several I have interviewed as a way of explaining the conversation. There are parallels to be made between statements made by Haudenosaunee community members and arguments against non-Indigenous U.S. women playing sports in the late nineteenth and twentieth centuries. These parallels are complicated because it is difficult to pull apart what are and are not colonial impositions of western patriarchy onto Haudenosaunee culture. There is a risk, as with Berg's representation, of superimposing western feminist history onto Haudenosaunee relevancies. Doing so first situates Haudenosaunee women as "behind" Eurowestern women in a fight for equality, which is not an accurate representation given the influence Haudenosaunee women had on women's suffrage in the United States. There is also the risk of conflating two sets of values ascribed to childbirth—Eurowestern and Haudenosaunee—while ignoring the ways in which the power associated with connection to creation has actual teeth in Haudenosaunee communities but that has, to varying extents, been colonized. (It bears noting that the contemporary women's lacrosse game is a noncontact sport.) Such statements suggest that if we only acknowledged and understood that women's power was reason enough for why they should not play, the questions would be answered. It also seems that such a statement ignores a history of colonial assaults on Haudenosaunee women's bodies and reproduction, specifically forced and coerced sterilization and stealing children and sending them to boarding schools.[18]

During an interview, two Oneida Elders employ this approach in discussing why some think girls and women should not play: "It just wasn't a function for women. There was no purpose for a woman to play. There were women there, but they were more or less to get the water and make sure the men were nourished and hydrated."[19] This approach to the conversation forecloses on the question of whether or not Haudenosaunee girls and women should play by ignoring contemporary issues that Haudenosaunee women and communities face, especially in relationship to a colonized past and present. Colonization is only implicitly named through the suggestion of assimilation connected to girls and women playing, as assimilation is only possible in relation to colonization.

I did not set out to write about boarding schools in this project, but they came up organically in all the early interviews I conducted. This influenced me to add a question set regarding boarding schools in all subsequent rounds of interviews. What follows is a brief description of boarding schools and what they took away from Haudenosaunee communities. This depiction is inserted here to intercede in this discussion of traditionalism, and to bring further context to the immediacy and urgency of Haudenosaunee communities holding tradition.

Boarding School and Cultural Memory

The act of remembering a colonized past is far more than an ethnographic exercise, being a political path toward shaping the present and future. Remembering, as a collective, communal act, is part of identifying how Haudenosaunee communities respond in the present day to a painful past. When a community acknowledges a painful past, according to Linda Tuhiwai Smith (Māori), "both healing and transformation become crucial strategies in any approach which asks a community to remember what they may have decided unconsciously or consciously to forget."[20] Haudenosaunee people remember the boarding school era from generation to generation, as a painful reality that nearly eradicated Haudenosaunee cultural practices and identities. Each generation of Haudenosaunee people share this painful past, though the approaches to healing and transformation vary. Michelle Schenandoah relays that when cultural leader Tom Porter (Akwesasne Mohawk) was a young man, Longhouse ceremonies were almost empty.[21] Today, they are burgeoning in many cases. Revitalization is engaged amid intergenerational trauma and collective memory.

Mommabear says, "Our ancestors were holding onto our culture by their fingertips."[22] This image conjures a people who are actively being pursued as targets of genocide, a people whose reality includes a settler nation-state that spends considerable resources and time addressing "the Indian Problem." This phraseology refers to the ways in which Indigenous peoples were positioned within U.S. expansionism and considered to be in the way of the Manifest Destiny. In order for Manifest Destiny to be executed, Indigenous peoples were positioned as barriers to civilization and progress within the settler nation-state imaginary. The "Indian Problem" was dealt with through breaking treaties, removal, and assimilation policies, state legislation and court rulings. Mommabear's statement reflects the reality of a people who are the target of a settler nation-state whose legislative and religious entities engage in pseudo-ethical/logical debates about which policies are simultaneously the most humane toward the Indians and best serve the nation-state. Boarding schools utilized some of the most insidious assimilation practices and reflect the ways in which the United States and Canada were forming their national identities and dealing with their guilt at their violence against Indigenous people by claiming to be benevolent—as opposed to violent—nation-states. The boarding school era, as assimilation policy, was informed by approaches that worked toward the outright corporeal destruction of Indigenous peoples. Indigenous fear of assimilation is rooted in the boarding school era. Regarding what her ancestors endured, Mommabear iterates, "With much reverence for the generation that suffered and went through those tortuous things—and the genocide—for them it was a time of survival."[23] This cruelty is encapsulated in General Philip Sheridan's language, "The only good Indian I ever saw was a dead one,"[24] or Theodore Roosevelt's: "I don't go so far as to think that the only good Indians are dead Indians, but I believe nine out of every 10 are."[25] Assimilation through boarding schools was purported as a kinder, gentler approach to "the Indian Problem."

The Carlisle Industrial Indian School, in Pennsylvania, which hundreds of Haudenosaunee young people were forced to attend, had been open for thirteen years when "The Friends of the Indians" made remarks at the Nineteenth Annual Conference of Charities and Corrections in 1892. In his report, "The Indian Policy and

Its Relations to Crime and Pauperism," Phillip C. Garrett reflects on the national angst regarding how containment policies, such as removal and the reservation system, had left Indigenous populations in a state of "pauperism and crime."[26] Pratt and others such as Philip C. Garrett, chairman of the conference, and president of Colorado College, William F. Slocum, encapsulate the role (and destructiveness) of boarding schools through the guise of benevolence; though to hear them tell it, they believe what they are saying in terms of their service to the Indians. Granted, the bar was low.

Commenting on "The only good Indian is a dead one," Pratt iterates, "In a sense, I agree with that sentiment, but only in this: that all the Indian there is in the race, should be dead. Kill the Indian in him and save the man."[27] This nuance distinguishes from the overt annihilation of Indigenous bodies and overt land theft in the form of outright massacres that were the backdrop of this assimilation policy but proves just as insidious in its goals and scope. At the same conference, William Slocum opines:

> We may differ in our opinions in regard to the amount of training they are capable of receiving, or in regard to the direction that training should take; but we are agreed that the national policy of pauperizing the Indian and keeping him as near to the brute life as possible, is a mistake, and a national disgrace to us.[28]

Slocum goes on to say that of course none of the friends of the Indians were proposing that Native peoples were qualified for industrial or agricultural schools, let alone the likes of Harvard. These statements reflect a subpar educational system, created to serve the avarice of the settler nation-state. Pratt saw organized physical activities, such as sports, as a way of "civilizing" those whose bodies he saw as impure and barbaric. This, however, was extremely gendered, and not surprisingly, the opportunity for girls and young women in boarding schools to play on sports teams was far less than the opportunity for boys and young men, a reality that mirrored mainstream society.[29]

Given the long history of U.S. and Canadian efforts to destroy Indigenous peoples physically and culturally, the Haudenosaunee determination to defend and revitalize their traditions is critical to their survival. Thus, the conversation over whether women and girls should play represents a struggle over sovereignty, and a lamentation for land, lifeways, and language lost. This is tied to how communities understand tradition in relationship to women and girls playing.

Experience of Tradition and Lacrosse

Amber Hill a Six Nations of the Grand River band member raised on the Tuscarora Nation Territory in New York, began playing women's field lacrosse in the mid-1990s, at seven or eight years old. She started on the team that would play in the 2006 World Championship in Prague when she attended Niagara Wheatfield Middle School, two miles from her home on the reservation. Amber has played on all-Haudenosaunee teams, such as the First Nations Elite team, and for teams with Indigenous and non-Indigenous players, such as the Saint Catherine's league in Ontario and for Syracuse University. She has played co-ed box lacrosse and on the Haudenosaunee women's team for the 2007, 2009, 2013, and 2017 World Championships. Growing up on the Tuscarora Reservation, she did not know that girls and women were discouraged from playing in some Haudenosaunee communities until, at age seventeen, she "went to Syracuse and met people from Onondaga."[30] Another player represented in this chapter, Corinne Abrams, a citizen of the Tuscarora Nation in New York, who began playing in 2000 at the age of eleven, remembers visiting Onondaga Nation and being told she was not supposed to play. Both Amber and Corinne started playing at a young age, played on teams where they were the only or one of a few Haudenosaunee girls, and played on the Haudenosaunee women's team and in World Championships. They also both shared that they did not know about the conversation over girls and women playing, citing Tuscarora as not as traditional as Onondaga or Tonawanda,[31] but naming decolonization and revitalization projects of which Tuscarora has been a part. Both are proud of their lacrosse background and were not exposed to the teachings about defined roles that men and women have in relationship to traditional lacrosse. However, now that they have come to know these teachings, Amber and Corinne articulate their respect for those who say they should not play, acknowledging the role that those who may oppose their playing hold in carrying Haudenosaunee culture. Simultaneously, Amber and Corinne see their own playing as part of Haudenosaunee culture.

Sandy Jemison, of the Seneca Nation in New York, coached both of these players and one of their mothers. Sandy started the Seneca Girls Lacrosse Club, a club in which over six hundred girls have played since its beginnings in the mid-1980s. Sandy learned to play lacrosse during her high school years at the Emma Willard School, a private boarding school in Troy, New York. She coached women's lacrosse at SUNY Fredonia and the Haudenosaunee women's lacrosse team that plays internationally. Sandy was part of the group who went to the Six Nations Council of Chiefs at the Six Nations Longhouse in 2005, in order to seek approval for the Haudenosaunee women's team to represent the Haudenosaunee people at an international level. Sandy's memory of lacrosse in Haudenosaunee communities spans several generations. She was at the center of the moment in the 1980s when Haudenosaunee girls were asked not to play at Onondaga. She has extensively fundraised and put together a group of volunteers to sew uniforms on a dime for a girls' team preparing to compete at an international level; and she has supported hundreds of girls and women to pursue lacrosse in their communities, in colleges, and at the international level. Sandy shares the following narrative of the impetus to bring lacrosse back to her community in the 1970s:

> And then I went to college. That was just at the time of Title IX. And it was like—we wanted to play lacrosse. A bunch of us girls wanted to play lacrosse, but we couldn't. I mean no one really recognized girls playing lacrosse. So what we did is we used a corner of the golf course. The [college] had a golf course. And it's a rich, private college and we had an area that was about the size of a lacrosse field. And that's where we would practice. And we'd practice. We were just a little club team. And we went up to Clarkson or Potsdam, tried to get some girls from up there to play. And that's what we did for about four years. And then when I finished college, I came home, and I played around here. And there was really nothing. I mean there was absolutely nothing for young women. I got so disappointed because I got home from college, and yeah, everybody was around, but they were all out partying, and doing this. And Lake Erie is just down the road and all the clubs that lined the lake, the big beach clubs they called them. They have the big dance floors, bars. And you'd go down the road, and there's another one, and there's another one, and there's another one. They were all along the lake. And if you're a college kid, it's a fun place to be. But I was also looking for something else to do. We had tennis courts over there so I would play tennis. But I still wanted to play lacrosse. So when I heard about the Iroquois Nationals, it made me frustrated. They had a men's team. And I kept saying, why not women? Why not women? We can do a women's team. We can teach them.[32]

Sandy's commitment to lacrosse and Haudenosaunee girls and women playing is palpable in interviews. She is from a community that is known for being traditional *and* for condoning girls and women playing, a seeming contradiction that I address in this chapter.

Tsiotenhariio Herne, from Akwesasne, played every sport possible "because my mom thought it was good for me to be in figure skating for all my life, and I hated it." Tsiotenhariio "never thought about girls being able to play lacrosse," until someone on her soccer team suggested it. At that time, they "played for the fun of it," and they "had a really weak program."[33] It was their coach, John Lazore from Akwesasne, who built up the new and fledgling program at the Salmon River High School, just east of the Akwesasne Nation in New York. Lazore has two daughters who, Sandy Jemison reports, made commitments to Dartmouth as high school sophomores. At the time that Tsiotenhariio Herne was playing on Lazore's team, his daughters were in sixth and seventh grades, playing varsity lacrosse for Massena High School, twelve miles southwest of Akwesasne. They transferred to Salmon River, and Lazore worked with the team year-round, playing tournaments in Rochester, Syracuse, Albany, and Long Island. Tsiotenhariio recalls:

> It was one of our last tournaments, and we had got beaten pretty bad, and we were getting beat by these good teams like constantly. And we got beat by this team by two or three points. And he turned to us and said when was the last time you guys got beat by twenty or ten? That's when I realized just how much he has put into us.

Tsiotenhariio said she kept playing for the sheer joy of it. "It felt right, and I loved it. I could run. Everyone told me how fast I was on the field and I loved that." Tsiotenhariio, who at the time was going through personal struggles and "making stupid choices," says that lacrosse saved her life and helped her feel important.[34] Tsiotenhariio's story comes through interviews I had with both her and her mother, Akwesasne Mohawk Clan Mother Mommabear, and also through the film *Keepers of the Game* (2016). In this film—which brings together women's contemporary lacrosse and the coming-of-age ceremony Ohero:kon—Tsiotenhariio shares how both lacrosse and Ohero:kon saved her life by bringing her closer to her culture.[35]

Mommabear frames the conversation with the following: "The game was given to the people." Mommabear asks, "At what point did it become a men's only game?"[36] Most would say that the medicine game never left the community, but that colonization and assimilation has changed lacrosse. The game that returns now to communities is a contemporary game, with traditional and medicinal roots. During the process of returning, the contemporary game has become a space whereby Haudenosaunee men can consolidate masculinity, after hundreds of years of having traditional roles diminished by settler colonialism. Mommabear says:

> And part of the reclaiming, there became an attitude with it. Because the more that the men were unable to hunt and fish, the more that they were unable to go to war, the more that their own environment and their roles and responsibilities got diminished, they had to hold fast to certain areas of the culture, and so lacrosse became a men-only sport.[37]

In understanding this conversation from a Haudenosaunee perspective, it is important to acknowledge how much colonization has taken away from Haudenosaunee men, informing a growing popularity of contemporary lacrosse as a cultural reclamation. A female player from Oneida Nation (New York) captures the manner in which Haudenosaunee communities in the 1980s, when lacrosse was dramatically increasing in popularity, staked their place as the original people to play the game. She says of her time playing at college, "I wasn't going to sit there and let white girls play my sport and not play."[38]

What it means to be traditional, and how Haudenosaunee communities define lacrosse in traditional terms, is at the center of the conversation regarding Haudenosaunee girls and women playing. Jeanne Shenandoah, Onondaga midwife and Elder, believes that it is a loss of tradition that is resulting in, and has resulted from, Haudenosaunee girls and women playing contemporary lacrosse. Jeanne, and those who share her hard line, says that this generation of Haudenosaunee girls and women who are playing are "disrespecting our true way for convenience." Jeanne expands: "Lacrosse has become a popular thing.... It's always been here, besides the fad that it is now—the college deal, and scholarships and awards.... It's always been here." She and others fear that the way contemporary lacrosse is being pursued mistreats the game. She states:

> I truly believe that you need to know who you are, have a good solid foundation about who your people are, who you are. And then you can go anywhere you want, all over the face of this earth. But that's the problem; people are not giving these young people this knowledge. We're at the point where we have several generations that are away from it, have been away from it, have not truly tried to be part of it,

or to be faithful to our way of life and our cycle of thanksgiving all year round. . . . So some people go to Longhouse for that day, and that's that.[39]

These concerns are directly linked to Haudenosaunee community members' sorrow for what has been lost through colonization—lifeways and cultural knowledge, specifically—and their fear that something so central to Haudenosaunee culture as lacrosse is that which is taking younger generations away from these knowledges and lifeways.

Jeanne Shenandoah and Berdie Hill, introduced in the introduction to this book, share similar, though not identical points of view when it comes to Haudenosaunee girls and women playing contemporary lacrosse. The following piece of our interview illuminates Berdie's and Jeanne's shared points of view, as well as why it is imperative for the two of them to be central to this chapter:

> Berdie was a good friend of mine. We didn't share the same views on everything, but they were similar. We were friends. She came from the older group of people teaching stuff. . . . So, it was comforting to be friends with them because we shared the same views, although I think that my lifetime of political experience and activism—always in some kind of movement—I'm not patting myself on the shoulder. I'm just giving a—it gave me a wider view of things. So, I was very curious. I did a lot of reading when I was younger and met up with people. I've traveled all over the world. Not on a vacation, ever. Always working. So, it helped me to understand a lot of the stuff that had happened to us. Most of our people don't even realize, you know? Intrusions into our thinking and people not realizing it.[40]

Jeanne and Berdie embody the sovereignty that the Onondaga Clan Mothers held when they decided in the 1980s to lay down on the field if Haudenosaunee women played.[41]

The internal conversation over girls and women playing crests at a particular moment in 1987 when Onondaga Clan Mothers asked a team of women not to play, creating fuzzy lines around what is and is not a medicine game. Did they see it coming, that these Clan Mothers would put their foot down? Sandy Jemison recalls preparing for a demonstration of girls' lacrosse to be held at Onondaga Lake, between the Iroquois Nationals women's team and "one of those Syracuse teams—CNS (Cicero-North Syracuse) or Fayetteville-Manlius." She continues, "It was going to be a big deal because they were really a powerhouse in New York State at that time." She was informed the night before by coach and supporter Carol Patterson that, "You don't have to pack, we can't play.... The Clan Mothers are real upset... and always been fighting that we shouldn't be playing, and they said that if we play, they will lay down on the field, so we can't play." So when Sandy protested, Carol continued, "No, we can't. They're going to go there in full force, and that's what they're going to do. So, I'm calling everyone and telling them just to stay home."[42]

Sandy did not stay home: "I got mad—very mad." While she was there, some asked her why they were not playing:

> And some of them could understand [the ban from playing], and some did not. And [some] said, look, we have videotapes of the games. We'll show the Clan Mothers what we're playing, and ... what's so different about it. And [the Clan Mothers] didn't even want to see it. They said, "No, we know it's still called lacrosse."[43]

Speaking about her mother who played for the team in the 1980s, Corinne Abrams (Tuscarora) relayed:

> I have the picture of my mom on the cover [of the *Turtle Quarterly*], sitting with her jersey on, but I don't know that she actually played. I think that it got up to the point where they had the team together and then they never actually played. I didn't realize it had been because the Clan Mothers protested.[44]

The caption next to the image of Kim Clause (now Kim Abrams) says, "Lacrosse Player, Iroquois Nationals." The article, which pictures Kim Clause giving instructions for a simple lacrosse workout, says, "The Iroquois Nationals Lacrosse Program, which includes both men's and women's teams, was begun [*sic*] after being sanctioned by the Iroquois Grand Council."[45] Not long after this went into publication, some Haudenosaunee leadership told this team's leadership that they would not be able to call themselves the Iroquois Nationals.[46] So decades later, when Haudenosaunee women again formed teams to play internationally, they called themselves the Haudenosaunee women's lacrosse team.

What is at stake for Haudenosaunee communities is respect for the integrity of the medicine game, and that is what frames the conversation. There is protection around the medicine game. Haudenosaunee people whom I interviewed ranged from not interested in sharing much about it to outwardly offended by questions about it. However, girls and women playing contemporary lacrosse calls for more precise definitions of what constitutes medicine and where medicine resides in relationship to the game.

The following piece of interview with Sandy Jemison illustrates the depths with which Haudenosaunee women are engaging these sets of questions, while demonstrating that Haudenosaunee tradition is, as the late John Mohawk described it, "a thinking tradition."[47] Sandy Jemison works to make distinctions between the contemporary and historical medicinal game and the contemporary game played with plastic sticks:

> The rules and all of it, it was developed in Scotland. It's just a whole different thing. ... We don't use protective [gear]. Our purpose isn't to go out and settle differences. [The men's] reason for doing it—we play for the Creator also but it's in a different way—for his pleasure.

She blends the historical and contemporary medicinal game that only men play:

> They play for his pleasure, but they also play to settle differences. That's what it was developed for—to settle differences, and for the Creator's pleasure.

She articulates the historical medicinal game:

> And they played for days, and sometimes weeks. Their game would go on and it would go from here to who knows where—wherever it took them.

And then she concludes about the contemporary game of field lacrosse played by women:

> And we just had it for different reasons, and we had all these different rules that were very different from the men."[48]

Here, Sandy Jemison wrestles with an articulation of the differences, echoed by one of the young women she coached: "But it's different when I guess you're playing with a regular stick because it's not the medicine game. I guess that's why it's okay."[49] How the contemporary game played by men and women is defined in traditional and medicinal terms is a deeply gendered conversation. Indigenous scholars' work on Haudenosaunee law and teaching illuminate the relationship between tradition and women's lacrosse playing.

Conceptualizing Tradition—Part Two

Theresa McCarthy names the capacity of the Great Law and its significance for the Haudenosaunee to address present difficulties:

> The Great Law is not meant to impinge on personal autonomy, but it encourages collective responsibility. It offers many orienting principles that can unify people, without requiring everyone to be the same. Historically, it has brought together people who were so at odds that they were killing each other, so it has accommodated enormous differences without being exclusionary. And it has continued to serve these functions since its formation. Over time, we have had Christian Chiefs and Clan Mothers; we have had leaders who have intermarried with non-Natives or other nations. We have the Mohawk Workers who are Christian proponents of the Great Law as well as staunch advocates of the Confederacy. The system can transcend diversity, and it is meant to be inclusive. It espouses thinking and practices meant for everyone to get behind.[50]

This understanding of the Great Law is incredibly vital for naming how the conversation regarding girls and women playing contemporary lacrosse functions within Haudenosaunee communities. As McCarthy states, personal autonomy is understood as part of Haudenosaunee teachings. Girls and women enact that autonomy regularly by playing lacrosse, even without full consent or approval from their communities. Collective responsibility comes into play when whole teams and their leaders look to the future of their sovereignty and decide to stay home instead of flying with settler state passports, as happened with the U19 girls' team in 2015. The Great Law holds within it "the things we hold sacred; our languages, cultures, beliefs, and rights. The people within the circle are to be of one mind and heart."[51] That there is not one clear opinion about if girls and women should play contemporary lacrosse does not indicate that some are traditional and others are not, but instead that the Great Law intends that the "one mind" of the people should be expansive and inclusive. As McCarthy purports, this "commitment [to futurity] long predates settler encroachment" and is grounded in present action.[52] Haudenosaunee tradition holds space to address changing times through a concept of adding to the rafters. The wisdom of this concept, found in the Great Law, accommodates changing times and needs.[53] Mommabear articulates the concept: "In the frameworks of our Great Law of Peace, they put in there a provision that says, when you come in times of change, and you need to change this law, you can add to the rafters."[54]

Culture is dynamic, not fixed. Fixed interpretations of what it means to be traditional threaten the health and longevity of any culture. And yet, Haudenosaunee community members sometimes employ this definition of tradition to explain why Haudenosaunee women and girls do not, or at least should not, play contemporary lacrosse. There are two primary positions people take in explaining the relationship between tradition and girls and women playing lacrosse. The first position is that traditional communities do not approve of or condone girls and women playing contemporary lacrosse. Within this framework, some articulate that traditional Longhouse communities do not endorse girls and women playing contemporary lacrosse, and their playing is understood as assimilation. In broad strokes, not accounting for individual differences within communities, Onondaga Nation, Tonawanda Seneca Territory, Oneida Nation (New York), and Tuscarora Territory hold this belief. In interviews, two young women from Tuscarora describe a direct relationship between support for girls and women playing contemporary lacrosse and a less traditional community. Amber laments, "My family, unfortunately, wasn't traditional . . . and nobody in our community that I knew of was outwardly against women playing lacrosse."[55]

While some talk about tradition as something that must be preserved, from a position that tradition was not and cannot be wholly lost, others talk about it as that which must be revived, further demonstrating how tradition is in flux. Corinne, also from Tuscarora articulates:

> So we don't have the Longhouse and traditional ceremonies as often as they do here [at Onondaga]. There's a small group of traditionalists on the Tuscarora Reservation who are trying to revive our culture and bring back the ceremonies. They're doing that more and more now than they ever have in the past thirty to forty years.[56]

A second tenet is that Haudenosaunee girls and women playing lacrosse is traditional, as it is embedded in the Great Law of Peace. The Great Law allows for adding new rafters when times call for it, and as Mommabear and others contend, colonization has called for it. Again, not accounting for individual differences, this is the point of view present at Six Nations, Akwesasne Mohawk Nation, and Cattaraugus Seneca Territory. From the perspective that it is possible to be a traditional Longhouse community and support girls and women playing contemporary lacrosse, women and girls who play are shaping what traditional means in this moment and for the future. Michelle Schenandoah reminds me that Indigenous peoples think out seven generations, or about 150 years, and adds, "I feel that we think even beyond that."[57] In order to define Haudenosaunee traditionalism and make connections to this conversation, I turn to Haudenosaunee scholars Theresa McCarthy (Six Nations, Onondaga, Beaver Clan) and Audra Simpson (Kahnawà:ke Mohawk) for the ways in which they conclusively demonstrate the limits of defining traditional along a linear timeline, illuminate the ways in which traditionalism informs essential discussions among Haudenosaunee community members, and define traditionalism as that which has continuity, is about futurity, and at times requires ethnographic refusal as a way of preserving that continuity into the future.

Both McCarthy and Simpson critique an understanding of Haudenosaunee tradition that is unchanging and relegated to the past, charging Iroquoianists such as J. N. B. Hewitt, Arthur C. Parker, Alexander Goldenweiser, Frank Gouldsmith Speck, Annemarie Shimony, and Wiliam Fenton with searching for a "pure" traditionalism, untainted by colonization. This approach to understanding Haudenosaunee tradition erases culture for the ways in which it firmly places it in the past. Simpson says, "[Fenton] focuses on the 'traces' of cultural knowledge and practice that appeared pure and unchanged from the past." The problems with this, Simpson contends, are many, not the least of which is that

> the people he worked with were knowledgeable about tradition and Iroquois lore, but that knowledge and lore was of "the New Religion" of Handsome Lake, the preacher/prophet who revitalized and reinterpreted the Great Law of Peace to adjust Iroquois people structurally and ritually to the demands of a settler landscape.[58]

What Fenton et al. miss in these representations of untainted, precontact Haudenosaunee traditionalism is traditionalism that deeply responds to colonization, traditionalism that Haudenosaunee communities reinterpret through the continuity of the Great Law. McCarthy demonstrates how Fenton's lifetime of work with the Haudenosaunee did not at all render him sympathetic to their labors toward sovereignty. For example, Fenton was actively against the intergenerational fight the Haudenosaunee engaged in to rematriate twenty-one wampum belts from the New York State Museum in Albany and the Heye Foundation Museum.[59] Haudenosaunee wampum belts represent the confederacy and agreements that Haudenosaunee have made with other nations, including the United States and Canada. They are incredibly important living records. Fenton's work toward preserving a past culture not only missed but was actively against the contemporary labor of ensuring sovereignty and how that labor is deeply connected to tradition.

Simpson and McCarthy demonstrate how the Great Law itself is an articulation of tradition as continuity and futurity. The Great Law came into being precontact to address discord among Haudenosaunee nations, demonstrating the fluidity of culture as needs arise. The Great Law disrupts the idea of a fixed tradition, precontact. The Great Law already names Haudenosaunee traditionalism as an intellectual, ongoing reality, a tradition that has the broad ability to deal with warring nations and extremely diverse points of view. The wisdom of the Great Law is rooted in the strength of its enduring structure and the flexibility to add to the rafters, add to the structure, as needs arise. This is a wisdom that has withstood colonization and will continue to withstand the effects of settler nation-states.

Haudenosaunee women lacrosse players demonstrate through their actions that simplistic representations of this conversation cannot and will not adequately capture that which is at stake for Haudenosaunee communities. Haudenosaunee women speak of the interdependence they have among the generations, how the wisdom of Elders is passed on from generation to generation, and the ways in which this conversation is tied to loss of language and land. To Berg's 2007 *New York Times* article, "Lacrosse: Cradle of a Sport Has Crossed the Gender Line," Amber Hill, of Six Nations of Grand River, responds, "Western media, people who are outside of our communities, that don't really understand what's going on, [can villainize] the Clan Mothers ... [when] they were standing up for what they believe in."[60] Another player, from Tuscarora Nation in New York, concurs, demonstrating what makes this conversation distinctly Haudenosaunee:

> Standing up for what you believe in is a fundamental in our culture. My grandmother always says, Indians are the most stubborn people you'll ever meet....

That's ingrained in us to stand up for our ideas and what we think is right, and how we think our future generations should live.... That's why we're still around today, right? Because maybe another culture would have... [assimilated] into your culture.... But we don't do that. And that's why we're still here today, although in smaller numbers because of the sad history that's happened... settlers taking our land.[61]

Amber also disagrees with Berg in that their cultural stance stood in the way of anyone playing lacrosse, stating:

You can't say that one incident held back anyone. Claudia Jimerson still played lacrosse at Fredonia and became an all-American and she's in that same age group. And she played on my World Championship team after having five kids... so I don't agree with this statement [that women were held back from playing].[62]

These young women are relying on the lessons learned from their Elders to make decisions for their own daughters: "I would never *not* allow my daughter to play.... I would always want her to go out, just because that's my identity and I believe that's a good thing for me and for future generations. But I can completely understand why someone would think the opposite, too. And I see where they're coming from... and I respect that."[63] Amber's daughter played on a Haudenosaunee, travel, co-ed box lacrosse team from the age of three until she had her first moon (first menstruation). When her team traveled to Onondaga or Tonawanda for games, her daughter could not play. When I asked Amber how this is understood and who enforces this, she responded: "It's an understanding [that she doesn't play]. Although if I wanted to push it, her team wouldn't let her, and if [her team] wanted to force the issue, the staff at Tonawanda and Onondaga wouldn't even let her on the floor."[64]

Amber says she is "sad that she has to see that and experience that being so young," but also glad "because she won't get slapped in the face with it when she's older and doesn't understand."[65] Amber says she and her daughter go to Longhouse, are very traditional, and play lacrosse. Here, Amber seems to be conceptualizing her and her daughter's participation in lacrosse as *in addition* to their participation in Longhouse. In our conversations, Michelle Schenandoah reflected that Amber's participation in lacrosse and traditionalism could be interpreted as adding to the rafters.[66]

Claiming the Narrative

The following discussion goes deeper into refusal as it pertains to Haudenosaunee tradition and women and girls playing contemporary lacrosse, specifically engaging Audra Simpson's generative theoretical category of ethnographic refusal. In short, generative authority is established by Haudenosaunee people through ethnographic refusal because communities decide what to include and not include in their own story production. This authority over Indigenous peoples' storytelling is highlighted by Diné scholar Jennifer Denetdale: "So it is that the Navajo in the very telling and retelling of their own stories, that their experiences under colonialism, have resisted Americans' representations of Navajo."[67] Denetdale further articulates, "Perspectives of the past are constructions that transmit cultural beliefs and values that allow for the reevaluation and revaluation of indigenous peoples' oral traditions as valid and legitimate histories."[68] In the following, I give three examples whereby Haudenosaunee community members determine the narrative, resisting colonization and transmitting cultural beliefs and values through ethnographic refusal.

The first example is the 2013 documentary *Sacred Stick*, directed by Michelle Danforth (Oneida, Wisconsin), which narrates Haudenosaunee reclamation of the contemporary game of lacrosse, rooted in the traditional game and medicinal ceremony. The film gives a narration of lacrosse that links the contemporary game played with plastic sticks, to the historical game played with wooden sticks, to the cosmological game played in the Sky World, and echoed in the medicinal game. The medicinal game, given to the Haudenosaunee as a ceremony to settle disputes and bring medicine, weaves in and out of the film, adding layers of complexity to how lacrosse is defined for future generations of Haudenosaunee people. In the film, Onondaga leader Oren Lyons says that in the medicine game, "all the participants are spiritual beings for the help of the person or community, the nation, the earth. We can do that with the game."[69] The medicine game, still played today during ceremonies for community or individual healing, is intimately linked to the traditional and contemporary game in the film. "Traditional" and "medicinal" are sometimes used interchangeably when referring to the contemporary game. Both, however, are meant to firmly position the contemporary game of lacrosse as a game that originated with the Haudenosaunee.

Sacred Stick tells the story of how Haudenosaunee communities claim lacrosse, focusing on how it never left the communities. Though some Indigenous claims are enacted at the formal level, passport disputes, for example, others are made through informal venues such as film. Such spaces of claiming, according to Māori scholar Linda Tuhiwai Smith, "teach both the nonindigenous audience and the new generations of indigenous peoples an official account of their collective story."[70] Haudenosaunee communities have been in the process of crafting the official account of lacrosse for broader audiences and new generations of Haudenosaunee people since the 1980s when the Iroquois Nationals men's team began preparing to play internationally, to claim sovereign spaces through *their* cultural game. The film relays that between 1887 and 1987, Iroquois men's lacrosse teams were officially banned from playing internationally, as they were deemed, "too professional." During that ban, many Iroquois men were recruited to play on U.S. and Canadian teams, but without the ability to openly identify themselves as Haudenosaunee or claim the game as their own. Prior to the ban, Haudenosaunee teams were encouraged to "dress up Indian" to add to the fanfare. This demeaning practice threatened to separate Haudenosaunee players from their communities and lacrosse through stereotyping and romanticization.

When Jeanne and Berdie, in their interviews with me, drew a hard line against Haudenosaunee women and girls playing contemporary lacrosse, they did so within a framework of refusal, speaking to what is at stake for Haudenosaunee communities. There is very little about the heart of their culture that these two women were willing to share. There has been too much damage, too much theft. I asked Jeanne if she could share something with me about traditional lacrosse. She responded:

> What do you want to know about it? Maybe I don't want to tell you about this stuff. I just got through telling you that it's such a hard time for us to protect what we have.... We're asking for respect, that you don't come walking in the door and say, "this is my house," and you come in, you want to know everything—you've got a right. People think they have a right to know everything and then do whatever they want, which ... is disrespect because people use knowledge as possession. Possession moves it away from spirituality.

Jeanne recalls a time when, in the late 1800s, the local newspaper would write about and share photographs of Haudenosaunee ceremonies:

I've seen those clippings. . . . They were appropriating . . . and that caused us to close the door here. Because it's our teaching that the door's open anytime and anybody's welcome, but stuff was going on . . . that caused us to close the door. [Lacrosse] is one of our original teachings. It's a very sacred medicine game that we use to help each other. Specific ways that they do it, that I'm not gonna say because if somebody hears it, they'll go running out there setting it up.

The one statement that Jeanne shared with me about Haudenosaunee lifeways was this:

My path in life is to be humble, compassionate, dedicate myself to the spiritual ways of thanksgiving, all the time; to appreciate the original teachings of my people, to keep them alive. Because if we don't have spiritual beliefs or behaviors, what are we?[71]

For those who oppose girls and women playing lacrosse, this is what is at stake. For those involved in traditional Longhouse communities, who oppose Haudenosaunee girls and women playing lacrosse, the integrity of the Longhouse and the future of tradition itself feels threatened.

The third example of ethnographic refusal is found in Tuscarora Seneca Clan Mother Berdie Hill's interview. I opened up the introduction to this project with Berdie's words: "There are just some things that I am going to say that you are going to have to accept."[72] Berdie was not going to spend the time, waste the energy, to help me to understand cultural difference. Simpson describes these interactions as "everyday encounters [that] enunciate repeatedly to ourselves and to outsiders that 'this is who we are, this is who you are, these are my rights.'"[73] From this theoretical base that Berdie created for our time together, she discussed her concerns about the physical risk associated with birth directly speaking to a culture very much concerned about carrying on into the future. This set of concerns speaks directly to an understanding that the traditional power that women hold in their communities must be regenerated because of the effects of colonization. Berdie Hill illuminates this concern, connecting the risk when she expresses fear that women playing any game of lacrosse, medicinal/traditional or modern renditions, could anger the Creator, thereby threatening women's ability to give birth and carry on the nations. Also present in her concerns is a pragmatic fear of a shift in balance, when she states, "I think it's very simple. There are some things that are meant for the women and some things that are meant for the males. Playing lacrosse is one that's meant for the males. You don't see males bearing children, do you?"[74] In fact, one of the women I interviewed was not able to have children and attributed it to her playing box lacrosse earlier in life.

A midwife, Jeanne Shenandoah has spent nearly fifty years seeing to the health and continuation of the Haudenosaunee people and culture through birth. Western medicine has pushed birth from the home into the hospital, diminishing the power held in women's bodies and midwifery knowledge for Indigenous and non-Indigenous women alike. Prior to 1920, most women had their babies at home. Jeanne Shenandoah recalls, "homebirth was not anything unusual. That's just how you did it." And then there wasn't a homebirth at Onondaga Nation for forty-five years, between approximately 1920 and 1965. Jeanne's great-grandmother was a midwife prior to 1925, but then stopped. I asked, "What was happening between your great-grandmother being a midwife and delivering babies and then you becoming a midwife?" to which she responded:

> They started going to the hospital because they frightened out those women.... Everyone who came in here did so with a mind to straighten up "those Indians." So, there wasn't much dialogue... because the medical establishment, they think they're the only ones who know.

Jeanne talks about the Onondaga Health Department coming to the Onondaga Nation and threatening midwives, including her great-grandmother:

> I guess they assumed they were going to be taking over here and were going to call the sheriff and arrest these midwives for doing homebirths here, when they were told not to. They said it was dangerous and dirty—anything you want to say bad about Indians.... So they did [stop the midwives], and my great-grandmother was one of those women—she was the last one. And they threatened her so much. They really frightened her.... And she stopped.

And then around 1965, there was an "accidental homebirth." "That's what they called it, and it was the first homebirth in forty or forty-five years."[75] Soon after, Jeanne joined a group of women in the area who were organizing around homebirth. Since then, Jeanne has traveled to many Haudenosaunee communities as a midwife and shifted the perception of homebirth from dangerous and dirty to natural and possible. She has worked to decolonize birth, bringing increased sovereignty to the Onondaga Nation and other Haudenosaunee communities. The work that Jeanne Shenandoah has done for Haudenosaunee women throughout her life undermines any possible binary representation of this conversation, as she has spent decades caring for Haudenosaunee women as they birth Haudenosaunee babies. For Jeanne, lacrosse is in contradiction to the health of Haudenosaunee women, their children, and the future of Haudenosaunee nationhood. The danger of placing this conversation over girls and women playing lacrosse along a binary of those opposed / those in favor is that we miss the nuances of how Haudenosaunee women fight for the integrity of women's bodies and national sovereignty.

Both Jeanne Shenandoah and Mommabear hold women's bodies at the center of Haudenosaunee culture and nations. Jeanne has spent her life working with the health and well-being of women and childbirth. Mommabear has supported traditional homebirths in her community, including her own and those of her daughters and daughter-in-law. Mommabear sees contemporary lacrosse as an avenue for healthy childbirth, stating:

> [Lacrosse] doesn't hinder ability to give birth. If anything, it helps it, because obesity is probably the number one thing that prohibits a healthy birth. So when you have a healthy, fit mother, her odds of having a healthy pregnancy and delivery are greater.... There's nothing more appealing, more healthy, than a woman with a fit body. And there's nothing that can help the reproductivity of our nations than ... our women having healthy bodies.[76]

What is central for Haudenosaunee people, the importance and integrity of the medicine game and women's health and well-being, is negotiated within shifting and colonized landscapes. The lived reality of Haudenosaunee women lacrosse players and their relationship to their bodies and tradition is what is shaping the cultural game of lacrosse. Tsiotenhariio Herne brings together tradition, playing lacrosse, and traditional homebirth. To some extent, the question of whether women playing contemporary lacrosse will hinder their ability to give birth—a question still quite unanswered in the mid-1980s at a pivotal moment in the conversation—has been answered. Many, many Haudenosaunee women lacrosse players have had children, and continue to have children.

Rematriating Lacrosse

Rematriation is an act of calling Haudenosaunee community members back to their culture after generations of genocidal acts against traditional cultural knowledge. The acts and movements of rematriation are centered on the female because of matrilineality, not so that women can dominate, as men dominate in patriarchy, but rather a turn to the female helps put things back into balance in the hypermasculinized spaces of colonization. A turn to the female helps to shatter stark binaries of good/evil or man/woman. Queer Indigenous theory also turns toward the feminine for balance, as a way of reestablishing healthy masculinities. We see this turn toward the female and how that turn opens the possibilities for radical belonging in Elizabeth Doxtater's artwork *Teiotiokwaonháston/Deyodyogwaǫháhs:dǫh* (It Encircles Everything), Theresa McCarthy's analysis of Doxtater's artwork, and a narrative that Diane Schenandoah and Michelle Schenandoah share about an Oneida women's gathering held in 2018. *Teiotiokwaonháston/Deyodyogwaǫháhs:dǫh* is a diorama that is a visual narrative of the Great Law. Belonging is depicted by a circle of about one hundred Haudenosaunee women surrounding a cultural fire. The women face outward, arms outstretched, ready to call in current and future generations. McCarthy says that "Doxtater's piece helps convey how the Great Law recognizes diversity by giving a three-dimensional sense of the magnitude of representation our people have within the system."[77] Art deeply reflects life, as in the narrative that Diane Schenandoah and Michelle Schenandoah shared with me about a 2018 Oneida gathering of women:

> D: At the Oneida gathering last year, were around this tree . . . everyone was expressing how amazing it was that we were together. When all the women came together around this tree, as we did these buses came, and they were filled with kids—our kids.
>
> M: Oneida kids. They were in a summer program, the summer program my son's in now.
>
> D: We had no idea they were coming. But here come all these kids from our territory. "Grandma!" And they joined our circle. And that circle grew and grew. . . . That's part of our prophecy, that we're supposed to share our teachings with our people. . . . The children will be the little ones who will carry that through.[78]

Arguments about who is and who is not traditional significantly limit what traditionalism is and does within Haudenosaunee communities. Both Jeanne and Amber make a distinction between defining traditional as existing within an individual identity and tradition as community engagement. Jeanne states, "There's a difference between theory and practice. A lot of people running 'round talking about theory. If you truly believe in something, then you practice and make it a part of your whole being."[79] Amber echoes that distinction:

> Maybe they say they're traditional and they don't go to Longhouse... when you're traditional, you're always supposed to have a good mind. And you're not supposed to... participate in any activities that would change your mind and give you a bad mind, so drinking, alcohol, anything of that nature. But people do that and then say they are traditional.... They like the badge of "I'm traditional, but I do what I want."[80]

Also, within this field of understanding, the community sees itself as fluid, and change not just assumptive of assimilation but traditional in and of itself, as communities make important shifts as needs arise, though the speed at which change is enacted and how is up for debate.

Haudenosaunee peoples, like all Indigenous peoples, held onto, and continue to hold onto, their cultures by their fingertips over and over again, through all of the difficulties of colonization; this ongoing history of survival, within a cultural context of respect and interdependence, must inform any discussion about the internal conversation about women playing lacrosse. It is this painful and recent past that is shared intergenerationally among Haudenosaunee women and their communities. With this collective, painful past, generations look to each other to hold the culture. At the center of this interdependence is the value of respect, which Linda Tuhiwai Smith says is

> consistently used by [Indigenous] peoples to underscore the significance of our relationships and humanity. Through respect, the place of everyone and everything in the universe is kept in balance and harmony. Respect is a reciprocal, shared, constantly interchanging principle which is expressed through all aspects of social conduct.[81]

In theorizing the Anishinaabemowin concept of chidibenjiged, Mark Freeland echoes this reality: "As a concept, chidibenjiged demonstrates a large sense of belonging, as we help to promote belonging in our web of relatedness. It is not so important what it is—power, energy or principle—only that we live in a way with the rest of life that promotes belonging."[82]

Conclusion

In this chapter, I have demonstrated how Haudenosaunee girls and women playing lacrosse presents an important challenge for communities in their efforts to name and claim the contemporary game of lacrosse that is played worldwide, and the work Haudenosaunee people do as ambassadors worldwide. Those who simultaneously are part of traditional Longhouse communities *and* support women and girls playing are at the forefront of making these distinctions, disrupting a presumed gendered prohibition and allowing for cultural change.

To carve out space to play the contemporary game, Haudenosaunee women work through the distinctions among traditional, medicinal, and contemporary lacrosse. Sometimes they use traditional and medicinal interchangeably when referring to the historical game of lacrosse played by men. Most effectively, they make a distinction between what they are playing and the medicine game. When I asked one player if what the Iroquois Nationals (now the Haudenosaunee Nationals) men's team plays is the medicine game, she said that what the women play is not a medicine game because they do not [detail about the medicine game] but was not sure if the men [detail about the medicine game]. She said she has had opportunities to go to medicinal games but has not. Another reason the definition of medicinal or traditional lacrosse is murky has to do with some not having access to the medicine game. When asked if she knew where the medicine game was held, one young Haudenosaunee player stated:

> I don't know because I've never heard of it happening. Only like years and years ago.... It's been described to me as precolonization. So they would have these medicine games that would go on for weeks.... And they would be without boundaries.... They would be in the woods ... in the whole forest. That's what I picture in my mind's eye the traditional game of lacrosse ... what it used to be in ancient times ... but I really can't say that I'm familiar with the modern medicine game at all.[83]

The turn of phrase, "modern medicine game" further connotes that tradition has a contemporary iteration, and change is understood to be part of tradition. While the medicine game being played only by men is not in dispute, that girls and women are playing opens the question of what constitutes medicine. When Haudenosaunee men play the contemporary iteration with plastic sticks and talk about it as their medicine game, they are not talking about the same game that is played within the community for healing purposes. Even though the contemporary game played with plastic sticks is not the medicine game in the strictest definition, it does provide medicine and healing for the men playing, perhaps especially when they are playing non-Indigenous teams. Michelle Schenandoah references Mommabear's articulation of the contemporary game as a medicine for those who play it, but not *the* medicine game.[84]

Mommabear speaks into this opened space with, "It only becomes a medicine when it changes a life." She expands by saying that it is traditional to adapt, change, and shift, without that automatically meaning assimilation. She reminds us that the Great Law of Peace has a provision that when the needs of the community call for it, rafters can be added to the Longhouse to make room. She says that men play the medicine game because it is their role to deal with sickness, death, and war for the community, but that if a time came and there were no men to play it, women would have to play the medicine game in order to keep that part of Haudenosaunee culture alive.[85] Mommabear makes sense of girls and women playing lacrosse by engaging tradition, attaching the medicine inherent in the game with the need to heal that Haudenosaunee girls and women face in colonized spaces.

A binary understanding cannot adequately access what is and is not traditional. What is traditional are the deep, sometimes frustrating ways in which community members wrestle through these discussions: deeply intellectual, philosophical, and heartfelt. From this set of voices from Haudenosaunee communities we can see three conflicting conceptualizations of how lacrosse and tradition are being defined and used. First, while a simplistic representation of controversy provides an entry point for some people, it can provide a mask of tradition with little to no cultural understanding behind it. This type of engagement provides for the maintenance of the status quo of prohibiting women from playing. While it is part of the conversation, it does not provide solutions to the problems Haudenosaunee communities face. Second, there is a definition of lacrosse as a Haudenosaunee game; it is a medicine game, and all iterations of that game are traditional lacrosse and should only be played by men. This view can be understood as understanding tradition as static and as resistant to change, as well as committed to holding onto understandings of Haudenosaunee teachings. While one can certainly argue that this perspective is also grounded in preserving culture for future generations, it does so by attempting to continue the culture regarding lacrosse as male only. While lacrosse may encompass multiple forms (i.e., medicinal and contemporary) it must continue to prohibit Haudenosaunee women from playing.

Finally, this is contrasted by a perspective that defines lacrosse as originating with Haudenosaunee peoples as a medicinal game played by men. This third way conceptualizes the contemporary games of lacrosse, played with plastic sticks, as significantly different from the medicinal game to allow for the lifting of prohibitions. This perspective allows for change in culture when it is for the well-being of communities. This conceptualization is also grounded in the future of tradition. It responds to the intergenerational trauma of colonization by connecting more people to healing—in this case, Haudenosaunee women—as active participants in a game that is evolving all over the world. They show up and intervene with Haudenosaunee culture. The women playing lacrosse are participating in the culture, and by conceptualizing contemporary lacrosse as a different game than the medicine game, they are engaged in a cultural phenomenon that brings them healing, closer to their culture. Through lacrosse they engage in Haudenosaunee expressions of sovereignty on an international stage, rematriating stolen lands. They break through the prohibitions around gender and lacrosse while continuing the culture into the future.

As McCarthy articulates above, the Great Law is grounded in inclusivity of multiple perspectives and provides a method of working through conflict. Considering the extraordinary changes that colonization has brought to Haudenosaunee communities, it should not be surprising that there are challenging conversations within and between communities about lacrosse. However, as communities undo the damage of colonization, they engage in their own cultural protocols to provide structure and guidance. While the tide is turning in many communities toward women playing the contemporary forms of lacrosse, this conversation is evolving. It is up to the communities to continue to engage in their own cultural methods to overcome challenges.

CHAPTER THREE

WOOD, PLASTIC, AND GENDER: CRAFTING THE STICK

Haudenosaunee women have always had a relationship with lacrosse and the wooden lacrosse stick. Akwesasne Mohawk Clan Mother, Mommabear remembers as a fourth grader, "sitting with my mother, weaving the webs of those sticks."[1] She describes soaking the cat gut and cow hide in preparation of weaving the web of those sticks. Tewaaraton (Mohawk) is the word for both the netting of the sticks and the game of lacrosse itself. Since it is women who traditionally weave the baskets, this word reveals an intimate linguistic relationship between women's action and lacrosse. And yet, there exists a protocol within Haudenosaunee communities that women are not to touch a man's lacrosse stick. Some say the protocol begins when the stick and the male player begin their relationship; some say it only applies to wooden, and not plastic, sticks. Respect for the protocol is closely aligned with a general agreement within Haudenosaunee communities that only men play the medicine game. While Haudenosaunee communities may offer differing degrees of support for women's lacrosse, most agree that only men play the medicine game.

The Haudenosaunee women I interviewed for this project make two critical interventions into the adage that women do not touch a man's lacrosse stick. First,

Wooden lacrosse stick. Photo courtesy of Lee Nanticoke.

they add to the naming and claiming of lacrosse as a Haudenosaunee ceremony via this protocol. Second, they demonstrate how that very protocol can flatten power by obscuring the colonization of women's bodies *even when* it is invoked to honor Haudenosaunee women's power, while calling into question internalized sexism in Haudenosaunee communities. For the first intervention—naming and claiming lacrosse as a Haudenosaunee ceremony—I examine the oft named explanatory clause, "because of the sacred nature of the game." For the second intervention—exposing the flattening of Haudenosaunee women's power and calling out internalized sexism—I examine an equally named explanatory clause, "because of the power that women have to give birth and menstruate." Through these two interventions, players and their supporters open space to name and frame the action of lacrosse play and the meanings therein. Through this power to name, a new category of healing and Haudenosaunee lacrosse emerges that includes *a medicine for oneself.*

Hearing the Stick Protocol

How one hears and understands the stick protocol depends significantly upon one's proximity to the culture. From a contemporary perspective, the rule that women do not touch a man's lacrosse stick might appear old-fashioned. Within Haudenosaunee constructions of time and space, however, this protocol is more about memory than history. Mvskoke poet Joy Harjo illuminates the nuanced differences between memory production and historiography: "Memory [is] not just associated with past history, past events, past stories, but non-linear, as in future and ongoing history, events, stories. And it changes."[2] This understanding of memory connected to the past in order to inform the present and future reflects my earlier discussion of tradition being as much about the present and future as it is about the past.

In *Silencing the Past: Power and the Production of History*, Michel-Rolph Trouillot posits that the production of history is dependent upon its contemporary relevance and the audience's particular relationship to that which is historicized. To interpret the convention from a western, settler-colonial perspective is at once to historicize the protocol and to lodge Haudenosaunee culture firmly in the past. Trouillot points to how what is represented as history makes its mark in particular, authentic ways for those who hold "an honesty vis-à-vis the present as it re-presents that past."[3] It is here that we can see a clear distinction between the protocol as heard by someone outside of Haudenosaunee social and ceremonial life and someone within. For Haudenosaunee communities, memory is shared relationally and intergenerationally and is more relevant than history. The protocol is a part of contemporary life and exists in relationship to tradition, which is based more in collective memory than in the past where history most often resides in western society.

The stick protocol exists within Haudenosaunee communities, holding traditional memory for contemporary survivance and for futurity. It holds a set of questions that are neither fixed nor universally answered. That the set of questions around the stick protocol exists further roots lacrosse into Haudenosaunee ethos. Some link Haudenosaunee women and girls playing lacrosse to a separation from Haudenosaunee culture. For example, Clan Mother Berdie Hill says, "They don't know. If they knew they wouldn't play."[4] Another interviewee thought women and girls play, "because they weren't from the very beginning of their life given that core feeling, that love of spirituality, of who we are, our very existence."[5] One mother of a player told me that after learning more about her culture she probably wouldn't let her daughter play, if she had to do it over again. A few conversations I had with Haudenosaunee women about the stick protocol in effect respond to these concerns. Additionally, they address perceptions that have the potential to disfigure the stick protocol through, say, a western feminist lens.

I asked one Haudenosaunee woman, "Is it possible that certain things that Haudenosaunee women do or not do is not about restriction, but about power?" She responded, "Yes. And about balance.... And I think a lot of modern feminism doesn't understand that well and positions it as a restriction for women in our culture when that's not how we understand that. Some people might misconceive that as well because they're not fully familiar with a lot of the roots of these teachings."[6]

Another woman describes her professor's "aha" moment when she was able to begin to see the cultural differences between western notions of gender equality and Haudenosaunee understandings of power and gender balance.

> I never felt growing up as a Haudenosaunee woman that I was any less than a man. Actually, I was made to feel that we have so much more to bring to the people as women. I'll never forget my first-year women's studies professor, and when I would try to articulate some of these things to her, she looked at me puzzled. And it wasn't until the end of the term when she figured it out, and she was just, "you really come from a different way of understanding, of being a woman." And I said, "yeah."[7]

Thus, the starting place for understanding the role of the lacrosse stick protocol is that it comes from a place of gender balance. In Haudenosaunee thought, gender constructs exist in a relationship of balance, not hierarchy as in settler logics. However, internalized western patriarchy in Haudenosaunee communities, through boarding schools, for example, risks obscuring women's power. The stick protocol sits at the juncture between the lived and real, cultural, political, economic, and social power that Haudenosaunee women hold and how that power is undermined even as it is heralded. To call Haudenosaunee women's power "traditional" without critically examining how it continues to be undermined both within and outside of Haudenosaunee communities only helps to uphold western hierarchies of gender, as I work to demonstrate in this chapter.

A Brief History of the Wooden Lacrosse Stick in the Haudenosaunee Context

Before the 1970s, all lacrosse was played with wooden sticks. Woodies, as they were called in interviews, were produced by Haudenosaunee artisans such as John Wesley Patterson, who started Tuskewe Krafts at Tuscarora Nation, Herb Martin (Six Nations Reserve), Enos Williams (Six Nations Reserve), and Alf Jacques (Onondaga Nation). In 1937, five years after the beginnings of box lacrosse, Canadian Robert Pool invented the double-walled lacrosse stick that would inform the plastic model commonly used today.[8] The popularization and westernization of lacrosse meant an increased demand for sticks, which were made by Haudenosaunee artisans, many of whom refused to commercialize production.

Alf Jacques began making lacrosse sticks with his father and then opened a small manufacturing house at Akwesasne. At the height of production, 1972 and 1973, the company produced 11,500 sticks each year. In 1970, an all-American lacrosse player at Johns Hopkins University, Richard Tucker, started the lacrosse stick manufacturer STX and patented the first plastic molded head. This synthetic lacrosse stick quickly became immensely popular, so that in 1974 Jacques's production of wooden sticks fell from nearly 12,000 to just 1,200. He sold off his stockpiled wood as firewood to deal with the devastating decline.[9] At the same time, the development of the synthetic stick contributed to the wooden lacrosse stick becoming that much more embedded within Haudenosaunee traditional and medicinal space. Today the wooden lacrosse stick is most closely associated with the medicinal and traditional game, and largely understood to be the sphere of men. The rule that women do not touch a man's lacrosse stick precedes this shift from wood to plastic, but this shift certainly informed and even solidified it.

That women do not touch a man's lacrosse stick does not always mean that they do not have their own woody. Corinne Abrams (Tuscarora) relays, "My great-grandma used to tell me that she used to play lacrosse all the time. She would pick up a [wooden] stick and run around because she was the fastest girl in the neighborhood." Though plastic sticks were available at the time, Abrams began using her mother's stick when she was a small child—a woody that had been crafted for her mother to match the contemporary sticks marketed to female lacrosse players across the globe: "My mom had this old wooden stick. A wooden one . . . it was a girls' stick. It was really hard, so I would get so frustrated trying to play catch with her stick.... She cut it down on the bottom, so it was shorter, and she painted it purple for me." I asked where her mother got her woody:

> On the Tuscarora rez, they have a lacrosse barn. It's called Tuskewe Krafts.... And at this place, they take the long wooden sticks, and they keep them for a year in this vat where they humidify them. And then they bend them and do the whole process of grinding them down. My mom got her stick there, and at the time, wooden sticks were a lot more popular.... The plastic sticks are easier to throw a ball and catch with, but the wooden sticks are a lot stronger.[10]

Corinne describes how she learned of the stick protocol:

> Tuscarora is a lot different. Each reservation has its mini culture. So, at home, I was allowed to play catch with my brothers... and I remember one time visiting Onondaga... I just picked up my stick and went outside... and my grandma came out and said, "you can't do that here."... Later I was with two friends, and we were sitting in their dad's pick-up truck, waiting. He went inside for something, and... he had a miniature lacrosse stick... and I went, and I touched it. And the girls, both of their faces dropped, and they were like... "why would you touch that? That's my dad's lucky stick."[11]

Another young player who grew up at both Onondaga and Oneida Nations, whose family member made her a wooden lacrosse stick, remarks, "It's unheard of for a woman to have a wooden lacrosse stick."[12] These diverse relationships to the wooden lacrosse stick speak to the diversity of Haudenosaunee communities and nations themselves. What they have in common is a deep relationship with the history of wooden lacrosse sticks and the contemporary use and meanings of those sticks.

Intervention 1: Because of the Sacred Nature of the Game

Haudenosaunee lacrosse and its ceremonial roots need to be placed within the context of the language and ceremonial loss through colonization. While boarding/residential schools instilled punitive responses that extend to cultural protocols, Haudenosaunee women remind the players of the ceremonial game by calling them to play with a good heart. It is the sovereignty that women enact to uphold the protocol, revitalize language, and make decisions to play or to not play lacrosse that rematriates language and lacrosse.

The sacred nature of the game is demonstrated through its use for the sick and dying. As one mother from the Oneida Nation explains, "Lacrosse is a very sacred game, and there are special games that are held if somebody's sick."[13] The Great Law of Peace (Haudenosaunee constitution) provides language from the funeral of a Chief that conjures the memory of what constitutes a good life: "Let nothing that transpired while you lived hinder you. In hunting, you once delighted; in the game of lacrosse, you once took delight, and in the feast and pleasant occasions, your mind was amused, but now do not allow thoughts of these things give you trouble."[14] Seneca anthropologist Arthur Parker records that before Haudenosaunee leader Handsome Lake's death in 1815, "a game of lacrosse was played to cheer him."[15] According to the anthropological study *Iroquis* [sic] *Foods and Food Preparation* (1916), "When a person has been suffering from some ailment such as rheumatism, lame back, fever, or headache, it may be decided . . . that a game of lacrosse is required."[16] Though as promised, I will not share details of the medicine game in the space of this book, one mother of a lacrosse player (Mohawk, Six Nations) gave a few details about how such a ceremony would be called into being. Her narrative further articulates the profound importance of the medicine ceremony.

When Haudenosaunee women explain the stick protocol accompanied by the explanation that it is "because of the sacred nature of the game," they firmly place lacrosse within Haudenosaunee ceremonial space. A 2007 *New York Times* article quotes Jeanne Shenandoah saying that it is "because of its deep spiritual significance, women are not even allowed to touch a stick."[17] When I asked Clan Mother Berdie Hill about this quotation, she said, "That's true," and added, "Instructions from all across the Haudenosaunee land was that no females should participate in the game. They shouldn't even touch the lacrosse sticks or their equipment."[18] Within Haudenosaunee logics of balance, not all in the community deal with death and illness; most often it is male-identifying community members. This means that the playing of the medicinal game of lacrosse is played by those members of the community. Something as important as a ceremony that deals with death and illness comes with protocols. The community works together to keep those protocols intact in order to facilitate ceremony.

Haudenosaunee communities articulate that the contemporary game should be played with a good mind, as with the medicine game. An Onondaga man who plays the medicine game explains how the medicine game overlaps with the contemporary game, and the role women have in shaping its execution:

> This one woman who I really respect, she's a language teacher. She's my teacher. She highlighted this one time when [a male lacrosse player] was getting up and getting ready to fight with this kid. She said, I just stood right up in the stands. And he grabbed this kid, and we went just like this to him [pantomimes threat], and he panned over to his mom. And his mom was standing up then. And she was just standing there. And he gets all sad, and he walks away. But I'm glad she shared that because then she followed up with, the way she looks at it is whenever you pick up that stick you are playing for the Creator.[19]

From the spectator stands, this Haudenosaunee mother and Onondaga language teacher compels the players to play the game in a good way, *for the Creator*. This moment represents the overlap that Haudenosaunee community members have in understanding the contemporary and medicinal game of lacrosse. As discussed later in this chapter, this understanding of the overlaps between contemporary and the medicine game of lacrosse is applied to men's lacrosse. Women's lacrosse requires a conceptual distinction between the contemporary and the medicine games in order to create the space for them to play, while aligning with Haudenosaunee cultural protocols.

When Haudenosaunee ceremonies were systematically pushed underground and outlawed by settler states, the ceremonial connections of lacrosse flew under the radar because it was perceived as only a sport. As a result, it retained much of its strength as a ceremony within Haudenosaunee communities, intervening in a history of colonization that grossly interferes with ceremonial space. However, with the growth of contemporary lacrosse worldwide, Haudenosaunee communities work to bring continuity to the ceremonial aspects of their lacrosse.

Compounding how communities fiercely defend ceremonial space is language loss during the boarding/residential school era. One Haudenosaunee community member laments the loss of language due to boarding schools:

> It's sad to say; my mother came from, her parents were the boarding school age and lost the language with her. They never taught her. They were fluent speakers and never taught her how to speak the language, and it was never passed to me.

And that's the saddest thing I've ever heard in my life, how the boarding schools, what they took from our people. It's just disheartening for me to think about. It's unfathomable to imagine that could even happen to somebody, or to a whole race of people.... They were just taken, well my grandfather was taken, and he was beat if he spoke the language.... How do you get taken somewhere and literally tortured? It was taught to him that it was wrong to practice anything that was native to our culture, especially speaking the language.... And so when he married my grandmother, she was a fluent speaker, and he would tell her, "don't ever teach these kids to speak Native because they don't ever need to use it. They'll just get ridiculed. They'll get punished." So, they never did. They never taught them the culture or anything. So . . . it was just gone. In one generation it was gone. Everything.[20]

In another interview, a young woman explains what language loss means for ceremony:

All of the ceremonies are done in the original languages. But once in a while, the speakers will speak English because not everybody knows it fluently, the language. So, they'll speak English and tell what's going on.... But you can tell the difference [between] who knows the language fluently and who doesn't because the speakers will joke, just joke around and then one crowd will be chuckling and laughing, and it will be quiet on this side.[21]

The stick protocol sits within the turmoil of colonized ceremonial space. It is embedded in the succinct and poignant way Mommabear reminds me that

we have to look at the turn of the century when the government began to outlaw a lot of our beliefs and practices and customs.... And then we have to look at the time when anyone who practiced them were considered witches. And we have to look at how those practices meant death and how harsh and brutal they were.[22]

These conversations and the interviews I had occur amid communities working to regenerate ceremonial space and revitalize language. There are times when this space is increasingly healthy—people travel from far and wide to attend ceremony at Tonawanda Seneca Territory and new language programs and immersion schools.[23]

Language and ceremony revitalization efforts mean communities look closely at how colonization has imposed and enforced a two-gender binary and associated roles. I spoke with Brandon Tehanyatarí:ya'ks Martin, the administrator of Onöndowa'ga:' Gawë:nö', the Seneca language immersion program for adults at the Cattaraugus Seneca Nation, about language revitalization and gender. Martin made a parallel between the recitation of the thanksgiving address—the central Haudenosaunee invocation that opens gatherings—and lacrosse. While it may be the case that historically only men recite the address and play lacrosse, revitalization projects necessitate that women participate in ways they may not have before. In the case of Onöndowa'ga:' Gawë:nö', most participants are women, and in order for the language to survive, women now also learn and recite the thanksgiving address.[24]

I witnessed the recitation of the address at a Haudenosaunee research symposium at the State University of New York, Buffalo, in the fall of 2015 by Jody Lynn Miracle (Mohawk), who opened the event while holding her small child in arms as he worked to say the words with her. Mommabear said that in her youth, her mother and aunts would burn tobacco, a job historically reserved for men alone, but there were no men around to do it. Now that both men and women from Haudenosaunee communities are playing lacrosse, a challenge is posed to a system of gender balance that prescribes strict roles, and communities are asking to what extent did boarding/residential schools undermine gender fluidity and impose strict roles. However, as demonstrated in this project, women's lacrosse has a distinct role in rematriation, or the returning to traditional relationships to land, water, and women's power. The following narrative is situated within the set of questions over whether Haudenosaunee girls and women should play lacrosse, a set of questions that only intensifies as they draw closer to their languages. It is a narrative that represents the ongoing challenge that communities face as they engage the work of cultural—and in this case language—revitalization.

Language and the Sacred Nature of the Game

This narrative demonstrates the work of Haudenosaunee women to root lacrosse more deeply into their communities, defining lacrosse as Haudenosaunee through language. When Haudenosaunee women travel far from their homelands to play this sport that has been taken up by the world, it is the work that is rooted in Haudenosaunee homeland that keeps these strong connections going.

In June 2018, I was invited to sit in during an immersion language class at Cattaraugus Seneca Territory, a program of first years that began in January 2018.

The eight students involved attend the program five days a week, from 8:00 a.m. to 4:00 p.m. The six women and two men, ranging from their twenties to fifties, went through an admission process whereby they were tested on their ability to translate twenty verbs from English to Seneca and twenty verbs from Seneca to English. One of their instructors, Gayanëö:wi' Jacky Snyder, a mother of four who has played lacrosse since she was five, says that the program is foregrounding the group's total comprehension instead of strict time frames, moving to the next lesson only when everyone is ready. As such, this group of first years will roll into the second-year program on no particular timeline and continue indefinitely.

There were two Elders, first Seneca language speakers, in the class I observed. Participants took turns sharing a narrative in Seneca based on what the instructor had written on a small piece of paper they drew. When language learners had questions, they directed them (in Seneca) to the two instructors, who, if they did not know or needed clarification, asked the two Elders. Jacky told me after the class that the two Elders are sisters, that one is silly and the other more serious, and that they balance each other. Their role as keepers of knowledge was palpable in the room. Those who are teaching and learning Haudenosaunee languages are dependent on that knowledge. After the class, Jacky told me that learning her language *saved her life*. As such, she feels indebted to the Elders who help her learn it, which means she sits deep within the questions of what it means to play lacrosse and become more entrenched in her tradition through language acquisition. Jacky shared a narrative of being in an immersion experience and struggling to tell the story of her lacrosse game from the night before and how she got slightly hurt. She looked to the Elders in the room to help her with the language to describe it, but they would not. Jacky says there is a woman lacrosse player in her class who speaks of her playing in Seneca. The two Elders in the room do not like it, but they do not stop her or refuse to help her when she needs it.

Jacky, who has been playing lacrosse since the age of five, decided in 2018 not to play, feeling that going deeper into the language, and working more closely with Elders, means that she more adequately understands why women and girls should not play. Because she understands this in the Seneca language, adequately explaining it in English seemed to fall short, nor did I ask her to. This, however, does not mean that she is not involved in lacrosse, but rather that she has found ways to integrate lacrosse and the Seneca language more deeply for her community.[25]

Jacky says lacrosse is her life. Jacky has decided to incorporate lacrosse into her life in ways that involve her passion for revitalizing the Seneca language, announcing local lacrosse games entirely in the Seneca language. She has expanded this to teaching her students to announce, as well as saying the North American Minor Lacrosse Association's code of conduct all in Seneca:

> O'tgwanö:nyö' niyögwe'da:ge:h eswadaja'te:' nëgë:h wënishä:de'.
> Ëswatši'wä:ne' gëjögwagëödö:nyö' hadiksAshley'shö'öh dewa'ë:ö' hënötga:nyeh.
> Sgë:nö' agwënohdö:nyö' honënijohgo:d ajänyonyAshley'shä' nijoiwayä'dahgöh.
> AjänyonyAshley'shä' o'wajä'dak ga'nigöë:i:yoh o'wa:do' ne'hoh ho'watgahdë' swaya'dade' swatga:nyeh swatši'waha' koh näh dëöwönä'nya:'.
> Jë:gwa:h da'deswadadasha:a', **ögwe:nyöh ëjëtšiya'ditgëh**. Gado:gëh heö:weh gaiwayëdahgöh.
> Ëyetšiyadë'gahdë' swëjöhgwa', ëwönotgädöshä' heswaiwajë:to'.
> Da:ne'hoh.

> *Welcome to the North American Minor Lacrosse Association Games. We are proud to be an association built on the foundation of respect.*
> *Respect for the athletes who compete, the fans who support them, and the officials who serve us. With this in mind, we expect all here today will act respectfully and demonstrate good sportsmanship. Inappropriate behavior or verbal harassment will be addressed by those assigned as security. A lack of cooperation could result in removal from the premises. Cheer for your team and enjoy the efforts of these athletes.*
> *Nya:wëh.*[26]

Haudenosaunee women lacrosse players connect to community and Elders who hold languages. Yes, there are challenging conversations over girls and women playing within the acquisition of language. Jacky's story demonstrates the inherent struggles, notably that Haudenosaunee women are not looking to disassociate themselves from their communities even as some do not support their participation. Assimilation is not the better option; sitting with the difficulty of the questions is. It is part of the way that they hold onto their nationhood and communities as they travel internationally to play. Jacky's voice and perspective carry tradition into the future, along with the set of questions about how Haudenosaunee women and girls are involved and will be involved in lacrosse. Rather than a linear progression toward increased support for their playing, Jacky's decisions regarding lacrosse—not to play, but to be increasingly involved through language—is part of the richness of this set of questions. Cattaraugus Seneca Nation is revitalizing the language, holding Longhouse, and offering quite a bit of community support for girls and women playing lacrosse.

Jacky Snyder says that Haudenosaunee tradition is full of contradictions. When discussing Jacky's narrative and decisions about language and lacrosse as a guest lecturer in a graduate seminar, one student asked what it is about learning her language that brought Jacky to the decision not to play. I responded that I did not press Jacky to explain it to me in English, and I do not know Seneca. I am comfortable with Jacky's narrative being part of this project as a way to demonstrate the complexity of the questions and how language revitalization is part of the conversation. In my time with Jacky, I was reminded of Clan Mother Berdie Hill's caution to me that if I were to continue with my inquiry, there would be some things I would hear that I would have to accept even if I did not fully understand. I was reminded of Audra Simpson's words about these "everyday encounters [that] enunciate repeatedly to ourselves and to outsiders that 'this is who we are, this is who you are, these are my rights.'"[27]

Intervention 2a: Revealing the Effects of Colonization on Women's Bodies

The second stick protocol explanatory clause—"because of the power she holds within her to give birth and menstruate"—refers to the medicinal power associated with the female body. Michelle Schenandoah explains: "As lifegivers, women hold an elevated status in our society. We have an equal responsibility with men to protect life, and that is they (men) protect us."[28] Haudenosaunee women demonstrate an ease, diminished in western society, about the power that they hold. Yet, as I demonstrate in this section and the next, this power functions paradoxically in the lived reality of Haudenosaunee women. One young woman explains, "I'm very familiar with women not touching the stick, [especially] not on your time, because [of the] power that you have ... especially during that time."[29] Two other Haudenosaunee women concur that women especially should not touch a wooden stick "when she's on her time" and "when [the stick] goes through ceremony."[30] A connection to creation informs how Haudenosaunee women articulate their roles and participation in ceremony: "When you're going through your menopause, and you're all done with your moon, you can go to the ceremonies. You can do all the things that you couldn't do when you had your moon. So, it's not like it's because you're a woman, it's because you have that medicine in you."[31] Finally, one young woman lacrosse player further connects power and medicine: "Being a woman and being able to give birth, that's a very, very powerful medicine.... When a woman is pregnant, she's seven times more powerful than anybody else.... There's a lot of energy right there. And it's a good medicine."[32]

It is enticing to reflect on this power and leave it intact as a given. However, assuming this power has remained intact glosses over, and has the potential to erase, the ways Indigenous women's bodies have been systematically attacked by colonization. I first heard the stick protocol at a Haudenosaunee research symposium at SUNY Buffalo in 2012. Since that time, whenever I asked about it in interviews, it is clear that the protocol is common knowledge within Haudenosaunee communities:

> I asked my grandma from Onondaga once why we couldn't play, why women weren't allowed to. She explained to me that the wooden sticks were medicinal.... She said, "when a woman is having her menstrual cycle, she is not allowed to touch a wooden stick because at that time a woman is sacred, and she'll put weakness on the stick."[33]

Others internalized the protocol, like "feeling it inside":

> It's a lot more than just the ability to give birth.... You're connected to the moon ... that is your medicine as a woman. You have a really, really strong medicine. And if you're around things that you're not supposed to be, that person could get really hurt, like, say, touching lacrosse sticks, like boys' lacrosse sticks. You don't because they could get really hurt because they have their own medicine.... It's just natural for me to think like that ... a lot of people sometimes feel offended when you're like, you can't touch the stick because it's bad luck or something. I've never thought of it like that.[34]

While this woman recognizes her power in relationship to the protocol, others illuminate how a simple utterance of the protocol, even with the explanatory clauses, can perpetuate internalized western patriarchy that interferes with rematriation.

For example, as mentioned earlier, at a Haudenosaunee research symposium at SUNY Buffalo, a young man relayed that he had always heard that women do not touch a man's lacrosse stick because of the power that they have to give birth and menstruate. Then, naming a lived reality that does not match the ideal of the protocol, a young Haudenosaunee woman responded, "Whenever I hear that I'm not supposed to touch a man's lacrosse stick, I feel dirty, tainted, shameful."[35] Another young woman lacrosse player echoed this sentiment in an interview with me: "I don't know that our ancestors would be proud of how we're conducting ourselves and treating women, and kind of thinking they're bad luck or weak for touching a lacrosse stick."[36] This small assembly of responses to the protocol reveals how women's traditional power and women's disempowerment through the lingering effects of colonization function side by side within Haudenosaunee communities.

A Tuscarora Haudenosaunee lacrosse player illuminates how an unreflective reference to women's traditional power obscures their disempowerment. She remarked, "There's a lot of things that they use 'women's energy' for. . . . And I do think that maybe there is some kind of base in that teaching but to promote it blindly is no different than Christians saying *you can't*."[37] Similarly, a community leader at Six Nations Reserve stated:

> We've found that too often our people have a very superficial understanding of what it is to be a Haudenosaunee person. So, we know we respect women, but do we know why we respect? I think every community member would tell you we have a high regard for women, but where does that value come from? How do we show that? How do we live that? We say these things, but we don't live them. Most people know about moon time, but why do we call it our moon time? What is it connected to? How is our cycle connected to the moon? Most people can't tell you how or why.[38]

The settler-colonial apparatus has colonized Haudenosaunee women's bodies with a particular sickness that has also infiltrated Haudenosaunee communities, resulting in layers of tension whenever the power of Haudenosaunee women's bodies is invoked. Take, for example, the influence of Dr. Holder, a physician who worked in a boarding school, who published his "research findings" in *The Medical and Surgical Reporter* of 1890. This white man kept intimate details of the onset, duration, and frequency of menstruation for ten Indigenous girls "under his supervision." In his report, titled "The Age of Puberty of Indian Girls," Dr. Holder opines:

> It is presumable that the early marriage and consequent sexual excitement, with the entire absence of modesty in Indian thought and conversation, would tend

to cause precocious menstruation, and *facts establish this impression*. Even in the girls who are in school til after puberty menstruation occurs earlier than among white girls in the same latitude.[39]

Dr. Holder established these "facts" through the close (and gross) examination of Indigenous girls between the ages of ten and fourteen and comparing the result to "the only American statistics" on white girls and menstruation.[40] His work to establish the "facts" of white women's piety and virtue and Indigenous women's promiscuity reflects the cruelty with which settler society approaches Indigenous women's bodies. This study is absurd, and yet his influence remains on the real, lived experiences of a Haudenosaunee woman when she hears about the power that she should feel but cannot shake the feelings of filth and shame.

Far less insidious interactions with young Indigenous women color how they experience the explanatory clause, "because of the power they have to menstruate and give birth." Diné scholar Laura Tohe recalls the stark differences between her community's approach to coming-of-age and the western version she learned in school:

> Throughout [our] ceremony, my body was acknowledged, celebrated, and made ready for the role of mature woman. Reaching puberty was not a shameful, dirty, and dreadful experience. Celebrating puberty with the Kinaaldá ceremony ushers the young woman into a society that values her. As I recall now, how different this experience was from the seventh-grade teacher who taped black construction paper to the windows and gave the boys a longer lunch break, so that he could show us "The Film" on female puberty.... When our young teacher from Wyoming finally turned on the lights, his face was flushed red with embarrassment.[41]

Any young person learning about menstruation can and should have a better experience than this. Tohe's narrative is applicable to how Haudenosaunee communities must work against the stream of western information coming at their young people at a systematic level.

Cutcha Risling Baldy (Hoopa) examines how menstrual taboos are enforced and reinforced and "how ceremony combats the ever-present systemic gendered violence of settler colonialism and (re)rites systems of gender in Indigenous communities through Indigenous ceremonies."[42] Baldy tracks the anthropological roots of menstrual taboos and lands, not surprisingly, on colonial perceptions of coming-of-age ceremonies that celebrate menstruation as "primitive." Baldy's project effectively demonstrates how the (re)riting of her ceremonies has meant healing and freedom from this internalized perception. In the Haudenosaunee context, one Six Nations community member, who has an influential role in rites of passage ceremonies, laments, "We were actually letting western culture define what kind of Haudenosaunee person they would become."[43]

When Haudenosaunee women hear about the power they have to give birth, the message comes entwined with a history of eugenics that robbed Indigenous women of the opportunity to have children through forced and coerced sterilizations in the 1960s and 1970s. There is a great deal at stake. Amber Hill, from Tuscarora Territory, tells a story that shows the eugenic undercurrent of settler nation-states.

> I will tell you this story . . . and I get so angry. When I played in the U19 World Championship, in 2007, we were in Peterborough, Ontario. And I didn't tell anyone except for Tia Schindler, who is my best friend forever, I was fourteen and a half weeks pregnant. And we didn't have another goalie, and my daughter's father didn't want me to play. But I said this is my team. This is my family. They don't have anybody else. It's only a couple games. I'll be fine. I believe we were playing Japan. And I came out of my net. I had let a girl behind me. They tossed the ball over my head. I was sprinting full speed toward her, so she didn't shoot at the net. And my feet were moving faster than my body, and I fell forward, and my legs came up over my head. I stood up, and I remember seeing Tia's face on the sideline because she was our assistant coach. And she was white. But she was the only one that knew. And I got up, and I said, I'm fine. I'm good. We're okay. And I didn't feel anything I was okay.

But she wasn't okay and needed to go to the hospital.

> We went to the hospital in Peterborough, me, Sam, and Tia, and they did an exam, and the doctor pulled his glove off and said, "you're probably going to lose your baby." Very nonchalant, don't care, like was just—I said, "I'm nineteen years old, I'm terrified, I'm really going to lose my baby?" He's like, "yeah, you're probably going to lose your baby."[44]

The doctor's comment, "you're probably going to lose your baby," uttered twice, is resplendent with judgment and indifference, masking subconscious cultural anxiety over Indigenous women birthing healthy babies who will become Indigenous adults that threaten the national fabric built on stolen land. Was that doctor thinking about the security of land he most likely owns, the land on which his practice and hospital sit, or on which his children's schools sit? Probably not. He doesn't have to. His derogatory response reflects the institutional racism of the settler state, which is adept at hiding such discourse from its citizens and even from itself, but it is nevertheless present and active.

My conversations with Haudenosaunee women about the lacrosse stick protocol reveal some of the power that is imbued in femaleness, which is connected to the life-giving power of the earth, water, and moon. Simultaneously, the conversations reveal the work that the players and their supporters are doing to make sense of this protocol given the history and contemporary realities of colonization to that very power. The labor they engage in to make the stick protocol comprehensible in settler colonialism helps to uphold the intended power of the protocol, while revealing the protocol's tendency to compress that power without fuller articulations of colonization. As demonstrated earlier, the recognition of female power that is intended by the stick protocol can be flattened by Haudenosaunee communities themselves, as discussed in the section that follows.

Intervention 2b: Exposing Internalized Sexism in Haudenosaunee Communities

In an interview, Mohawk scholar Dawn Martin-Hill speaks of the profound degree to which Haudenosaunee communities have internalized western patriarchy:

> What's so stinging about it is that it is coming from our own people. It's not coming from white men or white society. We can't blame them. They're not doing this to us; it's our own people doing this. And my theory is that they've been so acculturated, subconsciously absorbing for the last three hundred years the way in which our women are diminished in their authority, diminished in our power, diminished in our rights. I don't even think they're consciously aware that they're now carrying out what the oppressor had begun—they're finishing the job.[45]

In another interview, a young Haudenosaunee man echoes this point: "We have patriarchy in our communities . . . years of being impacted and influenced by it. . . .

It's not just men. There are women who have taken it on. . . . I really find myself trying to take a step back and think. And who do I go to? I can't even go to my Gran because she's internalized it. Who do you go to?"[46]

The challenge is to pull apart the strands of Haudenosaunee tradition from colonization, in a way that affirms tradition in contemporary life. Dawn Martin-Hill illuminates the difficulty of this work: holding onto what is truly traditional, accepting superfluous changes, and deciding what to reject as a western imposition.

> We evolve, and we change . . . but the roots are very deep and strong on the positions and the values, and the protocols are all in place. But you can't necessarily do what you need to do for a certain ceremony because those things you need are just not accessible. So you replace it with something else. But in the last couple hundred years, they've replaced it with western thinking. That's the danger, where the value of women, the value of Clan Mothers, the diminished authority that they now have to almost be subordinate to the Chiefs. And all of that is not traditional.[47]

It is within these strands—the core of tradition, how tradition has necessarily changed, and western impositions—that questions about the ceremonial aspects of lacrosse arise.

Ongoing colonization informs how women are treated in the Longhouse, and in Haudenosaunee communities more generally. When men teach girls and women how to be and become Haudenosaunee women, they usurp the role of mothers, aunties, grandmothers, and Clan Mothers. In 2006, for example, the Haudenosaunee women's lacrosse team went before a council of Haudenosaunee Chiefs from across the entire confederacy at Six Nations of the Grand River. Leaders from Onondaga Nation in New York were trying to convince those at Six Nations not to allow these women to represent the Haudenosaunee Confederacy at the World Championship in Prague. One mother describes a scene of drama when the good feelings the young women experienced at the moment of approval were dashed by colonial impositions of virtue:

> You're feeling all good. . . . All the parents are in Longhouse feeling relieved. And then [the Chiefs] get up and give them a lecture . . . if they travel with the flag, they must be virtuous. They must not embarrass, be ambassadors, basically don't drink, don't sleep around was more or less the subtext of what they were saying. So, they reprimanded them in a really fierce way. And we all know when the men go play

lacrosse anywhere, they're drinking. They're sleeping around. And they don't get told, "you're embarrassing the nation by your behavior." So, it was like, you just felt good and then boom you got clobbered. [The team] didn't like it. They knew it was wrong. But the bigger win was there, so they said, okay and promised they were going to be good.[48]

This moment in the Longhouse shows the long history of colonial sexism and misogyny, internalized by Haudenosaunee communities. A group of Elder men telling young women how to behave—with virtue—conflicts with Haudenosaunee coming-of-age ceremonies such as Ohero:kon, where aunties and grandmothers claim and enact the responsibility of leading girls into womanhood—as grandfathers and uncles usher boys into manhood—all grounded in the cultural values and teachings of the Haudenosaunee peoples.

Haudenosaunee women work to eradicate sexual and physical abuse within their communities by dealing with this internalization using methods and methodologies that come from their traditions and stories. Mommabear connects these teachings directly to lacrosse:

> If you don't want [your lacrosse stick] touched, put it away. It's like telling our sons not to rape and to take care of their sexuality, to be honorable men, to honor women. And in order for him to honor women, he's got to honor himself and his own stuff, to be able to take care of his own equipment and put it away. Men, put your lacrosse stick away and treat it like the sacred object that it is.[49]

Rematriation, an online storytelling platform centering Haudenosaunee and other Indigenous women's voices, released the short film *An Indigenous Response to #MeToo* in 2018, in which four Haudenosaunee women, one Haudenosaunee man, and one Chichemeca woman share their work to eradicate sexual and physical abuse from their communities. In the film, Chelsea Sunday (Akwesasne Mohawk) situates the discussion within a Haudenosaunee context with a set of challenging and provocative questions:

> We talk a lot about who we are Onkwe:honwe people, as Haudenosaunee people. In our community right now across our communities, people are being abused. We need to talk about this in a real way that acknowledges that these are real

people. These are our brothers. These are our uncles. These are our grandfathers. These are our leaders. These are our spiritual leaders. These are people running our ceremony. Would we be ready to have this campaign come to our community if we were to unload a list of all of those men who raped? Abused? Who hurt our people? Would we be ready because it would be the people we love? And it would rip apart our families. So, do we be quiet because it is somebody we love? Or do we say it because it will save somebody else from being hurt? How do we still create space for these women still to be heard? We need to listen and grasp what it means to be Haudenosaunee people. All of that. But put it in the real world of what's happening and come up with real solutions that address everybody who is being affected by abuse.[50]

Here, Chelsea Sunday names how challenging it is to call out abusers when spiritual leaders are needed to regenerate and revitalize culture, and colonization has dispossessed Haudenosaunee men of their ability to provide and protect. She also calls out a superficial understanding of Haudenosaunee women's power without dealing with real, contemporary lived experiences of violence.

Where the stick protocol can flatten the effects of colonization and hide internalized sexism in Haudenosaunee communities, the conversations about where medicine resides open space for healing through playing. What follows is an articulation of how Haudenosaunee women open space to play contemporary lacrosse through the stick protocol by first naming distinctions between their and the medicine game. Simultaneous to the opening of that space is the invitation from Mommabear to play lacrosse as a medicine for oneself. It is in the prying open of this space that Haudenosaunee women begin to articulate what lacrosse means to them: how it heals the effects of colonization that have also infiltrated their communities, and how it connects them to Haudenosaunee tradition.

Not *the* Medicine Game

As the number of Haudenosaunee women playing lacrosse has increased, players and communities have had to draw a distinction between what is and is not medicinal lacrosse. It is this discussion that continues to root the game within Haudenosaunee culture. When I asked one mother of a lacrosse player about the differences between wooden and plastic sticks she talked about this distinction: "There's a lot of difference. The wooden is made right from a tree ... it's cut right down and made right into a lacrosse stick which, if you do play traditional lacrosse—and which my daughter would never do—the men all play the medicine game and it's played for the Creator."[51] Another mother makes a further distinction between the traditional and medicinal game: "There's two kinds of lacrosse [girls and women] wouldn't play. One is in the Longhouse. It's a medicine game... they're not trying to play that. And then the second one is the traditional game with the wooden sticks. That's still somewhat of a medicine game—clan against clan. Those are still revered as belonging to the men."[52] One young woman who played at the college and international levels echoes this distinction: "I'll never touch a wooden lacrosse stick. I never have and I never will. I've never played with one. I don't even touch my husband's or my son's."[53] Where Haudenosaunee men quite seamlessly carry the energy of the traditional and medicinal game into the contemporary game, Haudenosaunee women work to make clear distinctions between them, as a way of both claiming the game as Haudenosaunee and claiming their space within it. Haudenosaunee women need to parse these distinctions in a way that Haudenosaunee men do not. Because of this need to define the game they are playing, and agreements women make with their communities to uphold lacrosse, women are at the center of articulating where medicine resides in the game, and therefore central to rooting lacrosse in Haudenosaunee culture.

In this present moment, it seems that the more community members question what constitutes medicinal lacrosse, the more deeply the game is woven into the fabric of their culture. An Onondaga mother of a lacrosse player (Oneida Nation, New York)—who makes sure to state that her daughter is not playing any kind of medicinal game—talks about her daughter's relationship to her culture through lacrosse:

> I really think it did help her choices when she was thinking about playing... and to really mentally think about the consequences of playing it, and really kind of grow up a little. And her culture—it brings her close because, "does this really mean a lot to me?" It kind of makes her question herself as a woman and her roles that she's going to play in her Nation in the future.[54]

An Onondaga man, who has been involved in many conversations with women about lacrosse, points out how women talk about lacrosse in order to stay close to their culture: "It's safer to say, 'I respect the game' if you're a woman lacrosse player. In my interviews, that's what I've gotten, 'but I respect the game, though.' 'But I respect the stick, though.'"⁵⁵

In addition to adding to broad conversations about lacrosse and culture, the stick protocol also helps open up space to ask where it is that medicine resides within the game of lacrosse and how women are engaging in, and in some cases revisioning, medicinal space. In many ways, the kind of stick a player uses informs the version of lacrosse being played. One young woman asks, "What's the game of lacrosse without the stick?"⁵⁶ She began playing on a girls' field lacrosse team in high school, and her coach could spot right away by her handling and cradling that she had played boys' box lacrosse to that point. Her mother continues the distinction: "Field is different. ... They're not playing with woodies. They're not playing against other men. There's no physical hitting in the girls' team so they're not jeopardizing their bodies."⁵⁷ While Haudenosaunee communities work to articulate where medicine resides in the game and how women participate in that medicine, they must do so amid the gender hierarchies in settler organized sports. The argument that women should not engage in sports because it could jeopardize their bodies was used to exclude all women from sports in general, from the late nineteenth into the mid-twentieth centuries. Discussions of upholding the integrity of women's bodies intertwine with mainstream histories of women in sports, further complicating already loaded discussions.

The distinction between wooden and plastic lacrosse sticks thus works to identify where medicine resides in the game and the gender constructs that surround it, in both Haudenosaunee and settler societies. One Haudenosaunee man who plays the medicine game explains the gender distinction this way:

> [The game women are playing is] not the medicine game. Even that's a fine line. Some people will say you give thanks every time you go out on the field. That's true. I do. But then I also heard perspectives on the medicine is in the stick. I heard the medicine is in the woody. ... But I also heard from a dad ... that the medicine isn't actually in the stick until the ceremony begins.⁵⁸

The wooden stick functions as a preservation of tradition and the location of medicine. That Haudenosaunee women must tease out these meaningful distinctions puts them at the critical juncture of maintaining and articulating tradition, as well as clarifying it in ways that do not violate it. Mommabear locates this medicine both inside of and beyond the stick:

And with the evolution with how the stick is made and it's more plastic and aluminum now. Does it make it less sacred? The medicine is in the Indian not the arrow.... It doesn't matter what you're holding in your hand. It comes from within. I think it becomes a medicine in how it is that they hold each other, because lacrosse is a team. And if one is in pain, everyone is in pain. And if one fails, everyone fails.[59]

This expanded version of where medicine resides names the medicine of lacrosse as connected to (not separated from) women's bodies, their connectedness to creation, their need for healing, and their inherent value in Haudenosaunee communities.

A Medicine for Herself

Mommabear connects the medicine of lacrosse to that which Haudenosaunee communities already firmly recognize within women's bodies. "It's just like the connectivity of our monthly moon time. Women are connected that way."[60] One mother who is also a player explains that women are not supposed to play the medicine game because they carry the gift of life, but she plays the game as a way to stay healthy for her son.[61] A mother of a lacrosse player points to the "dire circumstances" if lacrosse were to be taken away from women and girls: "to take something away from our girls right now is not going to be tolerated."[62] Again, Mommabear reorients the location of medicine, the role of medicine in healing, tying together the present conditions, the ability to give birth, and the cultural connection to lacrosse:

> A woman can play the game if it's *a medicine for herself*. Living in the current conditions.... I think for young women to pick up the stick and play lacrosse for a medicine for herself is absolutely right.... It doesn't hinder ability to give birth. If anything, it helps it, because obesity is probably the number one thing that prohibits a healthy birth. So when you have a healthy, fit mother, her odds of having a healthy pregnancy and delivery are greater. And when you have a young girl who has a belief embedded in her bloodstream, how can you deny her?[63]

Finally, one mother connects the healing women experience through playing to the healing of Haudenosaunee communities: "Those relationships are their medicine. The fact that all the parents go out and support these kids, you become

Tsiotenhariio Herne, playing with a contemporary lacrosse stick designed for women's field lacrosse. Photo courtesy of Jessica Sargent.

this mentoring support network. So that's medicine, all out supporting for life."[64] This collection of Haudenosaunee women's experiences defines medicine in particular ways. First, medicine helps individual Haudenosaunee women's bodies to heal from the *dire circumstances* women find themselves in due to colonization and associated intergenerational trauma. Moreover, the medicine of lacrosse leads to Haudenosaunee women being in top physical condition, better serving their ability to give birth and parent with health and energy. Finally, healthy Haudenosaunee women mean healthy Haudenosaunee communities.

When Haudenosaunee communities uphold a protocol in order to protect ceremonial space, they do so amid a history that has attacked this space through near linguicide, diminishing the land base upon which ceremonies occur (making it necessary for people to travel great distances), and the westernization of a ceremony that presents to the world as a sport. The medicinal game remains an important *traditional* ceremony for Haudenosaunee communities that includes men and women. The question is not whether women are a part of lacrosse, since the ceremony was given to the people, but in what ways women participate in its medicinal aspects. Communities are most in agreement that a particular iteration of the medicinal ceremony of lacrosse is played for the community by men. An expanded understanding of medicine opens up the ways in which women, whose bodies are under siege in settler nation-states, find, experience, and articulate this medicine, while asking why this particular medicine would be necessary for Haudenosaunee women and girls.

Conclusion

As increasing numbers of Haudenosaunee men and women play the contemporary iteration of lacrosse, the protocol that women do not touch a man's lacrosse stick has solidified. Until recently, the contemporary games of box and field lacrosse that are played at the high school, college, and international levels were dominated by white men. It is important to acknowledge the ways in which Haudenosaunee men playing contemporary box and field lacrosse are part of a larger cultural claiming of the game for Haudenosaunee communities. When non-Indigenous women play the game, they fight western patriarchy, along the trajectory of women making gains in male-dominated arenas such as sports, but colonization stays intact.

Far from a gendered prohibition, the stick protocol functions as a remembrance, whispering into the contemporary game played in colonized spaces, tying lacrosse to Haudenosaunee land, making it possible for Haudenosaunee women to play with cultural integrity, and protecting the sport from further appropriation and assimilation. Haudenosaunee women's engagement with the protocol allows for the decolonization of sexism in both western and Haudenosaunee communities, making particular kinds of claims on and decisions about lacrosse.

CHAPTER FOUR

REMATRIATION: A TURN TOWARD LOVE AND LAND

This final chapter focuses on Haudenosaunee women lacrosse players and how they rematriate land and culture through the decisions they make about lacrosse, how they shape and define lacrosse through their travel, and what they embody when they are in motion for the sake of lacrosse. In effect, the first three chapters are meant to clear the space necessary for this chapter where they can speak freely about how they represent Haudenosaunee nationhood, how they influence perceptions of and relationships to lacrosse on the world's stage, and how they work to restore a logic of balance within their communities. The first chapter names both what Haudenosaunee women are up against in settler society, as well as what is available to them within Haudenosaunee teaching to combat these social ills, including lacrosse. Chapter 2 names and contextualizes the internal conversation over their playing lacrosse in ways that include Haudenosaunee women as active participants in their traditions. Chapter 3 names the ways that Haudenosaunee women are working intergenerationally to further root lacrosse into Haudenosaunee ethos, heal from the effects of colonization, intervene in internalized sexism within their communities, all while clearing a path to play and define for themselves what is healing about the game they are playing. This final chapter expands on the definitional work throughout to posit a theory of rematriation, engaging several narratives of Haudenosaunee women and girl lacrosse players. I work toward this theory with the help of Indigenous queer theory and the theory of Indigenous worldview posited by Mark Freeland (Ojibwe).

Queer theory has worked to dismantle heteronormativity and hierarchy but, operating out of Eurowestern paradigms and frameworks, does not adequately interrogate how colonization and settler nation-states are built on these norms and structures. Two decades after "mainstream" queer theory took hold in academic programs and more explicitly informed community praxes, *Queer Indigenous Studies: Critical Interventions in Theory, Politics, and Literature* (2011) articulated some of what is possible when Indigenous ways of knowing (gender fluidity, all things belong, web of relatedness) inform queer theory and praxis. At this intersection, Indigenous efforts toward things like healthy masculinity, love, language, the body, and relationships to the environment work to unsettle that which settler nation-states hold within the soil, legislations, and informal institutions, such as the family: heteronormativity, gender binary, hierarchy, roles, and race-based politics.

Indigenous queer theory is rooted in Indigenous worldview. In *Aazheyaadizi: Worldview, Language, and the Logics of Decolonization*, Mark Freeland defines worldview as an "interrelated set of cultural logics that fundamentally orient a culture to space, time, the rest of life, and provides a methodological prescription for relating to that life."[1] Freeland demonstrates that an Indigenous worldview is represented by an intimate relationship to localized space, time primarily understood as cyclical, relationships to life understood as a web of relatedness, and a lens of balance to prescribe praxis with that life. Freeland's take on worldview is helpful for how it provides a theoretical vehicle to understand the land as having agency within Indigenous thought. In addition to this logical connection to land, understanding the logics of balance in Indigenous thought is crucial in understanding the relationship of Haudenosaunee and other Indigenous peoples to the land. In the Indigenous world, balance is best understood as a complex and dynamic process of many agents. This helps us to think outside of the prevalent heteronormative gender binary.

The piece of Freeland's theory of worldview I engage here is the logics of balance. Within the logics of balance is the goal of all of life flourishing. Rather than an end destination, balance requires ongoing action. The biological definition of equilibrium helps articulate a process of rematriation that works toward the health and well-being of not only humans, but humans in relationship to complex systems. Equilibrium is achieved by consistently engaging in the responsibility of ethical praxis. As Freeland states, "we see the use of equilibrium to denote the result of a complex system working effectively to balance itself out. Equilibrium is thought of as a system achieving its optional status."[2] It is from this understanding of balance as action and motion that we can contextualize a turn toward the female as movement across a large web of relatedness. The turn toward the female is a turn away from a binary gender system, and a system of ontology that focuses almost solely on human experiences. A turn toward the female is an embrace of a web of relatedness and diversity of relationships, including between human and land.

When the logics of balance within Indigenous worldview is applied to gender, helpful expansions are revealed and break free from the boundaries of a two-gender system. For example, Indigenous language systems reveal multiple gendered expressions and nongendered pronouns.[3] Freeland's discussion of balance demonstrates how humans are part of a larger web of balance that includes animal relatives, flora, rocks, fire, water, earth, the sun, and the moon. Within Haudenosaunee ontology, the earth is understood as holding female-ness. Within a multiple gender system, a turn toward the female does not mean flipping or moving from male to female. Instead, a turn toward the female is a move from an imbalance of maleness, an imbalance that permeates the logics and structures of settler nation-states. Queer Indigenous theory allows for the possibility of multiple locations of and actors in eros.

To expand on Indigenous constructs of balance, a turn to the female, and love, I turn to queer Indigenous thought as found in *Sovereign Erotics: A Collection of Two-Spirit Literature* (2011). In the introduction that frames the many pieces of prose and poetry by queer Indigenous authors, eros is defined as love in the realm of sexuality, certainly, but is not bound only to that realm. Within queer Indigenous theory, the erotic is achieved in the realm of the female. This does not mean that everyone need be female or love a female or females, but that a turn toward the female (and away from the hypermasculinity that permeates our world) is what is needed to accomplish love and balance. The female is found in bodies, in water, in land, and the moon, and "the erotic is a resource within each of us that lies in a deeply female and spiritual plane."[4] A turn toward the female means a rejection of heteronormativity and gendered hierarchies facilitated through a gender binary system. These Indigenous refusals, turns, and returns occur in the spaces between bodies and land and are at the center of rematriation. Driskill et al. name this return: "Within indigenous contexts, a return to our bodies as whole human beings can disrupt colonial gender regimes that have attempted to disavow and colonize indigenous genders and sexualities."[5] Within the Haudenosaunee context, it is understood that returning to wholeness must include a recognition of relationship to land, and that land holds memory and perspective. A turn toward the female—an ongoing set of actions—is a turn toward balance. Deborah Miranda (Ohlone-Costanoan Esselen Nation/Chumash) articulates this in *The Zen of La Llorona*: "an indigenous erotic is a perpetual act of balancing—always working toward balance through one's actions, intent, and understanding of the world. But both love and the erotic are at odds with the violence and domination that structures any colonizing or patriarchal culture."[6]

A Word about Stories

In an attempt to align with an Indigenous aesthetic of epistemology, I structure this chapter as a series of stories. In speaking about the Métis context, June Scudeler (Métis) quotes Jo-Ann Episkenew (Métis) who emphasizes the importance of stories as a way of healing for Aboriginal peoples: "Over the last three decades, Indigenous peoples have witnessed the healing power of stories as they have begun to reassert their individual and collective narratives."[7] Episkenew then goes on to say that stories are medicine and help share information with both Indigenous and non-Indigenous peoples. Scudeler also draws from Neal McLead (Cree) who acknowledges the intergenerational relationship of storytelling: "we also add to the meaning of [the Elders'] stories through our experiences and understanding, and add in small ways to the ancient wisdom."[8] In addition to being healing and intergenerational, stories share a matrix of memory and require care. I harken back to Thomas King (Cherokee) who speaks of stories as the center of our being and to Linda Tuhiwai Smith (Māori) who reminds us of the ethics involved in holding and sharing another's story. As a reminder, King states, "The truth about stories is that that's all we are."[9]

Haudenosaunee girls and women write their stories with their bodies on the land through their act of playing lacrosse. Haudenosaunee Elders become the interpreters of their stories. Rematriation can be seen through this lens as a collective act of remembering, writing stories through action, motion, and travel, and shared interpretations of that motion. It is from these lenses of love, land, a turn toward the female, memory, and meaning-making that I share this first narrative.

A Love Story

I was able to interview with Ashley Cooke, Mohawk from Six Nations of the Grand River Territory, after she was part of the panel presentation "Together We Rise: Indigenous Female Athletes and Contemporary Issues," held at McMaster University in Ontario, Canada, as part of the 2017 North American Indigenous Games (NAIG).[10] What became evident in our interview is that lacrosse is a part of Ashley. About

Ashley Cooke enjoying her game. Photo courtesy of Lee Nanticoke.

the decision she made to stop playing for a while when she became pregnant with her first child, she said, "It was hard. I cried. I played consistently for fifteen years. I never took a summer off. I cried at night. My husband knew; he knew it was hard for me because I loved it so much."[11] Ashley's many years of lacrosse play have been full of decision-making—moves toward balance and flourishing—none of which have been easy. Ashley's decision to play lacrosse for McMaster University and the experiences she had there—leading to her decision to stop playing for that team—reveal and disrupt settler logics, further clearing a path for what this chapter focuses on: what Haudenosaunee women feel and represent when they travel internationally to play lacrosse.

Being one of the top scorers on the teams for which she played, Ashley could have attended a Division 1 school in the United States, most likely on scholarship. Instead, to be close to home, Six Nations Reserve, in 2005, Ashley began playing lacrosse for the McMaster women's lacrosse team, just forty-five minutes away. I asked Ashley if McMaster recruited her. "I just walked on."[12] The following narrative is both shocking and not shocking, wholly embedded within the logics of settler colonialism:

> I didn't have a good experience. It was my first time playing with a different team, other than my team that I grew up with on the reserve. So, it was a risk I was taking, venturing out.... It wasn't very welcoming.... I thought it would be okay. ... They're probably going to like me because I am going to score a lot of goals for their team.... But I was very secluded. I was very alone. The coach never, he never respected me as a player or as a person.... I sat alone on the buses to our games. ... During practices and games, [the coach] would create a lot of plays for a lot of girls, who I felt that he wanted to be the superstars of the team. And they couldn't fulfill that role. And I just played the game that I know. And I was the top scorer on the team, and he'd give me no praise or congratulate me or thank me for my contribution to the team.[13]

To contextualize this narrative, I again turn to Mohawk cultural theorist Audra Simpson: "Settler colonialism requires an Indigenous elimination for territory." Simpson points to the ways in which Indigenous women have "historically been rendered less valuable because of what they are taken to represent: land, reproduction, Indigenous kinship and governance, an alternative to heteronormative and Victorian rules of descent."[14] Cultural theorist Anne McClintock (1995), speaking about African colonial contexts, points not to the lack of value, but the anxiety over land that must be subdued. In the project of colonizing Africa, the terrifying Black woman's body is mapped onto the land, understood as female so naturally subordinate based on Victorian codes of gender hierarchy, and raced as Black, exotic, foreign, and frightening.[15] While the land bases and contexts between the colonization of Africa and North America are unique, the logics of colonization that McClintock illuminates importantly bring anxiety and abjection to the conversation. Simpson and McClintock demonstrate how within settler colonialism, land functions dually: it is at once imperative and sought after, depended upon for its sustenance, required for the value it offers the colonizer's appetite for resources, immeasurably valuable, yet also positioned as Indigenous women are and have been—less valuable, rape-able. The land itself is abjected: desired for what it can provide, policed, held close, diminished in value as compared to the humans who subjugate it and craft their identity over and against it.

It is these layers that make up the space of a lacrosse field, onto which Ashley walks and exquisitely plays. She is at once exotic and threatening, her value to the team erased to make sense of anxiety. As Simpson posits, she has "been conflated with land and thus contaminating to a white, settler social order."[16] She disrupts settler space and contaminates the very land that has been rendered god-given through Manifest Destiny. The idea of conflation explains the settler perspective, but it is based on actual, lived realities of Indigenous women and connections to their land. They are indeed inextricably linked, and thus, that which must be disentangled from land for settler society to function. However, the land will not have it, continuing to reach out to her and inform her memories. Rematriation is facilitated through the relationship between land and bodies, both holding memory of what they work to restore, both longing for one another, loving one another.

The space between Indigenous woman and land is that which is most threatening to settler society. If she is conflated with land, she is ever part of the settler national project. It is the logics, anxieties, and endurance of settler society that accounts for thousands of missing and murdered Indigenous women. It is this same field of logics that support the killing, raping, and disappearing, violently ripping her from settler land. However, she can never be entirely dislodged from that relationship.

Simpson talks about the "strangulation of Indigenous governmental forms, philosophical practices, and gender roles."[17] It is despite existing within settler constructions of identity as a "strangulation" of being that Haudenosaunee women and communities negotiate and embody sovereignty. To discuss the pinched off, strangulated, diminished space through which Haudenosaunee women embody sovereignty, I turn to Black feminist theorist Katherine McKittrick. There are essential connections between McKittrick's theory of how space is controlled and constructed, and how Black women produce space despite these controls and constructs, and how Indigenous women decolonize space with their bodies in motion and in relationship to land. McKittrick theorizes Black women as shaping geography right in the heart of the most tightly bordered spaces. Through her analysis, McKittrick conclusively demonstrates that domination is not ever absolute and that Black women are producers of space even though dominant mapping and geography are set up for them not to be.

Cultural theorist Mishuana Goeman (Seneca) names the production of space by Indigenous women similarly to McKittrick: "Rather than stand on the periphery, Native women are at the center of how our nations, both tribal and nontribal, have been imagined."[18] Goeman talks about this production of space as "mental and material maps" and asks, "How might we (re)map the social, historical, political, and economical in these moments to include a critique of colonialism and imperialism?"[19] Thus, Ashley takes back and decolonizes the space of the lacrosse field, playing the game that she knows—her ancestral game—within and outside of the boundaries determined by the modern rules of the game. McKittrick demonstrates the ways in which Black women's bodies are mapped as simultaneously placed (restricted) and placeless (erased and without the capacity to shape space), through their raced sexuality, stating, "Once the racial-sexual body is territorialized, it is marked as decipherable and knowable—as subordinate, inhuman, rape-able, deviant, procreative, placeless."[20] In the case of Haudenosaunee women, they are not placeless, but their racialized sexuality managed through the reservation system functions as a way to encapsulate Indigenous women's bodies onto marked, bordered space. Ashley then is out-of-place on the strict boundaries of the field from a settler logics perspective, and very much in relationship to space and land from a Haudenosaunee reality. Pushing past boundaries has consequences, as McKittrick states: "Challenging these knowable bodily markers—asserting, for example, that blackness does not warrant rape-ability—was/is punishable."[21] In Ashley's case, asserting herself as a Haudenosaunee woman who has deep connections to land, community, and all of creation, demonstrating her prowess on the field and the love for *her* game, all become punishable.

I begin this chapter with Ashley's narrative for how it exposes the settler logics that are layered throughout the land onto which Haudenosaunee women travel and play lacrosse and will return to her narrative at the end of this chapter to articulate love for lacrosse as a bridge across space and difference. Her story helps to open these questions: How do Haudenosaunee women embody sovereignty when they travel throughout their ancestral homelands to play lacrosse? How is this sovereignty experienced when they play on Turtle Island outside of Haudenosaunee ancestral homelands? When they play on a different continent? What kinds of obstacles do Haudenosaunee women experience in these diverse locations and how do they mitigate them? In the case of overt racism and an environment that worked to diminish Ashley's value, *on* her ancestral homeland and so close to her present-day home, Ashley decided to stop playing for the college team in Canada, stating, "after a while, I just couldn't do it,"[22] turning her attention instead to playing with the Haudenosaunee women's team preparing for their first World Championship. This was a powerful refusal, followed by a turn away from the destructive masculinist ideologies imbued in settler colonialism, and a turn toward love, balance, and flourishing.

A Leadership Story: How a Haudenosaunee Girls' Lacrosse Team Inspired Support

To articulate how a Haudenosaunee girls' lacrosse team, their coach, and supporters shifted the consciousness of their community, I turn to Indigiqueer theorist Lisa Tatonetti and again to Mishuana Goeman. Placing these two theorists' work in conversation cultivates a lens that helps frame Haudenosaunee girls' and women's bodies as texts that map and rematriate space. Tatonetti's theory of felt knowledge articulates the body as text, a location of transformative possibilities. Speaking about pushing the colonial boundaries of gender, Tatonetti articulates the body's "ability to persuade, influence, to function as both text and canvas."[23] Applied to Haudenosaunee girls and women playing lacrosse, they push on the boundaries through collective action of play, travel, defeat, thousands of hours that result in championship wins, their individual and collective bodies shaping narrative and thought. Tatonetti's articulation of body as text applied to Goeman's analysis of Native women's text as a map creates a loop whereby Native women's bodies create texts that map nationhood. It is this framework—body creating text, which maps Indigenous nationhood—that I wish to apply to the following narrative.

A girls' team from Cattaraugus Seneca Nation in the early 1990s collectively wrote a text with their bodies that mapped a rematriated consciousness about Haudenosaunee female leadership. This collective team body, coach Sandy Jemison's tenacity, and growing support from their community mapped a field of questions—affect and text—that had gone underground or was not there before. The questions that Haudenosaunee women must struggle with, *should I play* or *should I not*, are only possible because of the Haudenosaunee women who put their bodies in motion to play. The fight to exist is a turn toward eros, a turn toward the female, a turn toward land. The next narrative is about a collective set of moves to engage in space, a collective demand to exist.

Coach Sandy Jemison (Seneca) has seen many fits and starts with Haudenosaunee women and girls playing lacrosse. After the team that was asked not to play in the 1980s disbanded, Sandy started the Seneca Girls Lacrosse Club at the Cattaraugus Seneca Nation. In 1991, through some finagling, Sandy helped the club team join the Midwest School Girls Lacrosse Association, playing as many as five games a weekend in Ohio, Michigan, Pennsylvania, Massachusetts, Maryland, and New York. These weekend tournaments were the seeds of staking their claim in the growing lacrosse world. These young women made decisions on behalf of their communities that they were valuable. It was not easy. They were on the cusp of near full support from their community, but there was still quite a lot of opposition.

At that time, in the early 1990s, there was very little in the line of financial support from the Cattaraugus Seneca Nation for girls' and women's lacrosse, so all the money they needed for uniforms, equipment, and travel, they earned through fundraising. Some parents were in opposition to their daughters playing and would refuse to participate in fundraisers or to pick up their daughters from practices. Rather than an obstacle to the map the team was writing, this refusal was part of the text, part of the affect that spoke to Haudenosaunee nationhood. While words may have been spoken in both support of and refusal of Haudenosaunee girls and women playing lacrosse, the conversations happening because of and through bodies created maps toward articulating what this would mean for the community. As Tatonetti describes, "Affect, then, both relates to and exceeds language."[24] The conversation that was taking place through the action of bodies—bodies playing lacrosse, bodies sewing uniforms, bodies cooking for fundraisers, bodies not coming to pick up their daughters from practice, bodies traveling distances to tournaments—created an interactive affective circuit moving across a web working to reach balance.

The team practiced eight months out of the year and found creative ways to outfit themselves. Sandy shares the following narrative about putting together the uniforms and equipment on a dime:

> Now we needed uniforms. We had no money.... So we had the job program. They had welding classes, carpentry classes, plumbing. So we asked the welding class if they could make us some goals.... They welded us six-by-six goals. And up until about three years ago, we used those goals. We've used them all these years.... And the nets—someone donated the nets. And then we needed uniforms. I didn't know where you get uniforms.... What are our team colors? What's our team name? Well, we never had a team name. We were just Seneca. Seneca Girls.... So I started on a hunt and went up to Nichols [High School]. Not very far from the school, just a couple of blocks, there was a warehouse.... They had clothes that would come in from schools, like boarding schools or prep schools.... And they had kilts, skirts back then, and Polos.... And I said I can't believe it! I asked what they had the most of. And the shirts at that point were two dollars each, and the kilts I think, were three dollars each. They had kilts just like you see the other teams wearing. So, I bought them all.... And I came back, and the girls were so excited.... But then I couldn't afford the kilts, so I took the kilts back, and one of the mothers said, we could make some. So, I went and got a pattern and material.... And at my house, we sat there and made kilts.... And we had about three or four sewing machines around my dining room table.... And then the girls needed shoes. And we found out when we were playing in the mud that we needed cleats.... So we played at Nichols one day, and after the game, I took all of the girls in different cars.... So we went to this warehouse, and they were just thrilled. There was a little section filled with cleats. And they had ... all different colors. They didn't care, as long as they fit them.[25]

How lacrosse had become an elite sport, often excluding the very people it comes from, is enunciated by the fact that the tournaments were held primarily at private schools. The Seneca Girls Lacrosse Club team had to contend with noticeable class differences, the other teams being "fully clothed with matching knapsacks and matching stick bags, and matching socks," about which "the girls used to say, they probably have matching underwear." Sandy emphasized how stiff the competition was, that the girls kept an intense practice schedule eight months of the year, in order to successfully compete with privileged teams with girls who went to elite camps. "And here we are—we can't afford—we're fundraising just to get gas money."[26]

Haudenosaunee women's and girls' bodies through lacrosse reorganize space that has never been fixed, shape geography, movement, a turn toward, a return home, ushering in a space of their doing. The Seneca Girls Lacrosse Club team is responsible for the turn that took place at Cattaraugus Seneca Nation regarding girls and women playing lacrosse. Early on, the girls would get dropped off at the practice fields and Sandy would drive them home, with some parents refusing to pick them up. Sandy recalls, "I constantly had to explain the game and the differences from the men's game." A shift occurred in 1991 when the team won a championship at a weekend tournament. At that time, the Seneca Nation of Indians began matching their fundraising efforts; Sandy recalls, when that happened, "we became more popular and acceptable in the community."[27]

This shift in support was evident two years later when the team won the Division 1 championship. At this large tournament with nearly thirty teams playing, the Seneca Girls Lacrosse Club team entered the winner's bracket and into the semifinals. Over fifty parents of the girls drove to Ohio to see the girls in the final games telling Sandy, "Get us a room. We'll find a way to pay for this." Sandy continued:

> We were all bunked up together. And we sat down, and I told the girls look, this is the biggest event you've ever gone to, biggest thing for the Seneca. We represent the Senecas, and we've got to show them the good side. They have all these perceptions of us being Seneca. Indian. And what it's like.... We're gonna show them that it's not like that. We can be here. And we can play at the same level. We may not have all the fancy things you have but we have that skill, and we have the commitment and dedication.[28]

In this moving narrative, Sandy leads us through a journey of what it was like for these girls and those supporting them to start something from nothing, to find the material requirements necessary to be part of something that is rooted within the Haudenosaunee Creation Story, and then to travel to and be part of space and to make the statement, WE CAN BE HERE. Mishuana Goeman aims to "think through the gendered colonial constructions of space and place in order to address regimes of power that have positioned Native women as insignificant."[29] Haudenosaunee women and girl lacrosse players render themselves significant and their connection to culture and land intelligible through the texts of their bodies. They map a narrative of a traditional Haudenosaunee community supporting women and girls playing lacrosse, rooted in nationhood.

The next part of the narrative was devastating to hear, but Sandy shared it with a calm resolve, perhaps because she was able to begin our interview with a long list of girls she had coached who now still play, or their children play, or they have an all-American from college play, or all three. In 1993, they won the Midwest School Girls Lacrosse Association championship:

> And here we were, the big 1993 Seneca School Girls won the Midwest championship, which was a huge deal. Huge. And I'll just never forget that time. It was just the culmination for what we'd worked for—and we did it in such a short amount of time. So, teams coming after that had a big deal to live up to.[30]

And then two years later, in a move reminiscent of the elimination of Haudenosaunee men from competing internationally for one hundred years, they changed the rules allowing club teams to participate and they eliminated the Seneca Girls Lacrosse Club team. I asked Sandy if she thought it had anything to do with their success, to which she responded, "Oh yeah. I'm sure it did. Yep."[31] The message was clear: YOU CANNOT BE HERE if you are going to win games and make our elite teams not have the championships on their record. This leads to a conversation about uneven external recognition. With Sandy's leadership, the Seneca girls' team had worked tirelessly to gain the support of their traditional community. Throughout and into the next decades, they would have to contend with uneven recognition of their claims, *we can be here*, and we can be here as a sovereign people. The Seneca girls' team must be credited for shaping external recognition of lacrosse as a Haudenosaunee game. The next narratives demonstrate further fits and starts that Haudenosaunee women's teams experienced in their pursuit of playing the Haudenosaunee game.

Uneven Recognition

Before gaining official recognition from the Council of Chiefs in 2006, the Haudenosaunee women's lacrosse team came together to play exhibition games at the

World Women's Championship in Maryland. By 2005, over sixty Haudenosaunee women tried out for these games. This number was cut to eighteen, demonstrating just how strong girls' and women's lacrosse was by that time. The team proudly (though tenuously) walked into the arena in Maryland with the Haudenosaunee flag, and it was hung with the rest of the nations' flags. Sandy Jemison described the disappointment when the Federation of International Lacrosse (FIL) first put up the flag *and then took it down*:

> The woman who was president of the [FIL] put it up. The second day, all those darn rules, because we were not technically members of the federation, we couldn't have our flag flying. So, they took our flag down. And we watched the USA and Canada team as they took the flag down. So, we all went out there with our little cameras taking pictures of it. And they took it down. And it was a sad time. And they brought the flag over to us.[32]

After this occurred, the team experienced a magnificent win when a representative of the FIL approached Sandy:

> The woman who was president came to me and said, would you be interested in joining the federation? Because of your level of play, we think you can do it. And that you can play as a country. And we will recognize you as a sovereign nation. And I was like, are you kidding? And I said, we would love to. I told the girls all about it.[33]

It was because of their skill and dedication, hours upon hours of practice, that the Seneca Girls Lacrosse Club team shifted the perspective at Cattaraugus Seneca Nation. It was for that same prowess that the FIL extended an invitation for this First Nations team to join, leading to their seeking and gaining endorsement from the confederacy and playing in the first World Championship four years later. These narratives define embodied sovereignty as a connection to nationhood and community, in direct response to the logics of settler colonialism. Haudenosaunee women work tirelessly to disrupt settler logics and clear paths. Embodied sovereignty is also positioned within a deep love for land, homeland, and the game of lacrosse. A similar contest over national sovereignty occurred ten years later when the U19 (under-19) Haudenosaunee women's team tried to fly to Scotland for the World Championship, using their Haudenosaunee passports.

The Haudenosaunee women's team has an official endorsement from the Haudenosaunee Confederacy Council in Six Nations to carry the flag and represent their nationhood. This does not mean that they are free from the sexism in sports reporting that we see in mainstream society. In 2010, England denied the Iroquois Nationals men's team entry with Haudenosaunee passports. In 2015, Scotland denied the U19 Haudenosaunee women's team entry with Haudenosaunee passports. Both teams made the decision not to travel on U.S. or Canadian passports, forfeiting their place in the games, making pointed statements about Haudenosaunee sovereignty. In 2010, there were over two hundred newspaper articles about the Iroquois Nationals men's team and their statement of sovereignty. In 2015, there were *two* newspaper articles about the U19 Haudenosaunee women's team and their statement of sovereignty. This cursory glance at the media coverage of both events speaks to the sexism in sports coverage in general, but also to the emphasis on men's participation in lacrosse and engagement with lacrosse as a platform for sovereignty, both within and outside of Haudenosaunee communities. Below is the official statement from Kathy Smith, Haudenosaunee Nation Women's Lacrosse Board Chair:

> After months of trying to find a way into Scotland that was acceptable to both the United Kingdom and our Haudenosaunee Confederacy, we have been unsuccessful. This is a long-standing political issue based on the lack of recognition of our Haudenosaunee people as a sovereign nation by some countries. The United Kingdom, being one of these countries, required our team to travel on Canadian and American passports. This is unacceptable to the Confederacy because we are not Canadian or American citizens. Our ancestors were on Turtle Island, known today as North America, before Canada and the United States were created. We continue to exist today as a separate, sovereign nation and we cannot undermine this position by using other countries' passports. However, we understand and respect the right of the United Kingdom to protect their country and citizens.[34]

Smith's is a clear statement representing the Haudenosaunee's stance on passports and sovereignty. When I asked Corinne Abrams about women being discouraged from playing in general, she situated the conversation within this moment of sovereignty:

> The under-19 division was supposed to send a team to Scotland. And they had everything set up. All the funding was done. The team was set up. They had been

playing in tournaments and really, really doing well. We have a lot of talented girls who are playing at the college level, so they are extremely talented, representing their Nations. And [team managers] did not send them because they weren't allowed to go with their passports to Scotland.... And there's always the argument from the other side, that we're just not letting these women—or we're limiting them in their abilities. But I think, more importantly, we're looking farther down the line to the future generations and what we want for our people as a whole, not just the one group who's playing lacrosse.[35]

Corinne illuminates that Haudenosaunee girls and women, now having full endorsement from the confederacy to represent nationhood, carry community responsibility. Clear in Corinne's statements is that Haudenosaunee communities look to these women's teams to enact sovereignty, even as mainstream society, and at times Haudenosaunee communities, diminish this contribution.

A Shared Love for Haudenosaunee Lacrosse

The following three narratives demonstrate what is possible when teams from nation-states recognize open space for Haudenosaunee women to play their game, seek them out to play, and support their playing. The first narrative is about Ashley playing on a Canadian team for one summer, the second is about a team from Japan seeking out a match so they could play with the game's originators, and the third about a group from the Czech Republic financially supporting a team in their first World Championship in Prague in 2009.

Canada

I began this chapter with Ashley's narrative to clear a path, and I begin this section with her narrative to demonstrate how love for the game connects Haudenosaunee women to their land and to a growing international community of lacrosse players. Haudenosaunee women who play lacrosse are not going to sit by while people from all over the world take up the stick. Instead, they pick up the stick and share their game with the world. This narrative is about a Haudenosaunee woman's love for lacrosse as a bridge. Ashley attributed her horrible experiences playing for McMaster University as the coach's and team's *lack of love* for the game. She places her experience of being erased from the team alongside an experience she had a few years earlier, playing one summer for her rival team:

> I also played one year for ... who is our rival, and the other top competitor in the league—and who were also very racist to us in our early years ... the coach loved me and loved the way I played and always applauded, loved watching me play against them, and in the league as well. And the one year we didn't have a team they asked me to play ... and I went. ... They treated me amazingly well. They understood that I had to travel two hours just to go to practice out there. And they were just so welcoming and happy and would pass me the ball and set up plays. They utilized my strengths, which a coach should do. We set up plays around [my strengths]. They knew where my strengths were, and they took advantage of them. And it was amazing. That was my first time playing for a different team. And I was the only Native on that team.[36]

In both this and her experience at college, Ashley represents a connection to land and culture through her love of lacrosse. She is willing to share that space (keep showing up and scoring goals) with others who love the game. Love for the game becomes the bridge, the intersection between this team of non-Haudenosaunee players and Ashley's ancestral game.

To understand how love for the game holds decolonizing potential, it becomes necessary to name and then dispute Ashley as merely serving western feminist goals having to do with a history of women and participation in sports. This happens when Ashley participates in this non-Haudenosaunee team, indeed, but that is not her primary focus or necessarily her non-Haudenosaunee teammates' focus. What becomes central in Ashley's play is the relationship that she has with the land, and that she is moving about the space of the lacrosse field with Haudenosaunee conceptualizations of land. When Ashley makes the decision not to drive forty-five minutes east to McMaster University to be punished for being Indigenous, female, and stellar at her game, she embodies sovereignty. When she decides to travel two hours each way to and from Orangeville, Ontario, for practice each day, she embodies sovereignty.

Japan

In Maryland in 2005, amid the turmoil of having their flag taken down and then being invited to play as a sovereign nation, the team was able to share their nationhood with the team from Japan uniquely and importantly. The Haudenosaunee and Japanese teams were not scheduled to play each other. Japan sought out the Haudenosaunee team to express their disappointment that they were not on the schedule to play each other. The two teams decided to play a pickup game, finding a field—just like Sandy and her colleagues found a field, decades earlier at college—claiming space. Sandy describes:

> At one point Japan's coach came to me and said through a translator, we want to play you, but you're not on our schedule. So, she goes, let's play at this time. Do you have a game then? And I said, no. She said, let's find a field, and we'll play. Okay! So, we found a field, and we found an official who said she would come with us. And it was way off somewhere in the back part of the games in the park. And we played and about halfway through the field, all of a sudden, a woman comes running out and says, you can't play this game! And we were like, why not? She said, because it's not a scheduled game, there's no insurance for you. If anyone gets hurt—and they started to take the goals away on us. And we said, no just leave the goals. We'll put them back. *Yeah, right.* So, we waited until the woman left. We had sat down amongst ourselves with the Japanese players trying to understand them. And we sat among them. And as soon as the woman left, we all looked at each other and said, let's play! So, we got up, and we played some more. We didn't know the score. But we were just playing and having such a great time. And we decided it was time enough and so we all sat down among each other, and we just tried to talk to each other, even though we couldn't understand. But they knew limited English, and we knew no Japanese. But they were just so excited to be able to talk to Natives, and they just thought it was the greatest thing. And they asked us a lot of things about our culture. How we lived and where we lived and what was it like? And it was just such a fun time.[37]

This is a story about Indigenous recognition at a global level; it is about finding a field and playing anyway. It is a story about shared love for the motion that lacrosse creates in relationship to land. It is the hundreds of Haudenosaunee girls and women who played anyway who worked to clear the way for a full endorsement to carry the Haudenosaunee flag from the confederacy in 2006. They would not have been endorsed if they waited to play, and they would not have played if they waited to be endorsed.

Countless Haudenosaunee women and girls told their communities, it is time. We can be here. On this hidden field, uninsured and unendorsed, young Haudenosaunee women made meaningful international exchanges with young women from Japan—through translators. Japanese to English. English to Japanese. Perhaps one day the translation will be to a Haudenosaunee language, which leads to the next narrative, a story about language revitalization and lacrosse.

Czech Republic

By 2009, when Haudenosaunee women played for the first time at the World Championship, the international competition had been underway for women's lacrosse teams for twenty-seven years. By the time Haudenosaunee women began playing in the World Championship, there were sixteen teams, and to date that number has more than doubled. Given the settler logics that works to render Haudenosaunee women's three-dimensionality nonexistent and an internal conversation that is a very real part of their decision-making, what it took for that first team to make it to Prague was nothing short of remarkable.

Dawn Martin-Hill (Mohawk), Ashley Cooke's mother who went with the team to Prague, said, "They had enough [money] to go: the plane tickets, their equipment and all that. They just didn't have any money to see anything." Dawn laments the lack of community support the women's team received that first year, even though "that team won gold after gold." Dawn was worried that they would be "stuck in [their hotel] room for the whole time and eat at McDonald's," so she reached out to contacts she had from the Czech Republic who "were always going to South Dakota." Dawn shared her concern about reaching out to them, but then found it to be an important learning moment for the team about connecting with people from different parts of the world *from the space* of knowing who you are:

> [The men from the Czech Republic] knew the [Lakota] language and there was this big controversy about, are they co-opting our culture? Are they pretending to be Indians? And so, I was so shocked when I ... [met] them. Where you thought, you were not going to like them and they're ... just these gentle sweethearts. And

you wanted to hate them and say you are co-opting our culture. And then I just decided . . . I know the people in front of me are good people. So, I called [them]. Since they love us so much, now they can actually help us.

The two men from the Czech Republic rented vans and brought the team around Prague seeing sights and going to peoples' houses for dinner. Dawn explained to the team what a significant gesture this was:

I tried to explain . . . to the girls; this is a year's worth of money they're spending on us. They're not out of communism yet and so for them to do—the artwork they gave me, the beadwork they gave me—they could have sold for a lot of money. They were really generous, and I think it was a really good teaching moment for everyone involved. They don't have much, but they gave everything they have.[38]

These three narratives demonstrate what it looks like when Haudenosaunee women move through space, playing lacrosse, knowing who they are. Through tenuous recognition of sovereignty, uneven monetary support, colonization and the resultant attacks on their bodies, Haudenosaunee women lacrosse players carry memory in their bodies that connects their feet to land. For decades, Haudenosaunee women have quietly been working to embody sovereignty through their game. They have endured uneven recognition of their tribal sovereignty through the subtle and persistent communing with the land, which holds memory and endorses their identity. It is this connection that is recognized by others, and this connection that is the work of rematriating Haudenosaunee culture back to mother law.

Conclusion

The 1980s and 1990s are two decades in which Haudenosaunee women were holding onto their ability to play lacrosse by their fingertips. Three decades before the 2009 World Championship, Haudenosaunee girls were forging their parents' signatures in order to play, scraping together uniforms and gas money, practicing for countless hours, playing without endorsement, and traveling far and wide to play anyway, to demand that their communities, mainstream society, and the international teams picking up the stick see them as valuable. Of the generation of Haudenosaunee women coming up, Akwesasne Mohawk Clan Mother Mommabear contends,

"There's no doubt they're going to be great. And they're going to be remembered because they had the courage. They had the courage. And so, for me, that tells me that the ancestors are telling us it's time. It's time to usher in a new consciousness. ... And those girls are leading that new consciousness in."³⁹

Even without much material support for their first World Championship in Prague, Haudenosaunee women playing on the world stage marked a poignant moment for Haudenosaunee sovereignty, a sovereignty connected to Haudenosaunee grandmothers, nationhood, community support, and visual sovereignty. These young women, their coaches, and supporters knew who they were, and what and to whom they were connected. By 2009, Haudenosaunee women had been engaged in a struggle to play their game since the 1960s, if we begin with Sandy Jemison's narrative of carving out space at college and then bringing it back to her community at Cattaraugus Seneca Nation.

It is a relationship to land, and the land's sense of love and being, that moves through Haudenosaunee women's journeys, calling (or not) non-Haudenosaunee players and coaches into a relationship with the game that originated on Turtle Island. To articulate this set of realities, I conclude with Mark Rifkin's analysis of Cherokee poet Qwo-Li Driskill's poem, "Stolen from Our Bodies." In this poem, Driskill centers the Cherokee's embodied emotional realities of removal, their land's response of mourning to losing them, and the welcoming that the new land offers its new Cherokee inhabitants. In centering embodiment, Rifkin demonstrates Driskill's suggestion of the erotics of feeling that calls into question state-sanctioned/ dominant articulations of Indigenous national sovereignty. Engaging two pieces of Rifkin's analysis in relationship to Ashley's cyclical journeys from and back to her home reserve of Six Nations enlightens what she embodies when she moves through these spaces and makes these decisions. The first piece has to do with centering feeling, and the second with the feelings that the land might have, in other words, how the land might experience Ashley's journeys and movements.

Like the ways in which Indigenous women's bodies are mapped onto and omitted from settler space, so too are their emotions mapped in particular ways, mainly as irrelevant, invisible, private, and a "collective subjectivity rendered unintelligible."⁴⁰ According to Rifkin, this mapped emotional field is perpetuated by the "somewhat hollow recognition of Native presence in U.S. policy," which certainly can be extended to the logics of other settler nation-states, such as Canada. By centering physical sensation and affective relation to a relationship to land and space, "the primacy of lived connections to land and one's people" replaces "a view of self-determination as primarily the administration of a jurisdictional grid (one that follows U.S. [and Canadian] principles, just on a smaller scale)."[41] Moving through and over colonized land, with what are supposed to be private feelings—love for land, community, self, and game—makes visible and remaps deep feelings about Haudenosaunee sovereignty.

Through Haudenosaunee women's love of the game and their excellent ability, they disrupt the boundaries and grid marks laid out for them. Those who play their game, who appreciate their prowess, who set up plays based on their skill, are drawn into the project of rematriation, however unwittingly. And in these journeys, these sets of movements, the land is a subject that also feels. The players rematriate and embody sovereignty because they are connected to a collective memory of what is held in the land. These memories "do not remain buried, safely sealed into a *then* fully sequestered from *now*."[42] The ongoing memory of removal, of torched villages, of displacement and bordered reserves, as well as the unbordered (by time or space) ancestral game of lacrosse, all sit within the land, sharing love with the players as they move through space on and off the field, inside and outside of a game played. Their bodies traveling through and around Turtle Island map Haudenosaunee sovereignty, disrupting colonized borders, rematriating. Even when recognition of Haudenosaunee national sovereignty is shaky or nonexistent, Haudenosaunee women and girl lacrosse players are still remembered by and recognized by their lands.

CONCLUSION

Lacrosse is deeply important to Haudenosaunee peoples: how it is represented, how it is claimed. When the Onondaga Nation hosted the 2015 men's World Indoor Lacrosse Championships (WILC), the Mohawk, Oneida, Onondaga, Cayuga, Seneca, and Tuscarora were able to share the origins of lacrosse, artistically and visually, on a world stage. Through dance, beautiful lighting, and music, Haudenosaunee people enacted a telling of the Creation Story, which included a depiction of two men playing with wooden sticks. The connection that the Haudenosaunee made for an international audience was that the game the thirteen teams were about to play originated as a medicine game. The Onondaga Nation built a $6-million arena for this competition. Many resources are going toward the claiming and representation of lacrosse, and that funding represents a particular point of view. When talking about the men's Haudenosaunee Nationals (formerly the Iroquois Nationals), it is possible to make broad statements such as *Lacrosse is essential to Haudenosaunee communities*, because whole communities support men playing. I was not able to secure any interviews with Haudenosaunee women during WILC, as they were busy attending games. Everyone was excited that this was taking place at Onondaga Nation. Men's participation in international lacrosse marks a considerable shift from their omission for a hundred years, and an important claiming for Haudenosaunee sovereignty.

However, the same cannot be said for Haudenosaunee women's lacrosse. It is not possible to make broad statements about supporting lacrosse when invoking the Haudenosaunee women's teams that presently play in the women's world competitions. Some of this has to do with the reality of sexism in sports in both the United States and Canada across the board. That women have less monetary resources allotted to them than men is not entirely due to Haudenosaunee lack of support. Other questions become necessary to ask in the context of Haudenosaunee women playing lacrosse: How does Haudenosaunee women's participation in lacrosse intervene in the social ills that Indigenous women experience in settler nation-states? How does their participation lend to the understandings of tradition and medicine? How does their participation speak to sexism within Haudenosaunee communities and speak back to western feminist representations of Haudenosaunee women's power? How is this engagement in lacrosse connected to a larger project of sovereignty, decolonization, and rematriation? In this book, I represent the space that Haudenosaunee women lacrosse players are carving out for themselves, how they are claiming the space to play, how community leadership is responding by clearing space for them to define what they are doing and why it is essential.

There is a dialectic relationship between Haudenosaunee women's bodies in motion as they play lacrosse and the words and actions leadership is taking in clearing a path for them to name and define what they are doing. Ultimately it was Clan Mothers through Chiefs who endorsed the Haudenosaunee women's teams to the Haudenosaunee Confederacy and allowed them to carry the flag. A Tuscarora lacrosse player reflects:

> When the decision came from the Clan Mothers at Six Nations, they said that lacrosse was given to all of our people and not just the men. That was their thoughts on it. I haven't heard good arguments to refute that. I just haven't from the people who don't want women to play. I'm not completely sure on their perspective.

She later added:

> I think you have to be allowed to question some things. You have to be secure in that. I'm from a different generation where I don't feel we're holding on by our

fingernails anymore. I think that I'm allowed to ask, Why? What's the teaching behind that? Where does it come from? And how was it impacted by colonialism?[1]

This player makes a note of this endorsement by the Clan Mothers and her ability to ask these questions as being reflective of a more stable time for Haudenosaunee culture and identity, more than previous generations who "may not have been able to ask because their concerns were not being massacred by the church."[2] Part of what makes this field of questions possible is the stable ground that the regeneration of ceremonies—such as the coming-of-age ceremony Ohero:kon—creates.

Discussions of self-determination are always clouded by dominant perceptions, based on settler logics. When Haudenosaunee women move through space, creating intersections of love centered around the integrity of women's bodies, rematriating connections to their homelands, communities, and traditions, they work to diminish the roar of colonial boundaries and prescribed identities. In *Make a Beautiful Way*, Winona LaDuke (Ojibwe) says it is the grandmothers and place that determine identity.[3] In 2005, a group of grandmothers, mothers, and aunties from Akwesasne came together to revitalize a coming-of-age ceremony they had not practiced for many generations. Concerned about the struggles their young people were facing, and the way in which western society seemed the loudest voice in determining young Haudenosaunee peoples' identity, Clan Mother Mommabear worked with her community to bring back Ohero:kon. In the 2016 documentary *Keepers of the Game*, Mommabear is shown sewing the dress her daughter will wear after her four-day fast. As she stitches, she says that the dress she is making is not only for her daughter, but for herself, her mother, and her grandmother, who were denied or beaten for engaging Haudenosaunee ceremony. Ohero:kon begins with young people, building them up while holding them close, leading them on a journey, a movement that brings them inward to identify their place in their communities. As Cutcha Risling Baldy articulates, "Continuing research shows that Native American cultural practices and community support are positive indicators that can address issues of self-esteem, poverty, school performance, and resilient adaptation in adverse situations."[4]

Ohero:kon works to restore balance, healthy communities, and embodied sovereignty. The revitalization of Ohero:kon began at Akwesasne and has traveled north to Kahnawake and east to Six Nations. Six territories practice it in their communities, with some traveling to participate. In nearly twenty years, over one thousand young people have participated. Each participant is asked to secure four supporting adults, aunties or uncles, meaning that to date, approximately five thousand people have participated. The focus is on language revitalization, self-governance, food sovereignty, reproductive justice and health, and community health. The impact on young people is profound. One young participant reflects, "I'm very proud of myself for completing my three-day fast and overcoming my fears. I'm very proud of my family and being a part of Ohero:kon.... It has kept me grounded and secludes me from all of the negative things that are around my community."[5] Another young woman says:

> Ohero:kon is really important to me. It's helped me in a lot of ways I didn't know I needed help. It's helped me learn a lot about myself and my culture, and my traditions.... We're the next generation of leaders in our communities, and it's really important to learn our languages, our songs, and our teachings.... It's taught me a lot of courage, respect, and empowerment.[6]

Baldy states, "In revitalizing ceremonial systems of healing like coming-of-age ceremonies, Native peoples are building a tribally specific decolonizing praxis."[7] Ohero:kon works to dislodge the grip that western society has on young Haudenosaunee people's lives, drawing instead on Haudenosaunee teaching, particularly around balance.

Part of the trick of colonization is that the impositions onto Indigenous communities, and their effects, end up being what dominant perceptions of Indigenous people are based on. The ways in which boarding schools have disrupted Haudenosaunee gender relations, healthy parenting, and community health lead to negative images perpetuated by dominant society. One woman from Six Nations, who has grandparents and great-grandparents who went to residential schools, talks about the effects as being not knowing how to parent. "Some of them were verbally, sexually, and physically abused. And that leads to drug and alcohol abuse. There are all of these side effects that have come from that one generation of people that have continued to trickle down to children, to the youth today."[8] A mother of a Haudenosaunee woman lacrosse player from Oneida Nation, whose mother, aunt, and uncle went to boarding schools, says:

> A lot of things that happened in the boarding schools that people can't get over. They can't forget it. And when they were let out of the boarding schools, these children didn't receive counseling they would now.... And when they got out of the

school, they were sent home to the reservation and expected to raise a family. They didn't receive any love or affection at these schools, so when they came home, they didn't know how to give love or affection to their children. So we grew up with this generation of children who really received no love or affection from their parents.[9]

This colonized reality then informs the negative images and perceptions put onto Indigenous peoples by dominant society. Young Haudenosaunee people see their communities struggling, and then see, hear, and feel the negative perceptions, compounding the difficulty. Dawn Martin-Hill describes the double bind of this colonized reality, and the resulting perceptions affecting her daughters and students:

> My daughter, many young women, my students from Six Nations, or other Native young women—they tell me constantly that if I Google search "Native women" or "Aboriginal women," all I get is missing and murdered women, raped, drug addicts. I can't find one positive story about an authoritative, modern woman. The only women we can find are in history, and these women are women who helped white men colonize.... Why can't I open a book and see a love story between a healthy Native man and a healthy Native woman? Or a healthy family?[10]

Ohero:kon is decolonizing bodies, kinship models, impositions of western patriarchy, and reclaiming Haudenosaunee space and time.

Later in the interview, Dawn Martin-Hill uses the word "sickness" to capture the insidiousness with which Indigenous women's bodies are harmed within settler colonialism. Present within the logics of the Haudenosaunee Creation Story is the importance of lifting up the people through ceremony, and that includes lacrosse. Lacrosse is functioning in many Haudenosaunee women's lives as a form of healing, of medicine. That Haudenosaunee women play lacrosse, that they invoke protocols around protecting the medicine game, works to safely tether lacrosse to Haudenosaunee communities, which in turn clears a path for their playing. Haudenosaunee women playing lacrosse has meant healing, leadership, and working with other women. One player elaborates:

> And so those types of lessons that the game itself provided us—being leaders, being able to take direction, working together, working towards a common goal, not tearing each other down—to me that was the most empowering aspect of the whole experience because so many times, even apart from a racialized understanding of

womanhood, women are pitted against each other in certain ways. Through this sport there were opportunities for us to work together, come of one mind and encourage each other along the way.[11]

The engagement with decolonization has taken multiple forms. Women picking up lacrosse sticks and staking a cultural claim for a Haudenosaunee game in their own communities is but one of many actions that Indigenous peoples are taking to rematriate their own cultural values, understandings, and actions. This project represents a slice of those efforts, positioning these young women as active agents of rematriation, embodying sovereignty and articulating definitions of tradition and medicine, in the midst of ongoing settler logics that work to silence them, disrupt their communities, and negate their voices and bodies. This rematriation and decolonization is represented in many mediums, including art, film, political action, ceremony, lacrosse, and daily activities that are too numerous to mention.

The most compelling part of this project was the conversations had with Haudenosaunee community members; the depths of what took place in those conversations were, by far, the most challenging to give justice to using the limited tool of words. How does one write such beauty, complexity, resiliency, thoughtfulness, refusals, and joy? I have done my best to represent the voices of these women and men who are at the forefront of cultural production in Haudenosaunee communities from within Indigenous frameworks of understanding. Those involved in these multiple sites of rematriation continue to craft an engagement with their ancestral homelands, calling out to the next seven generations of children to come back to their homelands and join their efforts.

AFTERWORD

Tewa'á:raton translates to "a net" or "veil." Ronata'arò:ron means "they are netted, webbed, or veiled." It is a sacred geometry woven from a universal and cosmic pattern, a zigzag weave that stabilizes the design with the ability to expand. A mother quickens the breath of life into her baby in the first moments of birth. She is the weaver and spinner of the life's web, breath in truth that celebrates the waters, the webbed veil, the caul, the netting. Babies are pulled from the primordial waters in which their spirits and first breaths of life are captured after leaving the web. This is the potency of the medicine when the game is played. Women are keepers of the game. It is the woman's heart and hands that gently shape the spherical nature of the ball into existence, and the game cannot begin until she tosses the ball back into the sky. The game was given by Creation to remind us how sacred the weaver is, and it must be played with the purest of mind, heart, and body.

I think about the mother spider, the sacred geometry, the cosmology, the octagonal patterns of her web. Our Sky Woman fell from a spherical opening in the Sky World. In the darkness of her fall, she spun delicate strands of stardust into a veil to capture the light. She was our first geneticist. The more strands she spun, the brighter she became. Like a falling star. However, her design wasn't complete until the male being, called the meteorite, sees Sky Women in her frantic fall to earth, and like a shooting star, he rushes to catch her. It is this moment when the powerful energy of procreation occurs. Every lunar month, a young woman in her fertility is a recreation of our original story: the fall, the capture, the ovum landing on a soft, fertile place to generate life. A women's purpose on earth is predesigned, and it becomes our work to honor and enact those stories, to ensure their application in our daily lives. In our story, Sky Woman becomes Grandmother Moon after her daughter dies giving birth to twin sons. The twins go on to become the poles of the earth, while the grandmother creates an oceanic tidal lock with the very earth she created for her daughter. It is the moon that stabilizes the earth and keeps our earth from spinning out of control. Our grandmothers' stories have deep profound meaning and continuity, making sure their wisdom weaves in replicated patterns throughout the generations.

When one thinks about playing lacrosse, the first thought is to reach for the stick, with little reference given to the net. Without the net, the ball cannot be captured. Together, the stick and the net replay the motion of creation. It is the magic of when the sperm meets the ovum; life is created. To me the stick is phallic; that is why this is considered to be the men's game. But really to me the net is the woman. The stick, weaved with the net, represents both the male and the female. Our grandmothers' wisdom says it is the sperm that chases the egg. The egg is absolute in her power, in her purpose, in her regeneration. She does not have to wonder about the earth or who she is. She does not have to chase anything. She already is! But the man, the ball, the sperm, must chase; he must find his way into the intricate weave of the net. Once he permeates the scared weave, he is then entrusted to protect it.

As a little girl about nine to eleven years old, I netted wooden sticks with my sisters. I remember the string and the reverse loops of the octogen that had to be pulled tight before the net could be complete. I can still see the smooth motion of my sisters' hands. We all took turns weaving the net. In the old days, elements of the earth made the stick and the net: the stick from the hickory tree and the net from cat gut. Making the net was a smelly, nasty job, but once it dried and hardened, it became firm.

When I think about the net, I think about birth. I think about our Creation Story and the thin veil that separates life and death. Mothers are the doorkeepers to life, and we guard that door vigilantly. We oversee life, and men are in charge of protecting that life. When the traditional game is played, it is done so to keep life going. It is how to settle the disputes of the people, to uplift the minds so that life moves forward in a good way, for the benefit of not one, but for all. Tewa'á:raton is the intricate weave of life; we are not one without the other.

Mommabear
Akwesasne Mohawk
Condoled Bear Clan Mother

GLOSSARY

As an academic writer, steeped in Indigenous and global gender studies, some of the language used in this work is admittedly geared toward an academic audience. For better or for worse, that is simply the way I know how to write. However, I have tried to make this an accessible piece, *not* just exclusively for an academic audience. I present here a glossary, which gives definitions of some of the field-specific language I use. Many of these concepts are difficult to pin down in quick definitional form, as they represent large fields of knowledge produced by multiple scholars across time. However, I do my best here to define them so that readers at least have a working understanding upon entry into the material. The complexities of these terms, I hope, will come through in the book's actual contents.

Note that the term "rematriation" is not defined below, as the book as a whole aims to build an explanation of rematriation and rematriative processes. The same is true of "embodied sovereignty."

abjection (*verb* abject): Ostracism; the state of being shunned by society, particularly for moral reasons, while being pulled close in order to define the identity of the group who is ostracizing.

articulation: Statement; putting something subjective, like a thought or an emotion, into words.

avarice: Greed.

benevolent: Kind, positive, charitable, unselfish, big-hearted; in short, "good."

corporeal: (Having) physical form, particularly referring to a person's body.

cosmology: Studies of and theories about how the world came and continues to be.

dialectic: The study of the truth of opinions, especially when people who hold different opinions hold conversations to try to reach a consensus about an issue.

epistemology: Knowing; in particular, *how* we know the things that we know (where that knowledge comes from, how we decide if it's true or not, et cetera).

equilibrium: A state of balance, where every element of a complex system (such as the human body or an economy) is at its ideal level.

eros: A word coming from Eros, the Greek god of erotic love and equivalent to Cupid; as used by Indigiqueer theorists, it refers not only to sexual love but to *passionate* love, including nonsexual passionate love like that demonstrated by Haudenosaunee women and girl lacrosse players for their game.

the erotic: A term coined by Black feminist Audre Lorde to describe a profoundly feminine, spiritual power; it is embedded in women and feminine people's joy and flourishing as well as their sexuality, and it, as a generative and empowering energy that is felt throughout the whole body, can be channeled into positive action such as Haudenosaunee women and girl lacrosse players do when playing their game and thus articulating their sovereignty and their cultural connections.

ethnographic refusal: The conscious decision, generally on the part of the research participant rather than the researcher, to establish the research questions and/or exclude certain information from official sources like academic publications; this is generally done to protect knowledge and culture that could be appropriated or otherwise misused by the general public were it to be taken from its home community.

ethos: A Greek word meaning "character" that refers to ethics and ways of understanding ethicality.

feminist standpoint theory: A theory in feminist studies that feminism needs to be considered and defined within the contexts of specific groups of women, rather than trying to apply one feminism to all women regardless of their location, time period, social class, race, dis/ability, et cetera.

generative authority: The power to create or produce (meaning, tradition, protocols, et cetera).

homeostasis: A state wherein the body (whether a human's or a nonhuman's) is in balance; all of its systems, including its temperature, its blood pressure, its heart rate, its oxygen levels, et cetera, are at the right level for the body to function well.

insidious: Something infiltrating (a community, a location, a relationship, etc.) in a way that is slow and difficult to notice at first, but that creates harmful effects in due time.

linguicide: The death of a language, which occurs when there are no remaining native speakers; languages can still "come back to life," though, through efforts of second-language speakers to teach it to younger generations and bring it back into community use.

methodological: Relating to the way that something is done and the lenses that inform method, particularly in relation to its structure and its action plan.

methodology: The way perspectives and lenses inform how inquiry is done (method), particularly if it is done in an organized and established manner, as in academic research.

ontology: A term from the field of metaphysics meaning "being," that is, how we exist in the world and in relationship to others (both human and nonhuman).

patriarchal: Having the characteristics of a patriarchy, that is, men having more power than women, and society and its institutions being organized for and around men.

patriarchy: A social structure where men hold power, with women generally having less power if any at all, and where large-scale institutions like courts and banks are organized for and around men; it functions both on the microlevel (in families, interpersonal relationships, workplaces) and on the macrolevel (in government, in industries, in law).

praxes (*sing.* praxis): Practice; generally contrasted with theory, which involves thought but not necessarily action.

prescribe (adj. prescribed) (d): Imposed; indicates that an outside force is making someone (or a community) do something against their will.

psychoanalysis: A European approach to psychology (the study of the mind) that believes that many of our mental processes occur without us realizing it, and that by tapping into those processes, psychologists can uncover our fears, hopes, desires, et cetera.

radical belonging: A bone-deep feeling of belonging in a place or space; it goes far deeper than basic belonging, where one feels welcome in a space but not extraordinarily so—rather, it embraces people wholeheartedly so that they feel not only that they're welcome, but that room is specially carved out for them in that space, and they are valued for being there and for all that they bring to the table.

revitalization: Bringing new life and energy to something in an effort to strengthen it after a period of struggle; bringing something "back to its former glory."

rheumatism: An old-timey word for joint pain and inflammation, most often due to what we now know as arthritis or rheumatoid arthritis.

subjugate: To oppress or control; to categorize someone or something as less than or inferior to another.

systemic: Large-scale; relating to a system, such as government (as a whole) or religion (as a whole) rather than an individual (a single court of law within a larger government; a single church within a larger religious system).

NOTES

FOREWORD

1. See Robin Wall Kimmerer, *Braiding Sweetgrass: Indigenous Wisdom, Scientific Knowledge, and the Teachings of Plants* (Minneapolis: Milkweed Editions, 2013).
2. Richard H. Pratt, quoted in Addison Kliewer, Miranda Mahmud, and Brooklyn Wayland, "'Kill the Indian, Save the Man': Remembering the Stories of Indian Boarding Schools," *Gaylord News*, https://www.ou.edu/gaylord/exiled-to-indian-country/content/remembering-the-stories-of-indian-boarding-schools.
3. "Outrage over Residential Schools Spurs Renewed Calls to Rename Winnipeg's Bishop Grandin Boulevard," *CBC News*, June 1, 2021, https://www.cbc.ca/news/canada/manitoba/bishop-grandin-boulevard-name-change-residential-schools-1.6048648.
4. Rachel Yehuda and Amy Lehrner, "Intergenerational Transmission of Trauma Effects: Putative Role of Epigenetic Mechanisms," *World Psychiatry* 17, no. 3 (2018): 243–57, https://www.ncbi.nlm.nih.gov/pmc/articles/PMC6127768.

PREFACE

1. Cherokee author Thomas King's theory of stories in *The Truth about Stories: A Native Narrative* (Minneapolis: University of Minnesota Press, 2003).

ACKNOWLEDGMENTS

1. For more of Michelle Schenandoah's work, see Michelle Schenandoah, "Indigenous Women's Influence on Modern Democracy and Women's Suffrage," PBS, September 25, 2023, https://www.pbs.org/native-america/blog/indigenous-womens-influence-on-modern-democracy-and-womens-suffrage.

INTRODUCTION

1. Berdie Hill has since passed away. My condolences to her family and community.
2. Sally Roesch Wagner, "Haudenosaunee Influence on the Women's Suffrage Movement," Discovering New York: Suffrage Stories, PBS, https://www.wned.org/television/wned-productions/wned-history-productions/discovering-new-york-suffrage-stories/haudenosaunee-influence-on-the-woman-suffrage-movement/.
3. Berdie Hill, interview by author, December 5, 2011.
4. Diane Schenandoah, interview by author, July 22, 2020.
5. Mike Cronin, *Sport: A Very Short Introduction* (Oxford: Oxford University Press, 2014), 48.
6. *The Day Book* (Chicago), February 5, 1913, *Chronicling America: Historic American Newspapers*, Library of Congress, https://chroniclingamerica.loc.gov.
7. *The Day Book* (Chicago), January 29, 1913.
8. Allan Downey, *The Creator's Game: Lacrosse, Identity, and Indigenous Nationhood* (Vancouver: University of British Columbia Press, 2018), 226.
9. Downey, *The Creator's Game*, 70.
10. For a detailed discussion of how race, class, religion, and Indigeneity played into the debate, see Downey, *The Creator's Game*.
11. Dawn Martin-Hill, interview by author, June 29, 2017.
12. Eric Rodrigo Meringer, "The Local Politics of Indigenous Self-Representation: Intraethnic Political Division among Nicaragua's Miskito People during the Sandinista Era," *Oral History Review* 37, no. 1 (2010): 14.

13. Thomas King, *The Truth about Stories: A Native Narrative* (Minneapolis: University of Minnesota Press, 2005), 9.
14. King, *The Truth about Stories*, 2.
15. Linda Tuhiwai Smith, *Decolonizing Methodologies: Research and Indigenous Peoples* (New York: St. Martin's Press, 1999), 26.
16. For example, women's box lacrosse made its first appearance at the 2017 North American Indigenous Games (NAIG). "Women's Box Lacrosse Makes History at NAIG | NAIG 2017," APTN News, July 19, 2017, YouTube video, https://www.youtube.com/watch?v=EQvcZxbvdC8.
17. The Haudenosaunee women's team, under-19 division (U19), played in 2007 in Peterborough, Canada, after the Haudenosaunee Confederacy met in Six Nations and endorsed the teams in 2006. The Iroquois Nationals U19 men's team began playing in world competitions in 1992.
18. Sandy Jemison, interview by author, June 27, 2017. Kim Clouse is now Kim Abrams.
19. Corinne Abrams, interview by author, September 21, 2015.
20. Australia, Canada, England, Scotland, the United States, and Wales played the first seven World Women's Championships. More on this history is found at the Federation of International Lacrosse website, https://worldlacrosse.sport/.
21. These four teams were the Czech Republic, Germany, Japan, and New Zealand.
22. The 2013 games included Finland, Hong Kong, Israel, Latvia, and Sweden. The 2017 games added Belgium, Columbia, China, Italy, Mexico, Spain, and Switzerland.
23. England, the United States, Australia, Scotland, Japan, the Czech Republic, and Canada have all hosted the World Women's Championship.
24. Sandy Jemison, interview by author, June 27, 2017.
25. David Treadwell, "Iroquois Are Returning to Their Field of Dreams: Team to Play Lacrosse on the World Level, 100 Years after Being Banned," *Los Angeles Times*, July 2, 1990.
26. The same set of questions about Haudenosaunee nationhood and sovereignty is being debated at the time of this publishing by the International Olympic Committee to determine if Haudenosaunee teams can participate in the 2028 summer Olympic games.
27. Tuscarora joined the confederacy in 1722, making the Six Nations of the Haudenosaunee Confederacy.
28. Brian Rice, *The Rotinonshonni: A Traditional Iroquoian History through the Eyes of Teharonhia:wako and Sawiskera* (Syracuse: Syracuse University Press, 2013), 180.
29. Rice, *Rotinonshonni*, 198.
30. Downey, *The Creator's Game*, 38.
31. Thomas Vennum, *Lacrosse Legends of the First Americans* (Baltimore: John Hopkins

University Press, 2007).

32. The International Federation of Women's Lacrosse Associations, formed in 1972, the Federation of [Men's] Lacrosse, formed in 1974, and the ILF merged as the Federation of International Lacrosse (FIL) in 2008. FIL was rebranded in 2019 as World Lacrosse.

33. In the summer of 2023, Haudenosaunee leaders went to Geneva to mark the one-hundred-year anniversary of the Cayuga Deskaheh Levi General's travels to Geneva to speak to the predecessor of the UN, the League of Nations. He was prohibited from speaking to the league. Unlike one hundred years ago, this time the Haudenosaunee were welcomed in Geneva with a large display of the Haudenosaunee flag. Today, the Haudenosaunee continue to fight for sovereignty and being recognized as a sovereign nation by the UN and not just a nongovernmental organization. One hundred years later, Deskaheh Steve Jacobs said he will not address the UN until the Haudenosaunee are recognized as a sovereign nation.

34. In *The Creator's Game*, Allan Downey discusses the complexity of this history that includes tenuous recognition of Haudenosaunee national sovereignty by the ILF, a brief history of Haudenosaunee passports, and responses from other nations to Haudenosaunee nationhood in the ILF.

35. Jeanne Shenandoah, interview by author, June 9, 2017.

36. Sarah Moses Buckshot, "Onondaga Nation Builds $6.5M Arena in Record Time for Lacrosse Championship," Syracuse.com, September 11, 2015.

37. Jeanne Shenandoah, interview by author, June 9, 2017.

38. Aimee Berg, "Lacrosse: Cradle of a Sport Has Crossed the Gender Line," *New York Times*, May 13, 2007.

39. An example of this is "Beyond Pocahontas," in *Beyond the Frame: Women of Color and Visual Representation*, ed. Angela Davis and Neferti Tadiar (New York: Palgrave MacMillan, 2005), 61–76, in which Joanne Barker critiques an advertisement put out by the U.S. Secret Service, titled "A New Kind of Warrior." The glossy advertisement features a photograph of a nameless Native woman wielding a warrior staff, U.S. flag pinned to her lapel, and is meant to symbolize diversity in the ranks of the U.S. government. Barker bridges the ways in which this Native woman has been cast without a name, homeland, community, or nationhood with the ways in which Pocahontas continues to be cast as a "quintessential American hero [in] the way such inventions render her without significance outside of her heterosexualized relationships to men and how they erase her identity and affiliation as a Powhatan, dispossessing Pocahontas of her sovereign identity, culture, and history" (65).

40. Bernedette Muthien, "Rematriating Love," in Jain and Meyer, *Connecting Contemporary*

African-Asian Peacemaking and Nonviolence, 419.
41. For an example, see George Hagman, *The Artist's Mind: A Psychoanalytic Perspective on Creativity, Modern Art and Modern Artists* (London: Routledge, 2011).
42. Bernedette Muthien, "Rematriating Love," in Jain and Meyer, *Connecting Contemporary African-Asian Peacemaking and Nonviolence*.
43. Barbara Alice Mann, "Rematriation of the Truth," Gift Economy, July 6, 2011, http://gift-economy.com/rematriation-of-the-truth/.
44. Steven Newcomb, "Perspectives: Healing, Restoration, and Rematriation," *News & Notes*, Spring/Summer 1995, Indigenous Law Institute, http://ili.nativeweb.org.
45. Eve Tuck, "Rematriating Curriculum Studies," *Journal of Curriculum and Pedagogy* 8, no. 1 (2011): 34–37, https://doi.org/10.1080/15505170.2011.572521.
46. Michelle Schenandoah, personal correspondence, September 15, 2023.
47. Michelle Schenandoah, Interview by author, July 24, 2019.
48. Rematriation, 2023, https://rematriation.com.
49. Michelle Schenandoah, interview by author, July 30, 2019.
50. Mommabear, "Indigenizing Spaces: Rematriating Leadership and Land" (speech, 2019).
51. Personal conversations with Mommabear, Jonel Beauvais, and Chelsea Sunday, November 2016.
52. Mark Freeland (Anishinaabe) coined the term "discursive mask" to encapsulate the ways in which ontology (in this case, individual and communal identities) can mask colonial realities. See more about discursive masking in Freeland's *Aazheyaadizi: Worldview, Language, and the Logics of Decolonization* (East Lansing: Michigan State University Press, 2021).

CHAPTER ONE. HAUDENOSAUNEE WOMEN LACROSSE PLAYERS AND HEALING

1. Mommabear, interview by author, September 9, 2015.
2. Albert White Hat Sr. and John Cunningham, "Our Origin Story," in *Life's Journey—Zuya: Oral Teachings from Rosebud* (Salt Lake City: University of Utah Press, 2012).
3. Mark Freeland, "A Logic of Balance," in Aazheyaadizi: Worldview, Language, and the Logics of Decolonization (East Lansing: Michigan State University Press, 2021), 140.
4. Mark Freeland, interview by author, May 20, 2022.
5. Freeland, "A Logic of Balance," 138.
6. Mommabear, interview by author, September 9, 2015.

7. Michelle Schenandoah, interview by author, June 6, 2021.
8. Ernest Gellner, *Nations and Nationalism* (Malden, MA: Blackwell, 2013).
9. Daiva K. Stasiulis and Nira Yuval-Davis, *Unsettling Settler Societies: Articulations of Gender, Race, Ethnicity and Class* (London: Sage, 1995), 17.
10. Audra Simpson, *Mohawk Interruptus: Political Life across the Borders of Settler States* (Durham, NC: Duke University Press, 2014), 156.
11. Simpson, *Mohawk Interruptus*, 11.
12. For additional interventions by Indigenous scholars on connecting race, gender, sexuality as spatially located within settler contests of desire, see Mishuana Goeman, *Mark My Words: Native Women Mapping Our Nations* (Minneapolis: University of Minnesota Press, 2013); Kathleen M. Kirby, "Re-Mapping Subjectivity: Cartographic Vision and the Limits of Politics," in *Bodyspace: Destabilizing Geographies of Gender and Sexuality*, ed. Nancy Duncan (London: Routledge, 1996); Bonita Lawrence, "Gender, Race, and the Regulation of Native Identity in Canada and the United States: An Overview," *Hypatia* 18, no. 2 (2003): 3–31.
13. Morton J. Horwitz, "The History of the Public/Private Distinction," *University of Pennsylvania Law Review* 130, no. 6 (1983): 1423–28; available at Penn Law: Legal Scholarship Repository, https://scholarship.law.upenn.edu.
14. Dawn Martin-Hill, interview by author, June 17, 2017. Emphasis mine.
15. For more on how U.S. legislation undermined matrifocal societies, particularly Hopi, see Wendy Wall's chapter, "Gender and the 'Citizen Indian,'" in *Writing the Range: Race, Class, and Culture in the Women's West*, ed. Elizabeth Jameson and Susan H. Armitage (Norman: University of Oklahoma Press, 1997), 207.
16. Rayner Wickersham Kelsey, *Friends and the Indians, 1655–1917* (Philadelphia: Associated Executive Committee of Friends on Indian Affairs, 1917), 17.
17. Kelsey, *Friends and the Indians*, 18.
18. Michelle Schenandoah, "Quakers, Indigenous People, and the Land," lecture, New York Yearly Meeting of the Religious Society of Friends (Quakers) (2018).
19. Schenandoah, "Quakers, Indigenous People, and the Land."
20. Zach Parrott, "Indian Act," The Canadian Encyclopedia, last edited September 23, 2022, https://www.thecanadianencyclopedia.ca.
21. For a discussion on the activism of First Nations women that pushed for C-31, see Janet Silman, *Enough Is Enough: Aboriginal Women Speak Out* (Toronto: Women's Press, 1997).
22. For information on the 2010 amendment to the Indian Act, "Gender Equity in Indian Registration Act," see Pam Palmater, "UPDATED—Bill C-3—Gender Equity in Indian Registration Act," March 12, 2010, blog post, http://www.pampalmater.com.

23. Luana Ross, qtd. in Renya K. Ramirez, "Race, Tribal Nation, and Gender: A Native Feminist Approach to Belonging," *Meridians* 7, no. 2 (2007): 28.
24. Dawn Martin-Hill, "She No Speaks: And Other Colonial Constructs of 'The Traditional Woman,'" in *Strong Women Stories: Native Vision and Community Survival*, ed. Bonita Lawrence and Kim Anderson (Longueuil: Point Par Point, 2009), 109–10.
25. Ramirez, "Race, Tribal Nation, and Gender," 25. Ramirez is referencing Mary Crow Dog and Richard Erdoes from *Lakota Woman* (New York: Grove Press, 1999), and Andrea Smith, "The Color of Violence: Violence against Women of Color," *Meridians* 1, no. 2 (2001): 65–72.
26. Martin-Hill, "She No Speaks."
27. Bob Holliday, "Bishop Disliked for Residential School Stance," *Winnipeg Free Press*, January 2, 2018, winnipegfreepress.com/our-communities/correspondents/2018/01/02/bishop-disliked-for-residential-school-stance.
28. Maria Yellow Horse Brave Heart, "The Historical Trauma Response among Natives and Its Relationship with Substance Abuse: A Lakota Illustration," *Journal of Psychoactive Drugs* 35, no. 1 (2003): 7–13.
29. N. Rosalyn Ing, "Dealing with Shame and Unresolved Trauma: Residential School and Its Impact on the 2nd and 3rd Generation Adults" (PhD diss., University of British Columbia, 2000).
30. Colonel Henry Pratt of the Carlisle infantry first said this. Richard H. Pratt, "The Advantage of Mingling Indians with Whites," in *Proceedings of the National Conference of Charities and Correction at the Nineteenth Annual Session Held in Denver, Col., June 23–29, 1892*, ed. Isabel C. Barrows (Boston: Geo. H. Ellis, 1892), 45–59; University of Michigan Library, Digital Collections, https://quod.lib.umich.edu.
31. For an incisive look at the connections between Indian boarding schools and the incarceration of Indigenous peoples, see the poetry collection by Laura Tohe, *No Parole Today* (Albuquerque: West End Press, 1999).
32. Bryan Todd Newland, *Federal Indian Boarding School Initiative Investigative Report* (Washington, DC: U.S. Government Publishing Office, 2022).
33. Rachel Treisman, "This New Canadian Holiday Reflects on the Legacy of Indigenous Residential Schools," NPR, September 30, 2021, https://www.npr.org.
34. "Native American Boarding Schools—What They Took Away: Reflections on Native Boarding Schools," Alchemicalmedia, May 3, 2015, YouTube video, https://www.youtube.com/watch?v=ZO38EUu-luA.
35. *We Were Children = Nous n'étions que des enfants* (National Film Board of Canada, 2012).
36. In 2008, Canada began the Truth and Reconciliation Commission to address the history

of residential schools. In six years, the commission heard 6,750 testimonials and 94 calls to action. For more on the calls to action and the stories that drive them, see "Truth and Reconciliation Commission of Canada: Calls to Action," Canadian Religious Conference, June 25, 2021, https://crc-canada.org/en/ressources/calls-to-action-truth-reconciliation-commission-canada/, and "We Know the Truth: Stories to Inspire Reconciliation," CBC News, September 30, 2021, YouTube video, https://www.youtube.com/watch?v=SEC_BoSS68E.

37. Rachel Shabalin, "The 'Sixties Scoop': A Dark Chapter in Canadian History," *LawNow Magazine*, March 2, 2017, Centre for Public Legal Education Alberta, https://www.lawnow.org.

38. "Claim Statistics," Class Action Sixties Scoop Settlement, https://sixtiesscoopsettlement.info/.

39. Daniel J. Rowe, "$25,000 Settlement for Sixties Scoop Survivors a 'Slap in the Face,'" CTV News, April 7, 2022, https://montreal.ctvnews.ca.

40. Christie Renick, "The Nation's First Family Separation Policy," *The Imprint*, October 9, 2018, https://imprintnews.org.

41. Allyson Stevenson, "Selling the Sixties Scoop: Saskatchewan's Adopt Indian and Métis Project," *Active History*, October 19, 2017, https://activehistory.ca.

42. It bears noting that ICWA was challenged through the courts to the U.S. Supreme Court. ICWA was upheld by the court through *Brackeen v. Haaland* (2023).

43. Charlotte DeClue, "To the Spirit of Monahsetah," in *A Gathering of Spirit: A Collection by North American Indian Women*, ed. Beth Brant (St. Paul, MN: Women's Press, 1988), 52. For another collection of Indigenous women authors, see Rayna Green, ed., *That's What She Said: Contemporary Poetry and Fiction by Native American Women* (Bloomington: Indiana University Press, 1984).

44. Louise Erdrich, *The Round House* (New York: Harper Collins, 2017), 12.

45. For an in-depth discussion of how federal, state, and tribal courts fail Indigenous women due to what Sarah Deer terms a "vacuum of justice," see Sarah Deer, *The Beginning and End of Rape: Confronting Sexual Violence in Native America* (Minneapolis: University of Minnesota Press, 2016).

46. Angeline Boulley, *Firekeeper's Daughter* (New York: Henry Holt, 2021), 97.

47. *Rape on the Reservation*, produced by John Henion, performed by Mariana Van Zeller, Wallace House, 2013, Vimeo video, https://vimeo.com/54786283.

48. Amnesty International, *Maze of Injustice: The Failure to Protect Indigenous Women from Sexual Violence in the USA* (New York: Amnesty International USA, 2007), 4.

49. Amnesty International, *Maze of Injustice*, 1–2.

50. Deer, *The Beginning and End of Rape*, 37.
51. Deer, *The Beginning and End of Rape*, 37. State prosecutors are only involved in states where PL 280 (1953) is in effect. PL 280, part of the termination (of tribal nationhood) policies of the mid-1940s to mid-1960s, transferred federal jurisdiction to the state in Alaska, Oregon, California, Nebraska, Minnesota, and Wisconsin. PL 280 does not apply to the Haudenosaunee context.
52. This reality is poignantly and painfully illustrated in *Rape on the Reservation* (2013).
53. Chief Cook is also a certified Sexual Assault Nurse Examiner who has attended specialized Department of Justice Indian Country training at the National Advocacy Center, United States. *United States Attorney Richard S. Hartunian and the Saint Regis Mohawk Tribe Kickoff Cross-Border "Common Ground" Initiative for Indian Country Public Safety*, November 13, 2014, https://www.justice.gov, accessed July 13, 2018, webpage not active. How jurisdiction plays out within the Haudenosaunee context varies. For example, Akwesasne Mohawk Nation and the Oneida Nation have tribal police, while the Onondaga Nation has an agreement with Onondaga county sheriffs to only come onto the territory if invited.
54. Deer, *The Beginning and End of Rape*, 106.
55. Jeanette Rodriguez and Iakoiane Wakerahkats:teh, *A Clan Mother's Call: Reconstructing Haudenosaunee Cultural Memory* (Albany: State University of New York Press, 2017).
56. Kevin White (Mohawk) takes up the question of whether Sky Woman jumped or was pushed by a jealous husband in his dissertation, "Haudenosaunee Worldviews through Iroquoian Cosmologies: The Published Narratives in Historical Context" (PhD diss., State University of New York, Buffalo, 2007).
57. Michelle Schenandoah, interview by author, July 30, 2019.
58. Heather Dane-Fougnier, qtd. in Leslie Logan, "For Two Centuries These Lands Have Not Heard the Songs or Felt the Oneida's Feet on the Ground," *Indian Country Today*, July 22, 2019.
59. Brian Rice, *The Rotinonshonni: A Traditional Iroquoian History through the Eyes of Teharonhia:wako and Sawiskera* (Syracuse: Syracuse University Press, 2013), 154.
60. Rice, *Rotinonshonni*, 157; onkwe:honwe translates as "real human beings."
61. Rice, *Rotinonshonni*, 158.
62. Rice, *Rotinonshonni*, 159, 162.
63. This does not diminish individual choice regarding motherhood. It is the connection to creation that is associated with the power.
64. "Welcome to Seven Dancers Coalition," Seven Dancers Coalition, http://www.sevendancerscoalition.com/.

65. "Welcome to Seven Dancers Coalition."
66. *An Indigenous Response to #MeToo*, Rematriation Media, 2018, Vimeo video, https://vimeo.com/261177660.
67. Rice, *Rotinonshonni*, 198.
68. John Mohawk and José Barreiro, *Thinking in Indian: A John Mohawk Reader* (Golden, CO: Fulcrum, 2010).
69. Mommabear, interview by author, September 9, 2015. My emphasis.
70. Interview by author, March 20, 2013.
71. Amber Hill, interview by author, September 30, 2015.
72. Interview by author, November 22, 2014.
73. As a reminder, describing the medicine game in too much detail was a limit placed on this project by Haudenosaunee community members.
74. Amber Hill, interview by author, September 30, 2015.
75. Star Wheeler, interview by author, June 21, 2016.
76. Interview by author, March 31, 2018.
77. Interview by author, February 28, 2012.
78. Mommabear, interview by author, September 9, 2015. My emphasis.
79. Rice, *Rotinonshonni*, 190.
80. Mommabear, interview by author, September 9, 2015.
81. Mommabear, interview by author, September 9, 2015.
82. Tsiotenhariio Herne, interview by author, February 5, 2016.
83. Star Wheeler, interview by author, June 21, 2016.

CHAPTER TWO. THE COMMUNITY SPEAKS: A SHIFTING CONVERSATION

1. Judd Ehrich, dir., *Keepers of the Game*, prod. Aiden Tumas (Flatbush Pictures, 2016), DVD.
2. Michelle Schenandoah, interview by author, June 9, 2021.
3. Mommabear, interview by author, September 9, 2015.
4. Tsiotenhariio Herne, interview by author, February 5, 2016.
5. Mommabear, interview by author, September 9, 2015.
6. Corinne Abrams, interview by author, September 21, 2016.
7. Mommabear, interview by author, September 9, 2015.
8. Ethically, the ceremonial elements of lacrosse should only be engaged by

Haudenosaunee scholars, if community members decide such a text is appropriate. For the only published book on lacrosse (to date) by Haudenosaunee community members, see Michael Mitchell, ed., *Tewaarathon (Lacrosse): Akwesasne's Story of Our National Game* (Mohawk Nation: North American Indian Travelling College, 1978).

9. Root paraphrasing Pete Hill in Christopher P. Root, "An Examination in the Evolution of Iroquois Lacrosse" (master's thesis, State University of New York, Buffalo, 2016), 22.
10. Amber Hill, interview by author, September 30, 2015.
11. Mommabear, interview by author, September 9, 2015.
12. Amber Hill, interview by author, September 30, 2015.
13. In our discussions Michelle Schenandoah connected the concept of "futurity" with thinking about and doing work to uphold the next seven generations.
14. Theresa McCarthy, "Unpacking the 'I' Word," in *In Divided Unity: Haudenosaunee Reclamation at Grand River* (Tucson: University of Arizona Press, 2016), 83–109.
15. Aimee Berg, "Lacrosse: Cradle of a Sport Has Crossed the Gender Line," *New York Times*, May 13, 2007.
16. Interview by author, September 21, 2015.
17. Nancy Titus Napierala, "Pearl White and the Sidewalk Senecas: Faithkeepers and Twentieth-Century Haudenosaunee Regeneration" (PhD diss., State University of New York, Buffalo, 2014), 49.
18. One example of how Native women's bodies and rights are violated in regard to giving birth is the rampant coerced and forced sterilizations of Native women in the 1960s and 1970s, through Indian Health Services. See Jane Lawrence, "The Indian Health Service and the Sterilization of Native American Women," *American Indian Quarterly* 24, no. 3 (2000): 400–419.
19. Interview by author, March 15, 2012.
20. Linda Tuhiwai Smith, *Decolonizing Methodologies: Research and Indigenous Peoples* (New York: St. Martin's Press, 2012), 146.
21. Michelle Schenandoah, interview by author, June 9, 2021.
22. Mommabear, interview by author, September 9, 2015.
23. Mommabear, interview by author, September 9, 2015.
24. "Philip Henry Sheridan," *The West*, PBS, https://www.pbs.org/kenburns/the-west/.
25. Alysa Landry, "Theodore Roosevelt: 'The Only Good Indians Are the Dead Indians,'" ICT, June 28, 2016, https://ictnews.org.
26. Richard Pratt, qtd. in Philip C. Garrett, "The Indian Policy in Its Relations to Crime and Pauperism," in *Proceedings of the National Conference of Charities and Correction at the Nineteenth Annual Session Held in Denver, Col., June 23–29, 1892*, ed. Isabel C. Barrows

(Boston: Geo. H. Ellis, 1892), 23–34; University of Michigan Library, Digital Collections, https://quod.lib.umich.edu.
27. Richard H. Pratt, "The Advantage of Mingling Indians with Whites," in Barrows, *Proceedings of the National Conference of Charities and Corrections*, 46.
28. William F. Slocum, "The Education of the Indians," in Barrows, *Proceedings of the National Conference of Charities and Corrections*, 70.
29. For further information on sports and Indian boarding schools, see John Bloom, *To Show What an Indian Can Do: Sports at Native American Boarding Schools* (Minneapolis: University of Minnesota Press, 2000).
30. Amber Hill, interview by author, September 30, 2015.
31. Since this interview with Amber Hill, Tuscarora has built a Longhouse and holds ceremony.
32. Sandy Jemison, interview by author, June 27, 2017.
33. Tsiotenhariio Herne, interview by author, February 5, 2016.
34. Tsiotenhariio Herne, interview by author, February 5, 2016.
35. Michelle Schenandoah (Oneida) shares that this film was a turning point for her in understanding and supporting Haudenosaunee girls and women playing lacrosse. Manuscript retreat, June 8, 2021.
36. Mommabear, interview by author, September 9, 2015.
37. Mommabear, interview by author, September 9, 2015.
38. Interview by author, March 14, 2012. I interviewed this same Haudenosaunee woman again in the summer of 2023. I wanted to let her know that the book was soon to be published and to see if she still wanted to be anonymized. Before we spoke over video chat, I shared the pages where I had written about our conversation. During our conversation, she expressed a range of feelings. First, she said, "I don't talk like that anymore. I wouldn't say it so bluntly now. It's just really important to us. We can share; we just don't want to be excluded." She also couldn't believe it had been eleven years since the interview. She became emotional when she realized that she hadn't thought about her own playing in that time and really missed it. She relayed that she is a leader and does much to support her community. She struggled to decide if she wanted to be named.
39. Jeanne Shenandoah, interview by author, June 9, 2017.
40. Jeanne Schenandoah, interview by author, June 17, 2017.
41. On October 9, 2023, I met with Jeanne Schenandoah and our mutual friend Susan Derby in a diner near the Onondaga Nation. I read to Jeanne each paragraph representing our interview in 2017. This was to gain her consent to keep her voice and perspective in the

book. Jeanne asked me to read this sentence again and said to make sure it was clear that the Onondaga Clan Mothers saying they would lay down on the field was not part of her quote.

42. Sandy Jemison, interview by author, June 27, 2017.
43. Sandy Jemison, interview by author, June 27, 2017.
44. Corinne Abrams, interview by author, September 21, 2015. *Turtle Quarterly* is a Haudenosaunee-produced periodical that was published between 1986 and 2011 in Niagara Falls, New York. The publication featured news articles, letters to the editor, artwork, stories, and features of local interest. The issues from the 1980s are particularly vocal about the fear of assimilation, land rights, and Christian encroachment.
45. Tim Johnson, "Iroquois Nationals Workout," *Turtle Quarterly*, 1987, 10.
46. Sandy Jemison, interview by author, June 27, 2017.
47. Theresa McCarthy, *In Divided Unity: Haudenosaunee Reclamation at Grand River* (Tucson: University of Arizona Press, 2017), 83.
48. Sandy Jemison, interview by author, June 27, 2017.
49. Interview by author, September 21, 2015.
50. McCarthy, *In Divided Unity*, 91.
51. McCarthy, *In Divided Unity*, 92.
52. McCarthy, *In Divided Unity*, 277.
53. Brian Rice, *The Rotinonshonni: A Traditional Iroquoian History through the Eyes of Teharonhia:wako and Sawiskera* (Syracuse: Syracuse University Press, 2013), 190.
54. Mommabear, interview by author, September 9, 2015.
55. Amber Hill, interview by author, September 30, 2015.
56. Corinne Abrams, interview by author, March 13, 2012.
57. Michelle Schenandoah, interview by author, June 9, 2021.
58. Audra Simpson, *Mohawk Interruptus: Political Life across the Borders of Settler States* (Durham, NC: Duke University Press, 2014), 91.
59. Michelle Schenandoah informed me that Mommabear is encouraging a shift in the use of *repatriation* to *rematriation* when addressing these cultural pieces (personal correspondence, September 15, 2023).
60. Amber Hill, interview by author, September 30, 2015.
61. Interview by author, September 21, 2015.
62. Amber Hill, interview by author, September 30, 2015.
63. Amber Hill, interview by author, September 30, 2015.
64. Amber Hill, interview by author, March 31, 2018.
65. Amber Hill, interview by author, September 30, 2015.

140 • Notes

66. Michelle Schenandoah, interview by author, June 9, 2021.
67. Jennifer Denetdale, *Reclaiming Diné History: The Legacies of Navajo Chief Manuelito and Juanita* (Tucson: University of Arizona Press, 2007), 10.
68. Denetdale, *Reclaiming Diné History*, 133.
69. Michelle Danforth, dir., *Sacred Stick* (Vision Maker Media, 2010), DVD.
70. Smith, *Decolonizing Methodologies*, 144.
71. Jeanne Shenandoah, interview by author, June 9, 2017.
72. Berdie Hill, interview by author, December 5, 2011.
73. Audra Simpson, "On Ethnographic Refusal: Indigeneity, 'Voice' and Colonial Citizenship," *Junctures*, December 9, 2007, 73.
74. Berdie Hill, interview by author, December 5, 2011.
75. Jeanne Shenandoah, interview by author, June 9, 2017.
76. Mommabear, interview by author, September 9, 2015.
77. McCarthy, *In Divided Unity*, 90.
78. Diane Schenandoah, interview by author, July 22, 2020.
79. Jeanne Shenandoah, interview by author, June 9, 2017.
80. Amber Hill, interview by author, September 30, 2015.
81. Smith, *Decolonizing Methodologies*, 120.
82. Mark Freeland, *Aazheyaadizi: Worldview, Language, and the Logics of Decolonization* (East Lansing: Michigan State University Press, 2021), 100.
83. Interview by author, February 17, 2012.
84. Michelle Schenandoah, interview by author, June 9, 2021.
85. Mommabear, interview by author, September 9, 2015.

CHAPTER THREE. WOOD, PLASTIC, AND GENDER: CRAFTING THE STICK

1. Mommabear, interview by author, September 9, 2015.
2. Laura Coltelli, *Winged Words: American Indian Writers Speak* (Lincoln: University of Nebraska Press, 1990), 57.
3. Michel-Rolph Trouillot, *Silencing the Past: Power and the Production of History* (Boston: Beacon, 1997), 148.
4. Berdie Hill, interview by author, December 5, 2011.
5. Jeanne Shenandoah, interview by author, June 9, 2017.
6. Interview by author, June 28, 2017.

7. Interview by author, June 28, 2017.
8. "Robert B. Pool, Lacrosse Star, Dies at 82," *Baltimore Sun*, July 24, 1991, https://www.baltimoresun.com.
9. This narrative is shared in the 2010 film *Sacred Stick*, directed by Michelle Danforth (Vision Maker Media).
10. Corinne Abrams, Interview with the author, March 13, 2012.
11. Abrams, interview by author, March 13, 2012.
12. Interview by author, February 28, 2012.
13. Interview by author, March 1, 2012.
14. *Gayanerekowa: The Great Law of Peace; as brought to the Confederacy of the Iroquois by Deganawida the Peacemaker*, transcript of film produced by Ohontsa Films, 1993, Mohawk Nation News, https://www.mohawknationnews.com/index_htm_files/Gayanerekowa_The_Great_Law_of_Peace_OPT.pdf.
15. Arthur C. Parker, *The Code of Handsome Lake, the Seneca Prophet* (Albany: University of the State of New York, 1913), 12. Handsome Lake (Seneca) was a leader who worked to invigorate Haudenosaunee lifeways.
16. P. E. Blondin and R. G. McConnell, *Iroquis* [sic] *Food and Food Preparation*, Anthropological Series 12 (Ottawa: Government Printing Bureau, 1916)17.
17. Aimee Berg, "Lacrosse: Cradle of a Sport Has Crossed the Gender Line," *New York Times*, May 13, 2007.
18. Berdie Hill, interview by author, December 5, 2011.
19. Interview by author, June 30, 2017.
20. Interview by author, March 1, 2012.
21. Interview by author, February 28, 2012.
22. Mommabear, interview by author, September 9, 2015.
23. Berdie Hill elaborated in our interview about the health of ceremony: "You should see all the people who are getting ready to come ... we had a ceremony last night and they're just itching to put the ceremony forth and to be part of it ... the Longhouse is bulging, and it's wonderful. It's a rebirth." In interviews I learned of the language program, Onyota'a:ká, at the Oneida Nation Early Learning Center and Onwawenna, a community-based adult language immersion of Kanyen'keha (Mohawk language) at Six Nations. For more on language immersion in K–12 education, see Tehota'kerá:tonh Jeremy Green, comp., *Pathways to Creating Onkwehonwehnéha Speakers at Six Nations of the Grand River Territory* (Brantford, ON: Six Nations Polytechnic, n.d.); and Tom Porter, *And Grandma Said... Iroquois Teachings as Passed Down through the Oral Tradition* (Philadelphia: Xlibris Corp, 2008).

24. Brandon Tehanyataríːyaʼks Martin, personal correspondence with author, June 29, 2018.
25. Jacky Snyder, interview by author, July 9, 2018.
26. The North American Minor Lacrosse Association's code of conduct is read before lacrosse games. Jacky Snyder shared this and the translation with me during our interview on July 9, 2018.
27. Audra Simpson, "On Ethnographic Refusal: Indigeneity, 'Voice' and Colonial Citizenship," *Junctures*, December 9, 2007, 73.
28. Michelle Schenandoah, interview by author, June 9, 2021.
29. Interview by author, February 13, 2012.
30. Interview by author, February 10, 2017.
31. Interview by author, March 1, 2012.
32. Interview by author, February 28, 2012.
33. Interview by author, March 13, 2012.
34. Interview by author, March 1, 2012.
35. I received this feedback after presenting, "'The Best that Our Tradition Has to Offer': Haudenosaunee Women Lacrosse Players and Healing," *Haudenosaunee Research Symposium Program*, State University of New York, Buffalo, November 13, 2015.
36. Interview by author, March 13, 2012.
37. Interview by author, June 28, 2017.
38. Interview by author, June 30, 2017.
39. Holder, "The Age of Puberty of Indian Girls," *The Medical and Surgical Reporter* 62 (1890), 521, https://library.si.edu/digital-library/book/medicalsurgical621890phil; my emphasis.
40. Holder, "The Age of Puberty of Indian Girls," 521.
41. Laura Tohe, "There Is No Word for Feminism in My Language," *Wicazo Sa Review* 15, no. 2 (2000): 107.
42. Cutcha Risling Baldy, *We Are Dancing for You: Native Feminisms and the Revitalization of Women's Coming-of-Age Ceremonies* (Seattle: University of Washington Press, 2018), 9.
43. Interview by author, June 28, 2017.
44. Amber, interview by author, December 15, 2014.
45. Dawn Martin-Hill, interview by author, June 29, 2017.
46. Interview by author, June 30, 2017.
47. Dawn Martin-Hill, interview by author, June 29, 2017.
48. Dawn Martin-Hill, interview by author, June 29, 2017.
49. Mommabear, interview by author, July 21, 2020.
50. "New Film—'An Indigenous Response to #MeToo'—Is an Engaging Conversation Starter to Break the Silence and Lean into Cultural Teachings for Viable Solutions," Cheyenne &

Arapaho Tribal Tribune, April 4, 2018, https://cheyennearapahotribaltribune.wordpress. com.
51. Interview by author, March 1, 2012.
52. Dawn Martin-Hill, interview by author, June 29, 2017.
53. Interview by author, July 18, 2017.
54. Interview by author, March 1, 2012.
55. Interview by author, June 30, 2017.
56. Interview by author, February 28, 2012.
57. Interview by author, March 1, 2012.
58. Interview by author, June 30, 2017.
59. Mommabear, interview by author, September 9, 2015.
60. Mommabear, interview by author, September 9, 2015.
61. Interview by author, February 13, 2012.
62. Dawn Martin-Hill, interview by author, June 29, 2017.
63. Mommabear, interview by author, September 9, 2015.
64. Dawn Martin-Hill, interview by author, June 29, 2017.

CHAPTER FOUR. REMATRIATION: A TURN TOWARD LOVE AND LAND

1. Mark Freeland, *Aazheyaadizi: Worldview, Language, and the Logics of Decolonization* (East Lansing: Michigan State University Press, 2021), 23.
2. Freeland, *Aazheyaadizi*, 138.
3. For a discussion on multiple genders within Indigenous communities, see Qwo-Li Driskill et al., eds., *Queer Indigenous Studies: Critical Interventions in Theory, Politics, and Literature* (Tucson: University of Arizona Press, 2011), especially June Scudeler's essay, "Gifts of Maskinkîy: Gregory Schofield's Cree Métis Stories of Self-Acceptance."
4. Qwo-Li Driskill et al., eds., *Sovereign Erotics: A Collection of Two-Spirit Literature* (Tucson: University of Arizona Press, 2011), 3.
5. Driskill et al., *Sovereign Erotics*, 3.
6. Deborah Miranda, *The Zen of La Llorona* (Cambridge: Salt Publishing, 2005), 4.
7. Scudeler, "Gifts of Maskinkîy," 193.
8. Scudeler, "Gifts of Maskinkîy," 194.
9. Thomas King, *The Truth about Stories: A Native Narrative* (Minneapolis: University of Minnesota Press, 2005), 2.

10. The NAIG are held every two to three years in various locations in Canada and the United States. The 2017 games were held in Toronto, with athletes primarily housed at McMaster University. Much of the programming was held at McMaster, as well. Between five hundred and over one thousand Indigenous nations compete, with as many as 10,100 athletes playing sixteen sports, including swimming, badminton, soccer, and lacrosse.
11. Ashley Cooke, interview by author, July 19, 2017.
12. Ashley Cooke, interview by author, July 19, 2017. "I just walked on" indicates a university athletics department that is less competitive to acquire a spot on a team, compared to a Division 1 school where there are tryouts, recruiters, and/or accompanying scholarships.
13. Ashley Cooke, interview by author, July 19, 2017.
14. Audra Simpson, *Mohawk Interruptus: Political Life across the Borders of Settler States* (Durham, NC: Duke University Press, 2014), 155.
15. Anne McClintock, *Imperial Leather Race, Gender and Sexuality in the Colonial Contest* (New York: Routledge, 2015).
16. Simpson, *Mohawk Interruptus*, 155.
17. Simpson, *Mohawk Interruptus*, 155.
18. Mishuana Goeman, *Mark My Words: Native Women Mapping Our Nations* (Minneapolis: University of Minnesota Press, 2013), 2.
19. Goeman, *Mark My Words*, 204.
20. Katherine McKittrick, *Demonic Grounds: Black Women and the Cartographies of Struggle* (Minneapolis: University of Minnesota Press, 2006), 45.
21. McKittrick, *Demonic Grounds*, 45.
22. Ashley Cooke, interview by author, July 19, 2017.
23. Lisa Tatonetti, *Written by the Body: Gender Expansiveness and Indigenous Non-Cis Masculinities* (Minneapolis: University of Minnesota Press, 2021), 3.
24. Tatonetti, *Written by the Body*, 16.
25. Sandy Jemison, interview by author, June 27, 2017.
26. Sandy Jemison, interview by author, June 27, 2017.
27. Sandy Jemison, interview by author, July 27, 2017.
28. Sandy Jemison, interview by author, June 27, 2017.
29. Goeman, *Mark My Words*, 29.
30. Sandy Jemison, interview by author, June 27, 2017.
31. Sandy Jemison, interview by author, June 27, 2017.
32. Sandy Jemison, interview by author, June 27, 2017.
33. Sandy Jemison, interview by author, June 27, 2017.
34. Jim Windle, "Haudenosaunee Women's Lacrosse Team Will Not Travel on a Foreign

Passport," Warrior Publications, July 15, 2015, https://warriorpublications.wordpress.com.
35. Corinne Abrams, interview by author, September 21, 2015.
36. Ashley Cooke, interview by author, July 19, 2017.
37. Sandy Jemison, interview by author, June 27, 2017.
38. Dawn Martin-Hill, interview by author, June 29, 2017.
39. Mommabear, interview by author, September 9, 2015.
40. Mark Rifkin, "The Erotics of Sovereignty," in Driskill et al., *Queer Indigenous Studies*, 175.
41. Rifkin, "The Erotics of Sovereignty," 174.
42. Rifkin, "The Erotics of Sovereignty," 181.

CONCLUSION

1. Interview by author, June 28, 2017.
2. Interview by author, June 28, 2017.
3. Winona LaDuke and Barbara Alice Mann, *Make a Beautiful Way: The Wisdom of Native American Women* (Lincoln: University of Nebraska Press, 2008).
4. Cutcha Risling Baldy, *We Are Dancing for You: Native Feminisms and the Revitalization of Women's Coming-of-Age Ceremonies* (Seattle: University of Washington Press, 2018), 114.
5. "Ohero:kon," Mohawk Media Creations, October 14, 2015, YouTube video, https://www.youtube.com/watch?v=YKFWp0FmJbI.
6. "Indian Nations Rising Ohero:kon 'Under the Husk' Rites of Passage," Honoring Nations, July 25, 2017, YouTube video, https://www.youtube.com/watch?v=ceTgTqRctwg.
7. Baldy, *We Are Dancing for You*, 115.
8. Interview by author, December 10, 2012.
9. Interview by author, March 14, 2013.
10. Dawn Martin-Hill, interview by author, June 29, 2017.
11. Interview by author, June 28, 2017.

BIBLIOGRAPHY

Amnesty International. *Maze of Injustice: The Failure to Protect Indigenous Women from Sexual Violence in the USA*. New York: Amnesty International USA, 2007.

Baldy, Cutcha Risling. *We Are Dancing for You: Native Feminisms and the Revitalization of Women's Coming-of-Age Ceremonies*. Seattle: University of Washington Press, 2018.

Barker, Joanne. "Beyond Pocahontas." In *Beyond the Frame: Women of Color and Visual Representation*, edited by Angela Davis and Neferti Tadiar, 61–76. New York: Palgrave MacMillan, 2005.

Berg, Aimee. "Lacrosse: Cradle of a Sport Has Crossed the Gender Line." *New York Times*, May 13, 2007.

Blondin, P. E., and R. G. McConnell. *Iroquis [sic] Food and Food Preparation*. Anthropological Series 12. Ottawa: Government Printing Bureau, 1916.

Bloom, John. *To Show What an Indian Can Do: Sports at Native American Boarding Schools*. Minneapolis: University of Minnesota Press, 2000.

Boulley, Angeline. *Firekeeper's Daughter*. New York: Henry Holt, 2021.

DeClue, Charlotte. "To the Spirit of Monahsetah." In *A Gathering of Spirit: A Collection by North American Indian Women*, edited by Beth Brant, 52–54. St. Paul, MN: Women's Press, 1988.

Brave Heart, Maria Yellow Horse. "The Historical Trauma Response among Natives and Its

Relationship with Substance Abuse: A Lakota Illustration." *Journal of Psychoactive Drugs* 35, no. 1 (2003): 7–13.

Buckshot, Sarah Moses. "Onondaga Nation Builds $6.5M Arena in Record Time for Lacrosse Championship." Syracuse.com, September 11, 2015.

"Claim Statistics." Class Action Sixties Scoop Settlement. https://sixtiesscoopsettlement.info/.

Coltelli, Laura. *Winged Words: American Indian Writers Speak*. Lincoln: University of Nebraska Press, 1990.

Cronin, Mike. *Sport: A Very Short Introduction*. Oxford: Oxford University Press, 2014.

Danforth, Michelle, dir. *Sacred Stick*. Vision Maker Media, 2010. DVD.

Deer, Sarah. *The Beginning and End of Rape: Confronting Sexual Violence in Native America*. Minneapolis: University of Minnesota Press, 2016.

Denetdale, Jennifer. *Reclaiming Diné History: The Legacies of Navajo Chief Manuelito and Juanita*. Tucson: University of Arizona Press, 2007.

Dog, Mary Crow, and Richard Erdoes. *Lakota Woman*. New York: Grove Press, 1999.

Downey, Allan. *The Creator's Game: Lacrosse, Identity, and Indigenous Nationhood*. Vancouver: University of British Columbia Press, 2018.

Driskill, Qwo-Li, Daniel Heath Justice, Deborah Miranda, and Lisa Tatonetti, eds. *Sovereign Erotics: A Collection of Two-Spirit Literature*. Tucson: University of Arizona Press, 2011.

Driskill, Qwo-Li, Chris Finley, Brian Joseph Gilley, and Scott Lauria Morgensen, eds. *Queer Indigenous Studies: Critical Interventions in Theory, Politics, and Literature*. Tucson: University of Arizona Press, 2011.

Ehrich, Judd, dir. *Keepers of the Game*. Produced by Aiden Tumas. Flatbush Pictures, 2016. DVD.

Erdrich, Louise. *The Round House*. New York: Harper Collins, 2017.

Freeland, Mark. *Aazheyaadizi: Worldview, Language, and the Logics of Decolonization*. East Lansing: Michigan State University Press, 2021.

Garrett, Philip C. "The Indian Policy in Its Relations to Crime and Pauperism." In *Proceedings of the National Conference of Charities and Correction at the Nineteenth Annual Session Held in Denver, Col., June 23–29, 1892*, edited by Isabel C. Barrows, 45–59. Boston: Geo. H. Ellis, 1892. University of Michigan Library, Digital Collections.

Gayanerekowa: The Great Law of Peace; as brought to the Confederacy of the Iroquois by Deganawida the Peacemaker. Produced by Ohontsa Films, 1993 (transcript). *Mohawk Nation News*. https://www.mohawknationnews.com/index_htm_files/Gayanerekowa_The_Great_Law_of_Peace_OPT.pdf.

Gellner, Ernest. *Nations and Nationalism*. Malden, MA: Blackwell, 2013.

Goeman, Mishuana. *Mark My Words: Native Women Mapping Our Nations*. Minneapolis:

University of Minnesota Press, 2013.

Goeman, Mishuana. "(Re)Mapping Indigenous Presence on the Land in Native Women's Literature." *American Quarterly* 60 (2008): 295–302.

Green, Rayna, ed. *That's What She Said: Contemporary Poetry and Fiction by Native American Women*. Bloomington: Indiana University Press, 1984.

Green, Tehota'kerá:tonh Jeremy, comp. *Pathways to Creating Onkwehonwehnéha Speakers at Six Nations of the Grand River Territory*. Brantford, ON: Six Nations Polytechnic, n.d.

Hagman, George. *The Artist's Mind: A Psychoanalytic Perspective on Creativity, Modern Art and Modern Artists*. London: Routledge, 2011.

Holder, Andrew Bowles. "The Age of Puberty of Indian Girls." *The Medical and Surgical Reporter* 62 (1890): 521–22. https://library.si.edu/digital-library/book/medicalsurgical621890phil.

Horwitz, Morton J. "The History of the Public/Private Distinction." *University of Pennsylvania Law Review* 130, no. 6 (1983): 1423–28.

"Indian Nations Rising Ohero:kon 'Under the Husk' Rites of Passage." Honoring Nations, July 25, 2017. YouTube video. https://www.youtube.com/watch?v=ceTgTqRctwg.

An Indigenous Response to #MeToo. Rematriation Media, 2018. Vimeo video. https://vimeo.com/261177660.

Ing, N. Rosalyn. "Dealing with Shame and Unresolved Trauma: Residential School and Its Impact on the 2nd and 3rd Generation Adults." PhD dissertation, University of British Columbia, 2000.

Johnson, Tim. "Iroquois Nationals Workout." *Turtle Quarterly: Native American Center for the Living Arts*, 1987, 10–12.

Kelsey, Rayner Wickersham. *Friends and the Indians, 1655–1917*. Philadelphia: Associated Executive Committee of Friends on Indian Affairs, 1917.

King, Thomas. *The Truth about Stories: A Native Narrative*. Minneapolis: University of Minnesota Press, 2005.

Kirby, Kathleen M. "Re-Mapping Subjectivity: Cartographic Vision and the Limits of Politics." In *Bodyspace: Destabilizing Geographies of Gender and Sexuality*, edited by Nancy Duncan, 45–55. London: Routledge, 1996.

LaDuke, Winona, and Barbara Alice Mann. *Make a Beautiful Way: The Wisdom of Native American Women*. Lincoln: University of Nebraska Press, 2008.

Landry, Alysa. "Theodore Roosevelt: 'The Only Good Indians Are the Dead Indians.'" ICT, June 28, 2016. https://ictnews.org.

Lavine, Sigmund. *The Games the Indians Played*. New York: Dodd Mead, 1974.

Lawrence, Bonita. "Gender, Race, and the Regulation of Native Identity in Canada and the

United States: An Overview." *Hypatia* 18, no. 2 (2003): 3–31.

Martin-Hill, Dawn. "She No Speaks: And Other Colonial Constructs of 'The Traditional Woman." In *Strong Women Stories: Native Vision and Community Survival*, edited by Bonita Lawrence and Kim Anderson, 106–20. Longueuil, QC: Point Par Point, 2009.

Lawrence, Jane. "The Indian Health Service and the Sterilization of Native American Women." *American Indian Quarterly* 24, no. 3 (2000): 400–419.

Logan, Leslie. "For Two Centuries These Lands Have Not Heard the Songs or Felt the Oneida's Feet on the Ground." *Indian Country Today*, July 22, 2019.

Martin-Hill, Dawn. "Declining Authority of Haudenosaunee Women and the Emergence of 'She No Speaks.'" In *Historical Roles of Clan Mothers and Women in Haudenosaunee Culture and Their Diminishing Roles within Western Colonial Society*, edited by Dawn Martin-Hill, Theresa McCarthy, and Amber Hill, n.d.

McCarthy, Theresa. *In Divided Unity: Haudenosaunee Reclamation at Grand River*. Tucson: University of Arizona Press, 2017.

McKittrick, Katherine. *Demonic Grounds: Black Women and the Cartographies of Struggle*. Minneapolis: University of Minnesota Press, 2006.

McClintock, Anne. *Imperial Leather Race, Gender and Sexuality in the Colonial Contest*. New York: Routledge, 2015.

Meringer, Eric Rodrigo. "The Local Politics of Indigenous Self-Representation: Intraethnic Political Division among Nicaragua's Miskito People during the Sandinista Era." *Oral History Review* 37, no. 1 (2010): 1–17.

Miranda, Debora. *The Zen of La Llorona*. Cambridge: Salt Publishing, 2005.

Misztal, Barbara. *Theories of Social Remembering*. Philadelphia: Open University Press, 2003.

Mitchell, Michael, ed. *Tewaarathon (Lacrosse): Akwesasne's Story of Our National Game*. Mohawk Nation: North American Indian Travelling College, 1978.

Mohanram, Radhika. *Black Body: Women, Colonialism, and Space*. Minneapolis: University of Minnesota Press, 1999.

Mohawk, John, and José Barreiro. *Thinking in Indian: A John Mohawk Reader*. Golden, CO: Fulcrum, 2010.

Mommabear. "Indigenizing Spaces: Rematriating Leadership and Land." Speech given at South Dakota State University, Brookings, SD. September, 18, 2019.

Muthien, Bernedette. "Rematriating Love." In *Connecting Contemporary African-Asian Peacemaking and Nonviolence: From Satagraha to Ujamaa*, edited by Vidya Jain and Matt Meyer, 412–26. Newcastle-upon-Tyne: Cambridge Scholars Publishing, 2018.

"Native American Boarding Schools—What They Took Away: Reflections on Native Boarding Schools." Alchemicalmedia, May 3, 2015. YouTube video. https://www.youtube.com/

watch?v=ZO38EUu-luA.

"New Film—'An Indigenous Response to #MeToo'—Is an Engaging Conversation Starter to Break the Silence and Lean into Cultural Teachings for Viable Solutions." Cheyenne & Arapaho Tribal Tribune, April 4, 2018. https://cheyennearapahotribaltribune.wordpress.com.

Newland, Bryan Todd. *Federal Indian Boarding School Initiative Investigative Report*. Washington, DC: U.S. Government Publishing Office, 2022.

"Ohero:kon." Mohawk Media Creations, October 14, 2015. YouTube video. https://www.youtube.com/watch?v=YKFWp0FmJbI.

Parker, Arthur C. *The Code of Handsome Lake, the Seneca Prophet*. Albany: University of the State of New York, 1913.

Parrott, Zach. "Indian Act." The Canadian Encyclopedia. Last edited September 23, 2022. https://www.thecanadianencyclopedia.ca.

"Philip Henry Sheridan." *The West*. PBS. https://www.pbs.org/kenburns/the-west/.

Porter, Tom. *And Grandma Said... Iroquois Teachings as Passed Down through the Oral Tradition*. Philadelphia: Xlibris Corp, 2008.

Pratt, Richard H. "The Advantage of Mingling Indians with Whites." In *Proceedings of the National Conference of Charities and Correction at the Nineteenth Annual Session Held in Denver, Col., June 23–29, 1892*, edited by Isabel C. Barrows, 45–59. Boston: Geo. H. Ellis, 1892. University of Michigan Library, Digital Collections. https://quod.lib.umich.edu.

Ramirez, Renya K. "Race, Tribal Nation, and Gender: A Native Feminist Approach to Belonging." *Meridians* 7, no. 2 (2002): 22–40.

Rape on the Reservation. Produced by John Henion. Performed by Mariana Van Zeller. Wallace House, 2013. Vimeo video. https://vimeo.com/54786283.

Rash, Steve, dir. *Crooked Arrows*. Peck Entertainment, 2012. DVD.

Renick, Christie. "The Nation's First Family Separation Policy," *The Imprint*, October 9, 2018. https://imprintnews.org.

Rice, Brian. *The Rotinonshonni: A Traditional Iroquoian History through the Eyes of Teharonhia:wako and Sawiskera*. Syracuse: Syracuse University Press, 2013.

Rifkin, Mark. "The Erotics of Sovereignty." In *Queer Indigenous Studies: Critical Interventions in Theory, Politics, and Literature*, edited by Qwo-Li Driskill, Chris Finley, Brian Joseph Gilley, and Scott Lauria Morgensen, 172–89. Tucson: University of Arizona Press, 2011.

"Robert B. Pool, Lacrosse Star, Dies at 82." *Baltimore Sun*. July 24, 1991. https://www.baltimoresun.com.

Rodriguez, Jeanette, and Iakoiane Wakerahkats:teh. *A Clan Mother's Call: Reconstructing Haudenosaunee Cultural Memory*. Albany: State University of New York Press, 2017.

Roesch Wagner, Sally. "Haudenosaunee Influence on the Women's Suffrage Movement."
Discovering New York: Suffrage Stories, PBS. https://www.wned.org/television/
wned-productions/wned-history-productions/discovering-new-york-suffrage-stories/
haudenosaunee-influence-on-the-woman-suffrage-movement/.

Roesch Wagner, Sally. *Sisters in Spirit: Haudenosaunee (Iroquois) Influence on Early American Feminists*. Summertown, TN: Native Voices Book Publishing Company, 2001.

Root, Christopher P. "An Examination in the Evolution of Iroquois Lacrosse." Master's thesis, State University of New York, Buffalo, 2016.

Rowe, Daniel J. "$25,000 Settlement for Sixties Scoop Survivors a 'Slap in the Face.'" CTV News, April 7, 2022. https://montreal.ctvnews.ca.

Schenandoah, Michelle. "Quakers, Indigenous People, and the Land." Lecture, New York Yearly Meeting of the Religious Society of Friends (Quakers). 2018.

Scudeler, June. "Gifts of Maskinkîy: Gregory Schofield's Cree Métis Stories of Self-Acceptance." In *Queer Indigenous Studies: Critical Interventions in Theory, Politics, and Literature*, edited by Qwo-Li Driskill, Chris Finley, Brian Joseph Gilley, and Scott Lauria Morgensen, 190–210. Tucson: University of Arizona Press, 2011.

Shabalin, Rachel. "The 'Sixties Scoop': A Dark Chapter in Canadian History." *LawNow* Magazine, March 2, 2017. Centre for Public Legal Education Alberta. https://www.lawnow.org.

Holliday, Bob. "Bishop Disliked for Residential School Stance." *Winnipeg Free Press*, January 2, 2018. https://www.winnipegfreepress.com/our-communities/correspondents/2018/01/02/bishop-disliked-for-residential-school-stance.

Silman, Janet. *Enough Is Enough: Aboriginal Women Speak Out*. Toronto: Womens Press, 1997.

Silva, Noenoe K. *Aloha Betrayed: Native Hawaiian Resistance to American Colonialism*. Durham, NC: Duke University Press, 2004.

Simpson, Audra. *Mohawk Interruptus: Political Life across the Borders of Settler States*. Durham, NC: Duke University Press, 2014.

Simpson, Audra. "On Ethnographic Refusal: Indigeneity, 'Voice' and Colonial Citizenship." *Junctures*, December 9, 2007, 67–80.

Slocum, William F. "The Education of the Indians." In *Proceedings of the National Conference of Charities and Correction at the Nineteenth Annual Session Held in Denver, Col., June 23–29, 1892*, edited by Isabel C. Barrows, 45–59. Boston: Geo. H. Ellis, 1892. University of Michigan Library, Digital Collections. https://quod.lib.umich.edu.

Smith, Andrea. "The Color of Violence: Violence against Women of Color." *Meridians* 1, no. 2 (2001): 65–72.

Smith, Linda Tuhiwai. *Decolonizing Methodologies: Research and Indigenous Peoples*. New York:

St. Martin's Press, 1999.

Stasiulis, Daiva K., and Nira Yuval-Davis. *Unsettling Settler Societies: Articulations of Gender, Race, Ethnicity and Class*. London: Sage, 1995.

Stevenson, Allyson. "Selling the Sixties Scoop: Saskatchewan's Adopt Indian and Métis Project." *Active History*, October 19, 2017. https://activehistory.ca.

Tatonetti, Lisa. *Written by the Body: Gender Expansiveness and Indigenous Non-Cis Masculinities*. Minneapolis: University of Minnesota Press, 2021.

Titus Napierala, Nancy. "Pearl White and the Sidewalk Senecas: Faithkeepers and Twentieth-Century Haudenosaunee Regeneration." PhD diss., State University of New York, Buffalo, 2014.

Tohe, Laura. *No Parole Today*. Albuquerque: West End Press, 1999.

Tohe, Laura. "There Is No Word for Feminism in My Language." *Wicazo Sa Review* 15, no. 2 (2000): 103–10.

"Truth and Reconciliation Commission of Canada: Calls to Action." Canadian Religious Conference, June 25, 2021, https://crc-canada.org/en/ressources/calls-to-action-truth-reconciliation-commission-canada.

Treadwell, David. "Iroquois Are Returning to Their Field of Dreams: Team to Play Lacrosse on the World Level, 100 Years after Being Banned." *Los Angeles Times*, July 2, 1990.

Treisman, Rachel. "This New Canadian Holiday Reflects on the Legacy of Indigenous Residential Schools." NPR, September 30, 2021. https://www.npr.org.

Trouillot, Michel-Rolph. *Silencing the Past: Power and the Production of History*. Boston: Beacon, 1997.

Tuck, Eve. "Rematriating Curriculum Studies." *Journal of Curriculum and Pedagogy* 8, no. 1 (2011): 34–37. https://doi.org/10.1080/15505170.2011.572521.

United States Attorney Richard S. Hartunian and the Saint Regis Mohawk Tribe Kickoff Cross-Border "Common Ground" Initiative for Indian Country Public Safety. November 13, 2014.

Palmater, Pam. "UPDATED—Bill C-3—Gender Equity in Indian Registration Act." Blog post, March 12, 2010. http://www.pampalmater.com.

Vennum, Thomas. *Lacrosse Legends of the First Americans*. Baltimore: Johns Hopkins University Press, 2007.

Wall, Wendy. "Gender and the 'Citizen Indian.'" In *Writing the Range: Race, Class, and Culture in the Women's West*, edited by Elizabeth Jameson and Susan H. Armitage, 202–29. Norman: University of Oklahoma Press, 1997.

"Welcome to Seven Dancers Coalition." Seven Dancers Coalition. http://www.sevendancerscoalition.com/.

"We Know the Truth: Stories to Inspire Reconciliation," CBC News, September 30, 2021.

YouTube video. https://www.youtube.com/watch?v=SEC_BoSS68E.

We Were Children = Nous n'étions que des enfants. National Film Board of Canada, 2012.

White, Kevin. "Haudenosaunee Worldviews through Iroquoian Cosmologies: The Published Narratives in Historical Context." PhD diss., State University of New York, Buffalo, 2007.

White Hat, Albert, Sr., and John Cunningham. "Our Origin Story." In *Life's Journey—Zuya: Oral Teachings from Rosebud*, 29–36. Salt Lake City: University of Utah Press, 2012.

Windle, Jim. "Haudenosaunee Women's Lacrosse Team Will Not Travel on a Foreign Passport." Warrior Publications, July 15, 2015. https://warriorpublications.wordpress.com.

"Women's Box Lacrosse Makes History at NAIG | NAIG 2017." APTN News, July 19, 2017. YouTube video. https://www.youtube.com/watch?v=EQvcZxbvdC8.

INDEX

Page numbers in italics refer to figures.

A

Aazheyaadizi (Freeland), 3–4, 20, 90–91
abjection, defined, 122
Abrams, Corinne, xix, xxxvii, 39, 44, 65–66, 103–4
"Age of Puberty of Indian Girls, The" (Holder), 75–76
Algonquian Creation story, 3–4
American Indian Freedom of Religion Act (1978), 14, 134 (n.42)
American Indian Movement and Eurowestern gender roles, 10–11
Amnesty International, 16
Anaquod, Glen, 12
articulation, defined, 122
assimilation, 36, 37
avarice, defined, 122
Ayenwatha (Hiawatha), xxxix

B

balance in Indigenous societies: and gender, 4, 5, 56, 64; logics of, 90–91; and Ohero:kon, 113; rematriation to restore, 5, 56, 90–91, 92; and web of relatedness, 3–4, 20–21, 90
Baldy, Cutcha Risling, 76–77, 113, 114
Banks, Dennis, 12
Beauvais, Jonel, xlvii, 21
Beers, William, xxxvi
benevolent, defined, 122
Berg, Aimee, xxv, xliv, 33, 34, 49, 50
Bill C-31 (Canada, 1985), 10

155

boarding schools: and assimilation, 37; in Canada, 12, 13, 133 (n.36); Carlisle Industrial Indian School, 12, 37; Christianity and operation of, 12; early, 12; education at, 38; experiences of children at, xi; goal of, xi, 11, 38; and Haudenosaunee language, 68–69; and imposition of strict gender rules, 70; and inability of future generations to parent, 114–15; intergenerational trauma from, xi–xii, 11–12, 13–14, 36; methods used in, 12; number of, 12; sports at, 38
Boulley, Angeline, 15

C
Canada: Indian residential schools in, 12, 13, 133 (n.36); Indigenous people in, 10
Carlisle Industrial Indian School (Carlisle, Pennsylvania), 12, 37
Cattaraugus Seneca Nation, 70–72, 98, 100, 102
cellular healing, 18–19
ceremony and ceremonies: colonialism's effect on, 69–70, 76–77, 80; dealing with death and illness, 67; decolonization and revitalization of healing, 114, 115; health of, 141 (n.23); hidden, 22; images conjured by, xx; land where, held, 86; language used in, 69–70; Ohero:kon (coming-of-age), 22–23, 80, 113–14, 115; recitation of thanksgiving address, 70; and settler nation-states view of lacrosse, 68; time of empty Longhouse, 36–37; western coming-of-age, 76–77, 80. *See also lacrosse entries*
chidibenjiged, 57–58

childbirth, 34–36, 53–55, 137 (n.18)
Christianity, xi, xxviii, 12
Clan Mothers: authority of, 79; beginning and power of, 20, 135 (n.63); endorsement of Haudenosaunee women's teams to Haudenosaunee Confederacy, 112; as not understood by outside communities, 49; Onondaga, opposition to female lacrosse players, 43–44; responsibilities of, 22; as upholding oppressive western patriarchal structures, 34. *See also specific individuals*
Clan Mother's Call, A (Mommabear), 17–18
clan system, 19–20
Clause, Kim, xxxvii, 44
Clinton, Hillary, xli
collective responsibility, 46
colonialism and colonization: and assimilation, 36; and ceremonies, 69, 76–77, 80; and childbirth, 54–55; discursive marks to maintain status quo of at expense of Haudenosaunee women and girls, xlix, 131 (n.52); and dominant perceptions of Indigenous people, 114–15; dual function of land within, 95; and ethnographic refusal, 51; and farming as domain of men, 9–10; Haudenosaunee females healing limits from, by playing lacrosse, 5, 84, 86, 115–16; and Haudenosaunee tradition, 48, 79; Haudenosaunee women playing lacrosse as unpeeling layers of, 24; of Haudenosaunee women's bodies, 75–76; and Haudenosaunee women's relationship to land, 7, 9–10, 94–95; Indigenous women as threatening, 2, 7,

94, 95; intergenerational trauma from disrupted relationships with land, 23; and lacrosse as men-only sport, 41, 42; limits placed on Haudenosaunee women by, 2, 3, 5; and matrilineality, 29; and non-Indigenous women playing lacrosse, 86; racism in, xxviii; rematriation and healing from, xxvi–xxvii; researchers during, xix; settler nation-states as perpetuating, 6; and stick protocol, 69, 74–75; western coming-of-age ceremonies, 76–77, 80; western gender binary system, 4, 69, 91. *See also* western patriarchy

coming-of-age ceremony (Ohero:kon), 22–23, 80, 113–14, 115

Cook, Beverly, 17, 135 (n.53)

Cook, Katsi, xlvi, xlvii

Cooke, Ashley, *93*, 93–94, 96, 97, 105, 109, 144 (n.12)

corporeal, defined, 122

cosmology, defined, 122

creation stories, x–xi, 3–4. *See also* Haudenosaunee Creation Story

Creator's Game (Downey), xl

Cronin, Mike, xvii

Crooked Arrows (film), xxxiv

Czech Republic, 107–8

D

Dane-Fougnier, Heather, 18–19

Danforth, Michelle, 51

Day Book, The (newspaper), xvii–xviii

"Dealing with Shame and Unresolved Trauma" (Ing), 11–12

DeClue, Charlotte, 14

decolonization: potential of lacrosse for, 105; and revitalization of healing, 114, 115; of space Haudenosaunee female lacrosse players, 96; of western patriarchy, xxxi, 113. *See also* rematriation

Deer, Sarah, 6, 16–17

Deer Cloud, Susan, xlv

Denetdale, Janet, 33, 51

Derby, Susan, xix

dialectic, defined, 122

"discursive masks," xlix, 131 (n.52)

Downey, Allan, xl

Doxtater, Elizabeth, 32, 56

Driskill, Qwo-Li, 90, 91–92, 109–10

E

Elder Brother, men's emulation of, x

"Enigma of Federal Reform, The" (Deer), 17

Episkenew, Jo-Ann, 92

epistemology, defined, 122

equilibrium, 122. *See also* balance in Indigenous societies

Erdrich, Louise, 14–15

eros, defined, 122

erotic, the, defined, 122

ethnographic refusal: about lacrosse, 52–53; defined, 123; and futurity, 48; as method of preservation, 48; as way of establishing generative authority, 51

ethos, defined, 123

Eve (in Judeo-Christian creation story), x, xi

F

Federation of International Lacrosse (FIL), xxxvi, 102

felt knowledge theory, 97

feminism: and balance in society, 64; fascination with Haudenosaunee's women power of western, xliv; Haudenosaunee influence on, xxvi; and Haudenosaunee women playing lacrosse, xliv; imposition of western history of, onto Haudenosaunee, 35; and insertion of "I" into academic work, xvii; and internalized western patriarchy of Haudenosaunee people, 78–79; standpoint theory in, 123; and western creation story, 4
feminist standpoint theory, defined, 123
Fenton, William, 48–49
field observations, xxxi–xxxiii
Finley, Chris, 90, 91–92
Fire Keeper's Daughter (Boulley), 15
Freeland, Mark, 3–4, 20, 57–58, 90–91, 131 (n.52)
futurity: commitment to, 47; and defining lacrosse, 51; and ethnographic refusal, 48; Great Law and adding rafters, 26, 47–48, 49, 50, 59; and Haudenosaunee tradition, 32, 33, 48, 49, 56, 60, 63–64, 71–73; and Haudenosaunee tradition as continuity, 49; seven generations thinking, 48, 137 (n.13); in *Teiotiokwaonháston/ Deyodyogwaọháhs:dọh*, 56

G

Garrett, Phillip C., 37–38
gender: activities appropriate for only one, 53–54; and balance in Indigenous societies, 4, 5, 56, 64; erotic as in female plane, 91; female-ness of earth, 91; hierarchies and women's bodies in settler organized sports, 83; and recitation of thanksgiving address, 70; rematriation and binarism, 56; rules in boarding schools, 70; and sports in boarding schools, 38; and sports in mainstream dominant cultures, 34; and tobacco burning, 70; as a web of relatedness in Indigenous thought, 4, 91; western binary system, 4, 69, 91
General, Levi, 130 (n.33)
generative authority, xxxv, 51, 123
Gilley, Brian Joseph, 90, 91–92
Goeman, Mishuana, 96, 97–98, 100
Goldenweiser, Alexander, 48
Gradual Enfranchisement Act (Canada, 1869), 10
Grandin, Vital-Justin (bishop), xi, 11
Grandmother Moon, x
Great Law of Peace: and change, 26, 47–48, 49, 50, 59; and collective responsibility, 46; and conflict solution, 60; description of good life in, 67; inclusive nature of, 46; lacrosse as game of peace, xxxix; and personal autonomy, 46, 47, 50; recognition of diversity in, 56; and U.S. Constitution, vii; visual narrative of, 56

H

Handsome Lake, 67
Harjo, Joy, 63
Hart, Lyna, 12
Haudenosaunee Confederacy: Central Fire of, ix; Clan Mothers' endorsement of Haudenosaunee women's teams to, 112; endorsement of female lacrosse teams by, 102, 103, 129 (n.17); formation of,

ii, viii, xxxix; lacrosse and recognition of sovereignty of, xxxviii–xxxix, 129 (n.26); members of, 129 (n.27); and U.S. Constitution, vii; and wampum belts, 49 Haudenosaunee Creation Story, 3–4; and clan system, 19; connection to land and water in, 18; creation of lacrosse in, 23; enactment of lacrosse within, at WILC (2015), xxxviii; humans' placement in relationship to all other animals in, 3–4; lacrosse as healing ceremony, xxxv; Sky Woman and lacrosse in, 17–18; Sky Woman and land in, xlvi; and women's connection to land, 9–10

Haudenosaunee culture: absence of violence against women and girls in, x, 8; appropriation of, 53; communal nature of remembering, 36; dealing with death and illness in, 67; dynamic nature of, 47, 57, 59; generational interdependence and respect in, 57–58; Haudenosaunee female lacrosse players as danger to, 30–31, 53; Haudenosaunee women and girls' relationship to, through lacrosse, 82–83; home as public and private, 8; importance of sustaining, 29; and integrity of Longhouse, 53; language and understanding, 71; non-Native lacrosse as appropriation of, 30; personal autonomy as fundamental to, 49–50; rematriation and return to, 56; time of empty Longhouse ceremonies, 35–37; traditional family life, 8; traditions as critical to survival of, 38, 53; women's role in holding alive, 34–35

Haudenosaunee female lacrosse players: bodies of, as texts and canvases, 92, 97–98, 101, 109–10; as carving out space to play, 58; and childbirth, 34–36, 53–54, 55, 137 (n.18); as danger to Haudenosaunee culture, 30–31, 53; decolonization of space by, 96; defining game they play, 81–82; as disrupting colonialism and settler-nation states, 3; endorsement of teams by Haudenosaunee Confederacy, 102, 103, 129 (n.17); as examples of personal autonomy, 46, 50; and feminism, xliv; healing limits placed by colonization, 5, 84, 86, 115–16; high school teams, 39, 41; and intergenerational trauma, 60; Jemison and establishment of women's team, 40; lacrosse as rematriation project, xlix; lacrosse as way of claiming Haudenosaunee identity for, xliii; as mistreating tradition and true lacrosse game, 42–43; next generation of, 108–9; Onondaga opposition to, 39, 43–44; playing as different from men, xiii, xliii; relationship of, to culture through lacrosse, 82–83; and rematriation, xlix, 67; and sovereignty, 60, 67; spirit and ability of, xxix; as traditional, 47–48; as unpeeling layers of colonialism, 24; use of plastic sticks by, xlviii; use of wooden sticks by, 65–66. *See also specific individuals*

Haudenosaunee girls. *See Haudenosaunee women and girls entries*

"Haudenosaunee Influence on the Women's Rights Movement" (United Nations panel), xxvi

"Haudenosaunee Influence on the Women's Suffrage Movement" (Roesch Wagner), xxvi

Haudenosaunee men: and consolidation of masculinity by, through contemporary lacrosse, 42; and death, 5; internalized western patriarchy of, 78–80; modern roles of, 21; public speaking by, traditionally, xxxiii; traditional roles of, 8; and violence against women, 21. *See also* lacrosse, as medicine game

Haudenosaunee Nationals Men's Lacrosse team, xiii, xiii–xiv, xxviii, 111

Haudenosaunee Nationals Women's Lacrosse, xiii–xiv. *See also* Iroquois Nationals (women's team)

Haudenosaunee tradition: as based in collective memory, 63; change as part of, 59; and colonization, 48, 79; contemporary lacrosse as mistreating, 42–43; as continuity, 48; contradictions in, 73; as critical to survival of culture, 38, 53; different definitions of, 29; as enemy of progress, 33; fixed interpretations of, 47; and futurity, 32, 33, 48, 49, 56, 60, 63–64, 71–73; and Haudenosaunee women and girls playing lacrosse, 53; importance of sustaining, 29; and integrity of Longhouse, 53; near extinction of, 32; as not just in past, 33; as not synonymous with "precontact," 33; rematriation and return to, 56; as static and resistant to change, 59–60; theory vs. practice of, 57; thinking nature of, 32, 45, 59

Haudenosaunee women and girls: attending college, 30; choices faced by, xlvii–xlviii; colonization of bodies of, 75–76; connection to Mother Earth of, ix, x; dangers faced by, 2; generative authority of, xxxv; and Haudenosaunee understandings of power and gender balance, 64; and healing from trauma, xii; internalized western patriarchy of, 78–79; and language survival, 70; limits placed on, by colonization and settler nation-states, 2, 3; maintenance of colonial status quo at expense of, xlix, 131 (n.52); menopause and lifegiving power of, 73–74; monolithic western representations of, xliv; during "moon time" (menstruation), x, 74, 118; Onondaga Clan Mothers' opposition to female lacrosse players, 43–44; power of, as lifegivers, ix, xlvi–xlvii, 5, 34–35, 73–74; as promiscuous, 76, 80; relationship of, to culture through lacrosse, 82–83; role in holding Haudenosaunee culture alive, 34–35; roles of, in men's lacrosse, xxxv, 36, 68; settler nation-states' decentering of, 7–8; traditional prohibition against lacrosse playing by, xxvi; as unofficial lacrosse players, 31; western feminism's fascination with power of, xliv; in western patriarchal society, xi; and wooden lacrosse sticks, ix, 61–64, 67, 69, 74–78, 86, 118–19. *See also* Haudenosaunee female lacrosse players

Haudenosaunee women and girls, sexual abuse of: and erosion of tribal government authority, 16; jurisdictional issues, 14–15, 16–17, 135 (n.51), 135 (n.53); making public, 21–22,

80–81; by non-Indigenous men, 16; and patriarchal overtones in Haudenosaunee communities, 21; unresolved trauma from, xii
Haudenosaunee women and girls, violence against: absence of in, Haudenosaunee culture, x, 8; in Creation Story, 17–18; epidemic nature of, 6; as product of western patriarchy, 8; and SDC, 21; and settler nation-states conflation of Indigenous women with land, 95; and women's activism, 21; and women's connection to land, 7, 14
healing: limits on, placed by colonization of Haudenosaunee females by playing lacrosse, 5, 84, 86, 115–16; and rematriation, xxxv; and Sky Woman, xxxv; women using cultural practices for, 15. *See also* lacrosse, as medicine game
Herne, Harvey, 21
Herne, Tsiotenhariio, 22, 27, 29, 41, 55, *85*
Hewitt, J. N. B., 48
Hill, Amber, 39, 47, 49, 57, 77
Hill, Birdie: on acceptance without understanding, 73; boundaries for interviews with, xx, xxv, 52, 53; girls playing lacrosse due to ignorance, 63; on health of ceremony, 141 (n.23); and traditional prohibition against women playing lacrosse, xxvi, 43; on women not being allowed to touch wooden sticks, 67
Hill, Phoebe, 31
history vs. memory, 63
Holder (physician in boarding school), 75–76
homeostasis, 123. *See also* balance in Indigenous societies

human body, xvii

I

"I," insertion into academic work of, xvii
ILF (International Lacrosse Federation), xxxvi, xli
Indian Act (Canada, 1876), 10
Indian Child Welfare Act (ICWA, 1978), 13–14
"Indian Policy and Its Relations to Crime and Pauperism, The" (Garrett), 37–38
"Indian Problem, the," 37
Indigenous people: balance and web of relatedness in, 3–4, 20–21, 90; colonization and dominant perceptions of, 114–15; creation narratives of, 3–4; gender and balance in societies, 4, 5, 56, 64; and holding onto culture, 57–58; memory vs. history for, 63; oral traditions of, 51; status of, in Canada, 10; worldview of, 90
Indigenous queer theory, 90–91
Indigenous Response to #MeToo, An (documentary), xxxiv, 21, 80–81
Indigenous sports teams, xxviii, 129 (n.26). *See also specific teams*
Indigenous women: conflation with land by settler nation-states, 95; connection to land, 6, 7, 9–10; forced sterilization of, 77; limits place on choices of, by colonization, 2; promiscuity of, 76, 80; and settler nation-states' need for land, 2, 14, 94; settler nation-states' representations of, xliv; as threatening settler nation-states and colonization, 7, 94, 95; western patriarchal portrayal of, vii–viii

"Influence of Haudenosaunee Women, The," xxxii
Ing, Rosalyn, 11–12
insidious, defined, 123
intergenerational trauma, xi–xii, 11–12, 13–14, 36, 60, 133 (n.36)
interviews: boundaries for, xix–xx, xxv, 52, 53; ethics of, xxxi; Nations covered, xxx; one's body during, xvii; strengths of, xxx–xxxi
Iroquis [sic] *Foods and Food Preparation*, 67
Iroquois Nationals (men's team): as Haudenosaunee Nationals Men's Lacrosse team, xiii–xiv, xxviii, 111; and Haudenosaunee sovereignty, 52, 103; in international competition, xxxiv–xxxv, xxxvi, xxxviii, xli; and Thorpe's medals, xxviii; as "too professional," 52; WILC 2015 games, xxxiv
Iroquois Nationals (women's team): disbanding of, xxxvi; and Haudenosaunee National's Women's Lacrosse, xiii–xiv, 44; and Haudenosaunee sovereignty, xxxviii, xli, xlii, 102, 103; and Onondaga Clan Mothers, xliii, xliv; participation in international championships by, xxxviii
It Encircles Everything (Doxtater), 32

J
Jackson, Lydia, 9
Jacobs, Steve, 130 (n.33)
Jacques, Alf, 65
Japanese lacrosse team, 106
Jemison, Sandy: basic facts about, 39–40, 98; on Haudenosaunee flag at World Women's Championship (2005), 102; on impetus for bringing lacrosse to Haudenosaunee women and girls, 40; and Onondaga Clan Mothers' opposition to female lacrosse players, 43–44; on playing Japanese lacrosse team, 106; and Seneca Girls Lacrosse Club, xxxvii, 39, 98–100, 101, 102
Jemison, Thomas, 9
Jimerson, Claudia, 50
Judeo-Christian creation story, 4

K
"Kayeneren:kowa (Great Way of Peace), The" (Rice), xi, xxxix
Keepers of the Game (film), xii–xiii, xxxiv, xxxix, 22–23, 29, 41, 113, 138n35
Kelsey, Rayner Wickersham, 9
"kill the Indian, save the man," 12, 133 (n.30)
Kimmerer, Robin Wall, x–xi
King, Thomas, xxxi, 92

L
lacrosse: announcing, games in Seneca language, 71–72; college scholarships for, 30; conflating contemporary, with medicinal, 34; decolonizing potential of, 105; defining, 51, 59–60; as elite sport, 99–100; and ethnographic refusal, 52–53; field, xxxv–xxxvi, 86; as game of peace, xxxix; and Handsome Lake, 67; history of women's, 30; importance of Haudenosaunee being original players of, 42; kind of stick used as informing version being played, 83; as men-only sport, 23, 41, 42; non-Native teams,

xiii, xxxvi–xxxix, 30, 86, 129 (n.20), 129 (nn.22–23); and Ohero:kon (coming-of-age) ceremony, 22–23; origins of, ix, xxxviii, xl; and personal autonomy, 46; as predating humans, 23; and Sky Woman, 17–18, 23; traditional prohibition against women and girls playing, xxvi; as vehicle for Haudenosaunee sovereignty, xxxviii–xxxix, xli, xlii, 102, 103, 129 (n.26); viewed as sport by settler nation-states, 68. *See also* Haudenosaunee female lacrosse players; *and specific organizations and teams*

"Lacrosse"(Berg), xxv, xliv, 33, 49

lacrosse, as medicine game: as ceremony, xl, 67; for community healing and dispute settling, xxxv; conflating with contemporary lacrosse, 34; creation of, in Creation Story of, 23; dealing with death, 5; defining, xlvii, 58; as different from contemporary game, 45; healing intergenerational trauma from colonization, 23; historical examples of, 67; medicine's location, xl, 82, 83–84; and menstruating women, 74; modern game of, xl, 59; potency of, 117; as precolonization game, 58; in *Sacred Sticks*, 51; traditional, xxxvi, xxxix; women playing as different from men, xiii, xliii; women's roles, xxxv, 36, 68; and wooden sticks, ix

lacrosse, box: basic facts about, xxviii; contemporary rules for, xxxvi; dominated by white men, 86; origins, xxxvi; women's, 129 (n.16)

lacrosse, contemporary: and ceremonial connections of lacrosse, 68; and consolidation of masculinity by Haudenosaunee men, 42; as different from medicinal game, 45; mindset while playing, 67; originators of, 51–52; roots of, 41–42; in *Sacred Sticks*, 51; and traditional lacrosse, xxix, xlvii. *See also* Haudenosaunee female lacrosse players

lacrosse sticks: history of wooden, 65–66; plastic sticks, xlviii, 59, 65, *85*; and location of medicine, xl, 82, 83–84; and menstruating women, 74–75; protocol forbidding women to touch, ix, 61–64, 67, 69, 74–78, 86; sacredness of, xlvii; used by girls and women in past, 65–66; use of, in different nations, 66; women making web for, 61, 118–19

LaDuke, Winona, 113

Lakota Creation Story, 3

land: in Creation Story, xlvi, 18; dual function of, within settler colonialism, 95; Indigenous women's conflation with, by settler nation-states, 95; Indigenous women's connection to, 6, 7, 9–10, 94–95; in Indigenous worldview, 90; intergenerational trauma from disrupted relationships with, 23; recognition of all Haudenosaunee, xxxii; recognition of relationship to, 92; rematriation and reconnection to, xxvi; settler nation-states and private ownership of, 8; settler nation-states' need for, 2, 6, 7, 14, 37, 94; where ceremonies are held, 86

language(s): announcing lacrosse games in Seneca, 71–72; and boarding schools, 68–69; bodies in action as, 98–99;

Haudenosaunee female lacrosse players and rematriation of, 67; multiple gendered expressions and nongendered pronouns in Indigenous, 91; near death of Haudenosaunee, 86; non-natives speaking, 107–8; revitalization of, 70–71, 141 (n.23); and understanding Haudenosaunee culture, 71; used in ceremonies, 69–70

Lazore, John, 41

Lazore, Pray, 21

League of Nations, 130 (n.33)

linguicide, 86, 123

London Daily Citizen, xxviii

Lyons, Oren, xxviii, xxxviii, 51

M

Major Crimes Act (MCA, 1885), 16–17

Mann, Barbara Alice, xlv

Martin, Brandon Tehanyataríːyaʼks, 70

Martin, Herb, 65

Martin-Hill, Dawn: on adoption of Eurowestern gender roles, 10, 11; basic facts about, xviii; on internalized western patriarchy of Haudenosaunee people, 78, 79; on negative images of Indigenous women, 115; on spirit and ability of Haudenosaunee female players, xxix; on traditional Haudenosaunee family life, 8; on 2009 World Lacrosse Women's Championship, 107–8

matrilineality: in Canada, 10; and colonialism and colonization, 29; described, x; and Natural Law, xlv; and rematriation, xlvii, 30

matrilocality, x, xlv, 5

Maze of Injustice (Amnesty International), 16

McCarthy, Theresa: analysis of *Teiotiokwaonháston/ Deyodyogwaǫháhs:dǫh*, 56; basic facts about, xviii; on Great Law, 46, 60; on thinking nature of Haudenosaunee tradition, 32; tradition as continuity, 48, 49; on tradition as meant to inform future, 33, 49

McClintock, Anne, 94–95

McDonald, Louise. *See* Mommabear

McKittrick, Katherine, xxxii, 96

McLead, Neal, 92

memory/memories, 36, 63, 92, 110

methods and methodology: definition of methodological, 123; definition of methodology, 123; field observations, xxxi–xxxiii; interviews, xvii, xix–xx, xxv, xxx–xxxi; listening with one's body, xvii; materials produced by Haudenosaunee peoples, xxxiv; presentations, xxxiii

midwives, 54–55

Miracle, Jody Lynn, 70

Miranda, Deborah, 92

Mohawk, John, 23, 32, 45

Mohawk Institute Residential School (Brantford, Ontario), 12

Mommabear: on boarding schools, 37; on choices faced by Haudenosaunee women, xlvii–xlviii; on effect of colonialism on ceremonies, 69; on fragility of retention of Haudenosaunee culture, 37; on gender and tobacco burning, 70; on Haudenosaunee men's role in violence, 21; and Ohero:kon (coming-of-age) ceremony, 113; on rematriation and matrilineality, xlvii, 30; rematriation defined by, xlvii; responsibilities of, as Clan Mothers, 22

Mommabear, on lacrosse: as avenue for healthy childbirth, 55; Haudenosaunee female players, 84, 108–9; on location of medicine in, 83–84; making webs of sticks, 61, 118–19; as medicine game, 5, 59; as men-only sport, 23, 42; on sacredness of wooden sticks, xlvii; and Sky Woman, 17–18, 23; on using imagery of, to combat internalization of western patriarchy, 80

Monahsetah, 14

"moon time," x, 74, 118

Morgensen, Scott Lauria, 90, 91–92

Mother Earth, women's connection to, ix, x

Mt. Pleasant, John, 9

Muthien, Bernedette, xlv

N

NALA (National Amateur Lacrosse Association of Canada), xxviii, xli

Napierala, Nancy, 35

Natural Law, xlv

Newcomb, Steven, xlv–xlvi

New York Times, xxv, 67

NLA (National Lacrosse Association of Canada), xxviii, xxxiv

North American Indigenous Games (NAIG), 93, 144 (n.10)

North American Minor Lacrosse Association's code of conduct, 142 (n.26)

O

Ohero:kon (coming-of-age) ceremony, 22–23, 80, 113–14, 115

Okweta:she, 19–20

Oliphant v. Suquami (1978), 16

Olympic Games, 129 (n.26)

Onondaga Nation: activism events organized by, xxxi; Clan Mothers, xliii, xliv, 43–44; in Haudenosaunee Confederacy, ix; midwives on, 54–55; opposition to female lacrosse players, 39, 43–44; and use of wooden lacrosse sticks, 66; WILC held at, xli–xlii

Onöndowa'ga:' Gawë:nö', 70–71

ontology, defined, 124

oral history, strengths of, xxx–xxxi

P

Parker, Arthur C., 48, 67

patriarchy. *See* western patriarchy

Patterson, Carol, 44

Patterson, John Wesley, 65

peace, lacrosse as game of, xxxix

personal autonomy, 46, 49–50

Pool, Robert, 65

Porter, Tom, 36–37

Pratt, Henry, 133 (n.30)

Pratt, Richard H., xi

praxes, defined, 124

prescribe(d), defined, 124

presentations, as methodology, xxxiii

psychoanalysis, defined, 124

psychology of creativity, xlv–xlvi

Public Law 280, 16, 135 (n.51)

Q

Queer Indigenous Studies (Driskill, Finley, Gilley, and Morgensen), 90, 91–92

R

racism, xxviii, 75–76, 77–78
radical belonging, 56, 124
Ramirez, Renya, 10–11
relational research, described, xviii
rematriation: and bodies of Haudenosaunee female lacrosse players as texts and maps, 97–98, 101, 109–10; and decolonization of western patriarchy, xxxi, 113; defining, xlvii, 92; and generative authority, xxxv; and healing, xxxv; lacrosse as project of, by women and girls, xlix; and lifegiving power of Haudenosaunee women, xlvi–xlvii; and matrilineality, xlvii, 30; as process to restore balance, 5, 56, 90–91, 92; as reconnection and healing from colonization, xxvi–xxvii; and return to Haudenosaunee tradition and culture, 56; as rooted in contemporary reality, xlv–xlvi; and sovereignty, xlix, 67
Rematriation (online publication), xxxiv
Rematriation (online storytelling platform), 80–81
"Rematriation of the Truth" (Deer Cloud), xlv
researchers, during colonization, xix
revitalization, defined, 124
rheumatism, defined, 124
Rice, Brian, xi, xxxix, 19–20, 23
Rifkin, Mark, 109–10
Roesch Wagner, Sally, xxvi, xliv
Roosevelt, Theodore, 37
Ross, Luana, 10
Round House, The (Erdrich), 14–15

S

Sacred Stick (documentary), 51–52
Schenandoah, Diane, 56
Schenandoah, Michelle, vii–xiv; on ceremony, xx; and Dane-Fougnier's cellular healing, 18–19; on futurity, 137 (n.13); on Great Law and Haudenosaunee female lacrosse players, 50; on introduction of patriarchy, 9–10; on *Keepers of the Game*, 138 (n.35); on making public sexual abuse of Haudenosaunee women, 21–22; non-Native lacrosse as appropriation of Haudenosaunee culture, 30; on power of Haudenosaunee women as lifegivers, xlvi–xlvii, 73; on rematriation and matrilineality, xlvii; on seven generations thinking, 48; on sharing of Haudenosaunee tradition and futurity, 56; on time of empty Longhouse ceremonies, 36–37; on violence against women and women's activism, 21
Scudeler, June, 92
Seneca Girls Lacrosse Club, xxxvii, 39, 98–100, 101, 102
settler nation-states: decentering of women within family and imposition of western patriarchy by, 7–8; dual function of land for, 95; formal institutions and society of, 5–6; gender hierarchies and women's bodies in sports organized by, 83; and Haudenosaunee ceremonies, 68; history according to, 63; hollow recognition of Native presence in, 109; inability of, to totally penetrate social and ethnic enclaves, 6; and "the Indian Problem," 37; Indigenous women as threatening,

7, 94, 95; institutional racism of, 75–76, 77–78; limits placed on Haudenosaunee women by, 2, 3; and need for land, 6, 7; as perpetuating colonialism, 6; and private ownership of land, 8; representations of Indigenous people in, xliv; view of lacrosse as sport, 68
Seven Dancers Coalition (SDC), 21
Shenandoah, Jeanne: basic facts about, xix; boundaries for interviews with, 52; on contemporary lacrosse as mistreating tradition and true lacrosse game, 42–43; on importance of keeping Haudenosaunee tradition alive, 53; "The Influence of Haudenosaunee Women," xxxii; on location of childbirths, 54; as midwife, 54–55; on tradition as theory and practice, 57; on WILC, xli–xlii; on women not being allowed to touch wooden sticks, 67
"She No Speaks" (Martin-Hill), 10
Sheridan, Philip, 37
Shimony, Annemarie, 48
Silencing the Past (Trouillot), 63
Simpson, Audra, 10; on boundaries for interviews, 53; dual function of land within settler colonialism, 95; Haudenosaunee tradition as meant to inform future, 33; on Indigenous women's conflation with land by settler nation-states, 95; on relationship between land and Indigenous women's bodies during colonialism, 7; on tradition, 48; tradition as continuity and futurity, 49; on violence against Indigenous women, 6; on women and settler nation-states' need for land, 94. *See also* ethnographic refusal
Sixties Scoop, 13
Sky Woman, x–xi, xxxv, xlvi, 23, 117–18
Slocum, William F., 38
Smith, Kathy, 103
Smith, Linda Tuhiwai, xxxi, 36, 52, 57, 92
Snyder, Jacky, 71–73
sovereignty: and concurrent jurisdiction, 16–17; and Haudenosaunee female lacrosse players, 60, 67; Iroquois Nationals men's team playing internationally, 52; lacrosse and recognition of Haudenosaunee, xxxiv–xxxv, xxxviii–xxxix, xli, xlii, 102, 103, 129 (n.26); and League of Nations, 130 (n.33); and Ohero:kon, 113; and rematriation, xlix, 67; and United Nations, 130 (n.33); and wampum belts, 49
Speck, Frank Gouldsmith, 48
Spirit Game (film), xxxiv
Sport (Cronin), xxviii
sports: at boarding schools, 38; gender hierarchies and women's bodies in settler organized, 83; of mainstream dominant cultures and gender, 34; professional-amateur debate in, xvii–xviii, xli; sexism in coverage of, 103
Stasiulis, Daiva, 6
"Stolen from Our Bodies" (Driscoll), 109–10
stories, x–xi, xvii, xxxi, 3–4, 51, 92. *See also* Haudenosaunee Creation Story
subjugate, defined, 125
suffrage movement, vii, ix
Sullivan-Clinton Campaign, 32
sun (Elder Brother), x

Sunday, Chelsea: on calling out abusers of Haudenosaunee women, 80–81; on rematriation and matrilineality, xlvii; on role of Haudenosaunee men in family, 21 systemic, defined, 125

T

Tatonetti, Lisa, 97–98
Teiotiokwaonháston/Deyodyogwaǫháhs:dǫh (It Encircles Everything, Doxtater), 56
Tewaaraton. *See* lacrosse
Thorpe, Jim, xxvii, xxviii
"Together We Rise" (panel, 2017), 93
Tohe, Laura, 76
"To the Spirit of Monahsetah" (DeClue), 14
Treadwell, David, xxxviii
Trouillot, Michel-Rolph, 63
Tuck, Eve, xlvi
Tucker, Richard, 65
Turtle Quarterly, xxxiv
Tuscarora: membership in Haudenosaunee Confederacy, 129 (n.27); tradition in, 47; and use of wooden lacrosse sticks, 66

U

United Nations, xxvi, 130 (n.33)
"Unpacking the 'I' Word" (McCarthy), 32
U.S. Constitution, vii

V

Valentine, Thomazine, 9

W

wampum belts, 49
Washington, George, 32
water, connection to, in Creation Story, 18
western patriarchy: binary categories of, 4, 69, 91; as civilized, 9; Clan Mothers as upholding oppressive, 34; decolonization of, xxxi, 113; definitions of patriarchal and patriarchy, 124; effect of, on Indigenous peoples, viii; and farming, 9–10; and Haudenosaunee matrifocal society, 5; and hypermasculinity, 56; imposed by settler nation-states, 7–8; internalization of, by Indigenous people, 10–11, 64, 74–75; life giving and sustaining reduced to giving birth by, 34–35; and Natural Law, xlv; and obscuring of women's power, 64; Onondaga Nation Clan Mothers as, xliv; portrayal of Indigenous women by, vii–viii; and professional-amateur debate in sports, xxviii; separation of public and home life in, 8; and sexual abuse of Haudenosaunee women, 21; and "status Indians" in Canada, 10; violence against Haudenosaunee women and girls as product of, 8; women in, xi
We Were Children (documentary), 12
White, Pearl, 35
WILC (World Indoor Lacrosse Championships), xxxiv, xli–xlii
Williams, Enos, 65
women's rights movement. *See* feminism
World Indoor Lacrosse Championships (WILC), xxxviii–xxxix
World Indoor Lacrosse Championships (WILC, men's), xxxiv, xli, xlii, 111
World Lacrosse, xlii
World Lacrosse Women's Championships: and flying of Haudenosaunee flag, 101–2; Haudenosaunee women's team

in, xxxvi, xxxvii; nations represented, xxxvii, xxxviii, 129 (n.20), 129 (nn.22–23); number of teams, 107; 2005, 102; 2009, 107–8

Y
Yakima Indian Reservation (Washington state), 12
Yellow Horse Brave Heart, Maria, 11
Yuval-Davis, Nira, 6

Z
Zen of La Llorona (Miranda), 92